The Poetics of Noise from Dada to Punk

The Poetics of Noise from Dada to Punk

John Melillo

BLOOMSBURY ACADEMIC
NEW YORK • LONDON • OXFORD • NEW DELHI • SYDNEY

BLOOMSBURY ACADEMIC
Bloomsbury Publishing Inc
1385 Broadway, New York, NY 10018, USA
50 Bedford Square, London, WC1B 3DP, UK
29 Earlsfort Terrace, Dublin 2, Ireland

BLOOMSBURY, BLOOMSBURY ACADEMIC and the Diana logo
are trademarks of Bloomsbury Publishing Plc

First published in the United States of America 2021
This paperback edition published in 2022

For legal purposes the Acknowledgments on p. vi constitute
an extension of this copyright page.

Copyright © John Melillo, 2021

Cover design: Louise Dugdale
Cover image © Shutterstock

All rights reserved. No part of this publication may be reproduced or transmitted in any form or by any means, electronic or mechanical, including photocopying, recording, or any information storage or retrieval system, without prior permission in writing from the publishers.

Bloomsbury Publishing Inc does not have any control over, or responsibility for, any third-party websites referred to or in this book. All internet addresses given in this book were correct at the time of going to press. The author and publisher regret any inconvenience caused if addresses have changed or sites have ceased to exist, but can accept no responsibility for any such changes.

Whilst every effort has been made to locate copyright holders the publishers would be grateful to hear from any person(s) not here acknowledged.

Library of Congress Cataloging-in-Publication Data
Names: Melillo, John, author.
Title: The poetics of noise from Dada to Punk / John Melillo.
Description: New York : Bloomsbury Academic, 2020. | Includes
bibliographical references and index. |
Summary: "Frames the history of 20th-century poetry as a listening to
and writing through noise and outlines a history of noise through poetry
and poetic performance"–Provided by publisher.
Identifiers: LCCN 2020009107 | ISBN 9781501359910 (hardback) | ISBN
9781501359934 (pdf) | ISBN 9781501359927 (ebook)
Subjects: LCSH: Poetry, Modern–20th century–History and criticism. | Noise in literature.
Classification: LCC PN1083.N65 M45 2020 | DDC 809.1–dc23
LC record available at https://lccn.loc.gov/2020009107

ISBN:	HB:	978-1-5013-5991-0
	PB:	978-1-5013-7372-5
	ePDF:	978-1-5013-5993-4
	eBook:	978-1-5013-5992-7

Typeset by Integra Software Services Pvt. Ltd.

To find out more about our authors and books visit www.bloomsbury.com
and sign up for our newsletters.

Contents

Acknowledgments		vi
Introduction		1
1	(Re)Versing Noise: Ear-Witness, Metrical Form, and the Western Front	13
2	Dada Bruitism and the Body	33
3	The Persistence of "That Da-Da Strain": The Modernist Travels of "Da"	61
4	Projective Versification, Sound Recording, and Technologizing the Body	87
5	Noise and the City: Writing and Punk Performance, 1965–80	123
6	Noise Music, Noise History: Articulations of Sound Forms in Time	153
References		174
Index		188

Acknowledgments

For his generous guidance and conversation throughout this project, I am deeply indebted to Lytle Shaw. For their early reading and important contributions to parts of this book, I thank Patrick Deer, Jairo Moreno, Sukhdev Sandhu, Peter Nicholls, Martin Daughtry, Cyrus Patell, Lisa Gitelman, and Bryan Waterman. For their kind support and helpful comments at various stages in my work, I thank Martin Harries, Wan-Chuan Kao, Alan Golding, Edward Dimendberg, Craig Dworkin, Charles Bernstein, Jennifer Scappettone, Brian Kim Stefans, Gelsey Bell, Daniel Kane, Ada Smailbegovic, Chris Mustazza, Michael Nardone, Michael Coyle, Elizabeth Bonapfel, Leigh Clare La Berge, Julie Beth Napolin, Sara Marcus, Amy Cimini, Michael Gallope, Jessica Schwartz, Stephen Decatur Smith, and Clara Latham. I also thank Professor Jane Tylus and NYU's Humanities Initiative for the opportunity to think about and present this work in its early stages. Thanks go to Marvin Taylor at NYU's Fales Library for his help in navigating that library's extraordinary collection of materials.

For her insightful readings and brilliant questions, I thank Rachael Wilson. For their friendship and continuous encouragement, I thank Tracy Miller and Zach Holbrook. I also thank my colleagues and former colleagues at the University of Arizona, in particular Scott Selisker, Lee Medovoi, Tenney Nathanson, Kaitlin Murphy, Manya Lempert, Lynda Zwinger, Adela Licona, Farid Matuk, Susan Briante, Paul Hurh, and Allison Dushane. I also thank the editors and staff at Arizona Quarterly for inviting me to present some of this material at the Arizona Quarterly Symposium. Thanks also to colleagues for comments on presentations of this work at the Modernist Studies Association, Association for the Study of the Arts of the Present, and the Modern Language Association. For their questions and their inspiring work, I thank Brandon Shimoda, Dot Devota, Ricky Laska, David Sherman, Steev Hise, Bonnie Jones, Suzanne Thorpe, Ryan Wade Ruehlen, Lauren Hayes, and Reed Rosenberg. For their noise-making, I thank Steve Formel, Hannah Ensor, Christian Ramirez, Geoff Saba, Nate Affield, Akil Wilson, Jasper Avery, and the many other Algae & Tentacles collaborators. For their helpful reading of parts of this manuscript and for permission to quote extensively from their work, I thank Richard Hell and Clark Coolidge.

Acknowledgments

Works by Charles Olson published during his lifetime are copyright the Estate of Charles Olson; previously unpublished works are copyright the University of Connecticut. I thank the archivists at the University of Connecticut-Storrs for permission to quote from these works.

For her careful reading and for her inspiration from the beginning, I send my profound thanks to Lesley Wheeler. I also thank Marina Peterson and Lyn Goeringer for their important contributions to this project. Thanks go to Leah Babb-Rosenfeld, Amy Martin, Rachel Moore, Jessica Anderson, and the whole editorial team at Bloomsbury for their dedicated work on this book. Thanks also to Sudha Soundrapandiyan for careful copy-editing of the manuscript, as well as the project manager Viswasirasini Govindarajan.

The writing of this book was supported by a New Faculty Fellowship from the American Council of Learned Societies.

I want to thank my family—Barbara and Neil Melillo, Maria and Mike Mullane, Laura Melillo, my nephews Andrew and Jackson, Janet Shively, Kristin Ross, and the whole Ross clan—for their critical advice, love, and encouragement over the years. I thank Olive and Sol for their babble and beyond. And last: for her insight, her patience, her guiding example in the writing life, and her sustaining love, immeasurable thanks go to my wife, Johanna Skibsrud.

Introduction

The Poetics of Noise from Dada to Punk reinterprets the history of twentieth-century poetry as a listening to and writing through noise, and it constructs a history of noise through poetry and poetic performance. I argue that poetry continuously figures and refigures noise in relation to communication, meaning, and voice. In the context of information science, which judges communication's effectiveness through its ability to banish noise, poetry remains fundamentally noisy, with even the most normalized poetic sound effects like rhyme and meter acting as "noise" in the system. However, the poets and poetries I describe in this book—whether avant-garde, experimental, popular, or marginalized—make noise through a radicalization of the relationships between sound and sense in poetic texts. By selecting for different "outside" sounds—the sounds of war, media static, bodily emissions, urban soundscapes, nonsense syllables, electronic feedback—they reorganize a variety of seemingly fixed or essential "insides"—including meaning, subjectivity, grammar, social order, expressiveness, and voice. Even more, as poets produce effects of interruption, excess, and violence and take up the unvoiced sounds of difference, they also trouble the very structures of inside and outside, figure/ground that produce the relations between sound, noise, and significance.

This interpenetration of text and context—figures of noise and conditions of listening—is also a method by which writers and performers rearrange these communal systems of reference and sensation. This book describes these rearrangements in order to argue that historical changes in the poetics of noise also manifest new theoretical engagements with sound and listening. I focus on the twentieth century because the explosion of formal and technological apparatuses for making, storing, and transmitting sound invited new ways of thinking and feeling noise. I include a wide variety of written and sounded interventions into noise—such as verse by ear-witnesses to the First World War, Dadaist "verse without words," mid-century avant-garde poetry, ragtime and jazz performance, modernist and post-modernist epic poetry, rock 'n' roll music and early sound engineering, punk music, contemporary experimental poetry, sound art, and noise music—in order to show the range of social, material, and subjective interventions that poets make in relation to noise and listening. Noise manifests in the undersound of difference: in a technological and phenomenological reorganization of sound as a field of perception and action.

Cole Swensen describes poetry as "the one place where noise is not only organized into information but has value *in remaining noise*" because its concrete use of language allows it to collect and connect uncoded, alternatively coded, and otherwise unassimilable material (Swensen 2011: 9). The incorporation of noise allows poets to defamiliarize the given, unexamined modes by which cultures hear, understand, and thus produce noise. Poets can mark how noise influences—or flows into—poetic making at the same time that noise arises within—and emanates from—that same poetic making. In this way, a poetics of noise indexes changing relationships between listeners, environmental sounds, poetic form, and poetic performance, as well as the social practices of listening that organize social worlds.

The question of noise, then, is not a question of how sound echoes a pre-given or idealized meaning nor is it a question of how a "pure," unmediated materiality bursts through a linguistically mediated contact with "the real." Friedrich Kittler suggests the end of poetry through the discovery of noise in the medium of the phonograph: "the phonograph does not hear as do ears that have been trained immediately to filter voices, words, and sounds out of noise; it registers acoustic events as such. Articulateness becomes a second order exception in a spectrum of noise" (Kittler 1999: 22). After phonography, the symbolic gives way to the "real" of noise. Noise, however, calls up the very question of sense-making through phonographic effects: where, when, and how do sound and sense connect and articulate with each other? While listeners remain embedded within a sonic flux, they also access, experience, and live through that flux with the help (and hurt) of techniques, technologies, and channels that separate significance from insignificance, background from foreground. Jonathan Sterne's work on the history of sound reproduction shows how technologies emerge through practices and discourses that precede an "invention," and by the same token, what he calls "audile techniques" articulate bodies, postures, and ways of listening that reveal different ways of being in and organizing the sound world (Sterne 2003: 23). Taking their cues from media technologies and "audile techniques," as well as from the rhythmic and sonic affordances within language and the body, poets figure noise in order to ask: At what point do acoustic vibrations become addressed to sense? At what point do we hear sounds differently? Or, simply, hear different sounds?

Because poetry emphasizes language as a material construction in and with sound, and because it relies upon differentiated modes of address within different contexts, a poetics of noise combines a variety of generically separated forms of listening in order to suggest the provisionality and contingency of a given culture's sonic organization. Poets as sound artists actively play with, refuse, and reshape the address of sounds to listeners and social bodies. In most cases, the figuration of noise forms in the negative, as listeners cast out or ignore noise in the name of communication or poetic voice. But the poets I take up in this study actively write and perform the sound of noise, and they reimagine the ways of listening that define what counts as significant or insignificant sound. Rather than suggesting that poets simply overturn the hierarchical binary between signal and noise, I listen for the ways in which they implicitly and explicitly theorize listening, mediation, and responsibility through their figurations of noise.

Figuration, Voice, and Noise

Figuration is an important word in this account, and it encompasses two senses that I want to emphasize. First, from a rhetorical perspective, figuration is a blanket term that marks figures of speech, like metaphor and metonymy, as well as formal figures in sound, such as alliteration and rhyme. Second, from a phenomenological and art historical perspective, a figure arises from a background as a difference that focuses our gaze. In the case of noise, "figuration" can be a problematic term because noise either always retreats from presence (you can never "hear" it without transforming it into a figure) or noise is ever-present (it is, in the words of Hillel Schwartz, "everywhere and everywhen") (Schwartz 2011). The philosopher Michel Serres takes up the problem of noise's figuration in *Genesis* (1997 [1981]):

> The background noise never ceases; it is limitless, continuous, unending, unchanging. It has itself no background, no contradictory. How much noise must be made to silence noise? And what terrible fury puts fury in order? Noise cannot be a phenomenon; every phenomenon is separated from it, a silhouette

on a backdrop, like a beacon against the fog, as every message, every cry, every call, every signal must be separated from the hubbub that occupies silence, in order to be, to be perceived, to be known, to be exchanged. As soon as a phenomenon appears, it leaves the noise; as soon as a form looms up or pokes through, it reveals itself by veiling noise.

(Serres 1997 [1981]: 13)

To figure or make noise is, by this account, an impossibility. Noise remains resolutely beyond the frame. Serres explicitly connects this to "metaphysics," a "disturbance" of being.

I want to suggest, rather, that poets and musicians in the twentieth century and beyond work to render noise as an artifact of listening. In his *Noise: The Political Economy of Music* (1977), Jacques Attali connects this process of listening to the social world:

[M]ore than colors and forms, it is sounds and their arrangements that fashion societies. With noise is born disorder and its opposite: the world. With music is born power and its opposite: subversion. In noise can be read the codes of life, the relations among men.

(Attal 1985: 6)

For Attali, noise is both an index of power—for those who control what counts as noise—and a principle of subversion. Noise, a sonic materiality that is at once created by and prior to structures of listening, can also break through those very structures that define it. It is always outside (and yet defined by) the "codes [that everywhere] analyze, mark, restrain, train, repress, and channel the primitive sounds of language, of the body, of tools, of objects, of the relations to self and others" (Attali 1985: 6). The aesthetic push against these sonic codes both finds and creates noise—often by assuming different ways of analyzing, marking, restraining, and repressing sounds in relation to dominant codes. In Attali's hands, noise is an explicit figure of transgression and futurity. Its very historicity is what makes it precede and predict transformations in society.

Attali's teleology may be tempered by recognizing noise as neither totality: neither an unfigurable, unheard metaphysics nor a purely social artifact harkening transgression, change, and progress. "Noise" remains a subjective, mobile, and provisional term. As Douglas Kahn says, "The trouble is that noises are never just sounds and the sounds they mask are never just sounds: they are also ideas of noise" (Kahn 1999: 20). This is where poetry enters. Whereas Serres and Attali posit, in different ways, an unchanging "outside" that never ceases and continuously produces and reproduces noise, the poets I take up in this book, ranging from the First World War poets of the Western Front to contemporary sound poets, punk performers and noise musicians, take up different "ideas of noise" by moving or displacing sounds between differing abstractions of sonic form and between the ever-changing "outsides" and "insides" that these abstractions produce. They create figures that sound out and produce noise while also reimagining it as a category within sonic ways of knowing or "acoustemologies" (Feld 2015: 12).

In "Artifice of Absorption," Charles Bernstein suggests, "There is no fixed / threshold at which noise becomes phonically/significant; the further back this threshold is/pushed, the greater the resonance at the cutting/edge" (Bernstein 1992: 12). The "pushing back" of this threshold can also be figured as a constant renegotiation of boundaries as poets insert their languages, bodies, and performances into the space between "phonic significance" and "noise." The greater resonance is an intensifying of sonic echoes that move forward and backward in time: a multiplying of possibility beyond the sonic registration of indexical or referential facts. In a different context, the ethnomusicologist Louise Meintjes hears musical figuring as "a process of arguing musically, by means of repeated and varied motives, over ideas about social relations" (2003: 149). The separation between figure and ground, phonic significance and noise, inside and outside emerges through social relations embedded within texts. Jonathan Sterne describes noise as the "voicing of differences" (Sterne 1997: 44), and we hear such differences not only through "voicing" but also through the undersounds of social difference—unrecognizable, inchoate, difficult, or "other" sounds that demand a response.

This question of "voicing" is important not only because "voice" remains a figure intimately tied to poetry and poetic making but also because voice is implicit in concepts of personhood, citizenship, community, and value. Poets continuously work with and within figures of voice—metaphors and personifications but also recorded and performed sounds—that function as the point of contact between individuals, institutions, and audiences. Voice and noise intermingle, conflict, and cohabit throughout the history of twentieth-century poetry because voices remain channels and guarantors of meaning and speech. Figures of noise are the counter-figures of voice: noise emerges in sounds that disrupt the channel of voice and its faithful transfer of meaning from poet to reader, from sound-emitter to listener.

At the same time, a poetics of noise means that poetic making is not simply a textual symptom of a set of contextual conditions but rather an active mediator between ways of listening, material sounds, communications systems, rhetorical organization, and poetic and performance tradition. I have selected for works that offer important conjunctures between the mediation and remediation of noise and different conditions of sense and sensibility. As poets transform the felt and heard noise of the Western Front into broken verse or cut through the post–Second World War American media-sphere with experiments in recording and vocal performance, they not only act in accord with changing historical conditions but also work to reshape, theorize, and swerve from those conditions. By close listening to particular figurations in the inconsistent field of noise, by exposing the ways in which individual artists rework and destabilize the relations of voice and noise, I show how text and context interpenetrate in accordance with changing fields of sound and with the different ways of listening that organize and reorganize those fields.

My wide-ranging archive of texts and works focuses in particular on sonic figurations and disfigurations that react to or produce new theories and practices of noise. Noise has no transcendent definition. Noise works within—and against—the acoustic, sensory, political, and material conditions that produce and filter sonic experience. *The Poetics of Noise from Dada to Punk* shows how these wider conditions of sonic experience are embedded within the techniques and technologies of the poetic writing of sound—including metrical and free verse, "verse without words," sound poetry, popular song, tape experiments, studio recording, feedback, and electronic sound. It also shows that noise becomes audible in multiple ways: as excess sound unnecessary for communication; as "ugly" sound outside of aesthetic valuation; as racialized sound; as sounds that violate formal regularity or generic consistency; as sounds that trace the remaindered, the forgotten, the irreducible; and as sounds that rupture the physical, technological, and rhetorical filters that give shape to listening. Noise fluctuates in the "as" of these different audibilities.

In describing different noise figures through the century, I read and listen for the ways in which poetry moves between noise's ubiquitous presence and its fugitive absence. Jean-Luc Nancy has called poetry "the lipstick of noise," and this book investigates the means by which this "lipstick"—as surface, form, and texture—does not hide or cover over noise (Evans, "The Lipstick of Noise Project Note"). On the contrary, it patterns the manifold processes by which noise meets listening and listening meets noise. Close listeners to noise—ranging from the barest sense perception to the most technologically advanced mediation—attend neither to "sound itself" nor to "noise itself" but rather to the culturally encoded relationships between the transmission and reception of sound. The power of poetic experiment is to connect listening and making in ways that discover the limits of those relationships—and the motivations and powers within them.

Theorizing Noise through Poetry

The Poetics of Noise from Dada to Punk takes part in an ongoing conversation about the values and powers of noise and noise music. By describing how poetic organizations of sound self-consciously manifest their own framing, it seeks to insert poetry into the theory and practice of sound studies. Poetry is a sound art—if we imagine that term to indicate not a limited field of artistic endeavor but rather an art of and in sound. But more important than this ontological claim about poetry is the fact that the figure of the poet transformed during the twentieth century in answer to new conditions for mediation and performance. The new media litany—phonograph, telephone, radios, television, electronic amplification—transformed the speed and range of global communication utterly, but poets did not blindly reproduce the medium as message. Instead, they reshaped the conditions in which writing and performance occurred by embracing the differential of noise.

Rather than defining and defending a particular vibrational ontology, phenomenological objectification, or teleological hermeneutic, this book describes material and cultural frames that parse the flowing matrix of sound. Poetic making figures its own conditions of address—conditions of voicing, performance, responding, and listening—in the interplay between text and event. I read poetry, therefore, not through but *as* sound theory and noise theory. This allows me to attend to, and explore, the ways that modern and contemporary poetry—and its performance—returns again and again to problems in the production, representation, mediation, and recognition of voice, noise, and vibration.

That said, important recent works in the theory and practice of noise, such as the aforementioned works by Attali and Serres, as well as Paul Hegarty's *Noise/Music*, Salome Voegelin's *Listening to Noise and Silence*, Craig Dworkin's *No Medium*, Greg Hainge's *Noise Matters*, Hillel Schwartz's *Making Noise*, and Marie Thompson's *Beyond Unwanted Sound*, have engaged in a conversation about the ontology, ubiquity, and uses of noise. This book takes up and extends these conversations on noise by swerving into poetry and poetic performance.

Poetry does not admit to "noisiness" in any obvious way. Usually imagined as quiet, private, and interior, poetry seems to engage in a process of turning away from the world as well as from an assembled audience. But an expanded poetics in the twentieth century works outside of the isolated space of private reading. In taking up performance, theatricality, and popular genres, poets move away from the intimate relation of text and reader and into a noisy public world. The sound texts presented in this book take up the question of how textual production moves through a variety of different frames: versification, rhythm, medium, genre, and performance style.

The six chapters of the book are organized chronologically, beginning with the poets on the Western Front during the First World War and ending with contemporary noise music and performance poetry. The first three chapters take up modernist poetry and popular song written and performed prior to the Second World War, while the second three chapters take up the amorphous space of late- or postmodernity. The terms "modernism" and "postmodernism" provide heuristic value at times in the book, but rather than litigating them again, I am interested in recognizing two different noise regimes that emerge in the century. Two figures haunt these regimes: Luigi Russolo and John Cage. Their different and influential attitudes toward noise simultaneously undergird and contrast with the works I examine. Russolo's 1913 Futurist manifesto, "The Art of Noises," inaugurated the use of noise as a transgressive conquest: "We must break out of this limited circle of sounds and conquer the infinite variety of noise-sounds" (Russolo 1986 [1913]: 25). Russolo instigates and represents a modernist urge to escape limits, to discover the new, but he shapes that escape and discovery in terms of imperialist conquest and, ultimately, an act of regulation: "We want to give pitches to these diverse noises, regulating them harmonically and rhythmically" (27). All sounds—including most famously the sounds of war—can become the material for musical regulation and new forms of harmony. Noise represents a triumphal movement into the future, and we see in these words the germ of Attali's figuration of noise.

John Cage's 4′33″, on the other hand, rejected all forms of regulation, composition, and conquest in favor of silence: a performer of the piece merely marks time and the audience listens to an unexpected music produced in the absence of instrumental sound. Here the composer rejects both senses of "instrumental:" as in produced by a particular instrument and as in intended or directed. In the space of silence, the listener is invited to encounter new sound events: the environmental sounds of audience and theater, for example, become the content of the piece. 4′33″ was conditioned by Cage's well-known (even mythological) realization upon exiting an anechoic chamber at Harvard: "Until I die, there will be sounds. And they will continue after my death. One need not fear for the future of music!" (Cage 1961: 8). Cage's sense that all sound was potential music radically reformulates musical and poetic production through acts of listening and attention. Cage wanted to "let sounds be themselves." Douglas Kahn hears in this move a form of noise abatement, for in the urge toward total sound and toward sound "in itself," Cage also silences the differences that organize the social world of sounds (Kahn 1999: 185). Noise emerges from the sounds of difference, and while Cage radically opens music to sound "in itself," he also turns away from sonic significance because he hears only singular, continuous sound, not the differentiated play between meaning and non-meaning, writing and erasure that also conditions our encounters with sound.

In commenting on these two influential figures and the noise regimes that they embodied, I want to show how other artists work with and against the major interventions that these artists presented in the organization of sound. In the first half of the century, war poems, avant-garde performances, epic poetry, and popular music entail figures of noise as mimesis, infection, and fragmentation. Rather than the celebratory rhetoric of futurist progress, these other works make noise in order to keep noise at bay. These different modernisms work inside and against the disfiguring effects of modern life—particularly in the horrific violence of the First World War and Jim Crow America.

I begin with the extreme conditions of warfare on the Western Front in Europe, because they make a practice of hearing and figuring noise necessary and explicit. Noise works as an index of danger as well as an unrepresentable, unutterable experience. The mediation of verse form—in classical meters, fragmented free verse, and "verse without words" (or sound poetry)—could simultaneously defuse noise's invasive power and produce a starting point in the midst of the void of representation. Poetry paradoxically retreats from and makes noise. An anecdote recorded by Paul Fussell relates how soldiers in the midst of bombardments on the Western Front would often recite prayers, poems, or simple rote phrases. This conflict and contact between internalized speech and outside acoustic environment produces a homeopathic rendering of noise through the selection and repetition of particular sounds. This process carries over to the formalist poetry of the First World War poets on the front, where form begins to fall apart in the midst of the challenge of noise. At the same time, Dadaists like Tristan Tzara and Hugo Ball and jazz modernists like the lyricist Mamie Medina, T. S. Eliot, and Langston Hughes emphasize the arbitrariness of such selections and repetitions by foregoing straightforward representation for abstraction, nonsense, mediation, and distance. In place of lyric self-possession, they explore the reflection and refraction of language's noisy surfaces with new forms of sonic mediation—from sound poetry to (proto-)scat singing.

In the second half of the century, poets begin to write and perform sound in ways that transform this homeopathic structure into a reproductive one based upon forms of projecting, erasing, and tracing noise. In contrast with Cage's embrace of all sound, noise becomes general and generative. Rather than staging forms of resistance to noise, sound-makers actively construct work to discover its properties of resistance. No longer "out there," noise emanates from every point of contact between bodies and the mediums that would connect them—mouth sounds, aesthetic form, text, metaphorical and performed voices, instruments, and sound recording. From the "alien" effects of rock 'n' roll (and punk) lyrics, performances, and recording techniques to the poetries of Charles Olson, Little Richard, Clark Coolidge, Bernadette Mayer, Richard Hell, Patti Smith, Tracie Morris, and Susan Howe, I find artists contesting the pluralized relativism of information theory with the particularities of attention and sensation. While media theorists like Marshall McLuhan and Walter Ong fantasized about a "post-literary" orality—and while technological change has allowed for the proliferation of voices through new channels of recording and communication—the poets I take up amplify noise's disruptive and generative potential in a condition of ubiquitous mediation and universalizing dedifferentiation. These particularities of noise align to social differences of race, gender, and class while also producing counter-representations of such social differences through renewed forms of aesthetic experience, textual performance, and historical imagination. The final scene of analysis in the book is the collaborative work of Susan Howe and the musician David Grubbs. In these collaborations, every visual fragment of text becomes phonographic, and Grubbs's sound editing processes combine collaged mouth sound with field recordings and drones to create a ghostly soundscape. The radical frequency realignments that Howe and Grubbs create are inassimilable to the expected figures and orders of sonic organization we would call language—and yet they open up history, memory, and meaning to the uncompromising alterity and distance of the past. Here, the sound of noise remains unrelentingly transitional and provisional. Rather than resulting in a parasitical contamination of speech's signifying flow, these works figure noise as a productive incongruity between reading and listening in the articulation of sound forms in time (a title of one of Susan Howe's books).

At one and the same time the sound traces that Howe and Grubbs emphasize through their work dissipate into frequency scatter and let us hear (inside of the decayed, the inchoate, the inarticulate) what persists. They ask us: What do we continue to listen for but cannot hear? The sound experiments that I explore at the conclusion of this book—those of Howe and Grubbs along with the sound poetry of Tracie Morris and the psychoacoustic play of Florian Hecker's work—encapsulate the project as a whole because they begin by radically dispossessing the power of the utterance and investing the sound of that dispossession—noise—with a new aesthetic and conceptual force. If we listen in order to understand, noise would seemingly be the onrush of a materiality that would refuse any understanding. But noise does not simply foreclose, and its very intransigence and malleability make it an epistemological and speculative tool. Along with the artists whose work this book explores, then, I ask: What are the phonographic systems that undergird the meanings of sound? What other possibilities for recombination and response exist within those systems? And with them, I begin to answer: Listening to and writing noise uncovers not just forms of violence, exclusion, and loss but also other ways of articulating collectivity and other ways of knowing our environments, languages, and lives.

1

(Re)Versing Noise: Ear-Witness, Metrical Form, and the Western Front

You can't communicate noise. Noise never stopped for one moment—ever.
—Graves (1971: 86)

Robert Graves's inability to communicate noise does two things at once: it indicates the problem of representing the conditions of noise on the Western Front during the First World War while at the same time presenting noise as a special kind of knowledge that combatants experienced. The very fugitivity of noise—and its implicit sensory cost on the body and psyche—undergirds the authority of the soldier to depict life and death at the front. During the First World War, the experience of noise became a limit case for the senses, and combatant poets are both ear-witnesses for and exemplary sufferers of this experience. In this sense, reporting or relaying noise fits into the truth-telling that Wilfred Owen famously argues for in one of the first statements of a poetics of witness in the twentieth century:

> Above all I am not concerned with Poetry.
> My subject is War, and the pity of War.
> The Poetry is in the pity. ...
> All a poet can do today is warn. That is why the true Poets must be truthful.
> (Owen 1985: 192)

Owen inaugurates a position in which poetry becomes a mechanism for truth and warning. The poet's report on experience can create co-feeling as opposed to the indifferent forces of "Poetry" with a capital "P." Truth-telling resists a poetry that led to, and participated in, the destruction wrought by the First World War.

In this chapter, I want to examine the ways in which those who experienced noise at the front translated—carried over—that noise from experience to text, from sensory world to poetic form. Rather than suggesting that only certain poets and memoirists have a special access to a specific truth about the experience of war, a "combat gnosticism" that could directly express the truth, I want to describe the work of a variety of poets and writers at the front who used the impersonal mechanics of verse form to register the fact of noise. This is done not by directly communicating or reproducing noise so much as communicating its effects to create a space of empathic response. As an experience of sounds at the limits of human sensory, cognitive, and emotional capacities, noise indexes failure in language, sound form, and figuration. It also remains a site of potential connection in the midst of communication breakdown.

Soldier poets like Wilfred Owen, Siegfried Sassoon, and Isaac Rosenberg, as well as noncombatant poets like Mary Borden, do not use verse as a transparent medium of reportage nor as a symbol of an achieved tradition. Rather, they revalue the mechanisms of poetic form that can both verse and reverse noise. That is, they improvise metrical, rhythmic, and phonemic orders *against* the noise engendered by the chaotic totality of trench warfare while at the same time emphasizing the disfiguring effects of noise on the poetic organization of language. In this sense, the disfigurability of noise remains a constant "tactical" recourse for poets with a "profound suspicion of claims to represent the totality of battle, or to show the spectacle of modern warfare" (Deer 2009: 28). Ultimately, these writers refuse the creation of a comprehensive "voice" for communicating a fixed meaning or experience of the war. They reject the given means for figuring and enacting voice that they inherited from a broad nineteenth-century metrical and lyrical tradition. They embrace incommunicability, breakage, and muteness even as they continue to sound out poems against and within the noise.

Hearing Noise

Soldiers and civilians had to improvise new orders of experience in the midst of the war's unprecedented concentration of human bodies, industrial machinery, and destructive weaponry. After only a few months of combat, an ideal war of quick and easy victories taking place on fixed and delimited battlefields gave way to the reality of a defensive war of attrition in a vastly expanded zone of combat, a war zone. The trench "system" of the First World War was a 400-mile-long conglomeration of holes, ditches, and underground shelters stretching through France from the North Sea to Switzerland (Keegan 1976: 310). Soldiers dug into the ground in order to defend themselves from the rapid fire of machine guns and the explosions of heavy artillery. In light barrages, about half a dozen shells fell on a company sector (about 300 yards) every ten minutes. During heavier bombardments, thirty shells or more would land every minute (Ellis 1989: 62). A transformation from battlefield to war zone meant an expansion of the "front" of battle not only along the ground surface but also below ground and, with the advent of planes, in the air.

In this zone, "the link between sight, space, and danger" was broken (Das 2006: 80), and combatants and noncombatants alike had to adapt to a world where nonvisual senses—especially sound, smell, and touch—took on new importance. As Patrick Deer writes, "in the anti-landscapes of the trenches, seeing, in the traditional sense, has become defamiliarized, uncoupled from perception and emotion" (2009: 21). Here, a new "geography of senses" came into being: the Front created a phenomenology in which the body became a site of constant haptic awareness, where the relative denigration of sight created a new set of responses to touch imagined not simply as what one does with one's fingers but as a "sense spread all over the body that helps in the perception of space" (Das 2006: 73). In the closed-in world of the front, sound also became a kind of touch. Subjectivity transformed into an intensified and concentrated version of what Steven Connor calls the "modern auditory I:" an ego "defined in terms of hearing rather than sight, … imaged not as a point, but as a membrane; not as a picture, but as a channel through which voices, noises, and musics travel" (Connor 1997: 207). This stretched and sensitive membrane of the self becomes exposed and frail in a place where listeners perceive "every sound as physical collision and possible annihilation" (Das 2006: 81).

With their sense of space, safety, and self-awareness called radically into question, those at the front had to create new orders of meaning and narrative in conditions of utter passivity. Sound, in particular, took on new importance for combatants and non-combatants who had to listen closely in order to understand their surroundings. A passage from the French soldier Henri Barbusse's memoir novel, *Under Fire*, shows this mechanism at work:

> A dull crackle makes itself audible amidst the babel of noise. That slow rattle is of all the sounds of war the one that most quickens the heart.
>   The coffee-mill! [Military slang for machine-gun] One of ours, listen. The shots come regularly, while the Boches' haven't got the same length of time between the shots; they go crack—crack-crack-crack—crack-crack—crack—
>   Don't cod yourself, crack-pate; it isn't an unsewing-machine at all; it's a motor-cycle on the road to 31 dug-out, away yonder.

> "Well, I think it's a chap up aloft there, having a look round from his broomstick," chuckles Pepin, as he raises his nose and sweeps the firmament in search of an aeroplane.
>
> A discussion arises, but one cannot say what the noise is, and that's all. One tries in vain to become familiar with all those diverse disturbances. It even happened the other day in the wood that a whole section mistook for the hoarse howl of s hell the first notes of a neighboring mule as he began his whinnying bray.
>
> (Barbusse 1917: 217)

In the effort to "become familiar with all those diverse disturbances," those on the front became experts in categorizing and locating the different sounds of ordnance and gunfire. Listeners learned to identify the type of shell and gauge their relative danger.[1] They also could transform these sounds into an ironic music:

> A German shell came over and then whoo—oo—ooo-oooOOO—bump—CRASH! Landed twenty yards short of us. We threw ourselves flat on our faces. Presently we heard a curious singing noise in the air, and then flop! flop! little pieces of shell-casing came buzzing down all around. "They calls them the musical instruments," said the sergeant. ... Another shell came over. Everyone threw himself down again, but it burst two hundred yards behind us. Only Sergeant Jones had remained on his feet "You're wasting your strength, lads" he said to the draft. "Listen by the noise they make where they're going to burst."
>
> (Graves 1981 [1929]: 90)

This is a classic trope of war experience: the ability to hear in a way that can parse the ambiguous and ever-present noise of war in order to manifest a sense of safety and control. Shells become "musical instruments" and undifferentiated noise—the "babel of noise" in Barbusse's words—gives way to knowledge.

In his book on listening in wartime Iraq, Martin Daughtry discusses four zones of "belliphonic" audition: they range from the distant zone of the "inaudible-audible" to the ever-closer "narrational," "tactical," and "trauma" zones (2015: 77). In the zone of the "inaudible-audible," experienced soldiers have learned to shut out the sounds of war by recognizing which sounds demand attention and reaction and which sounds are merely in the background. War is not all noise but a differentiated set of possible reactions to sound in the midst of varying degrees of distance, danger, and attention. Noise comes to represent not the particular belliphonic

---

[1] The English used an enormous array of different guns and shell types; they fired 18-pounders, 4.5-inch howitzers, 60-pounders, 4.7-inch or 6-inch guns, and a variety of heavy howitzers of different caliber, ranging from 6 inches to 15 inches. These weapons dropped bombs of 100 to 1400 pounds (Keegan 1976: 231).

sounds of war but a complex set of relationships to randomness, violence, and unknowability. For the writers of the Western Front, figures of onomatopoeia, figures of indexing or referencing, and figures of ambiguous yet threatening presence model these relationships to the unknown and reproduce noise's effects in the body of the poem. Noise becomes the other of identification, a movement of sound between and outside of organizing zones of audition.

Barbusse moves through these figures in another description of noise from *Under Fire*:

> Crack! Crack! Boom!—rifle fire and cannonade. Above us and all around, it crackles and rolls, in long gusts or separate explosions. The flaming and melancholy storm never, never ends. For more than fifteen months, for five hundred days in this part of the world where we are, the rifles and the big guns have gone on from morning to night and from night to morning. We are buried deep in an everlasting battlefield; but like the ticking of the clocks at home in the days gone by—in the now almost legendary past—you only hear the noise when you listen.
>
> (Barbusse 1917: 6)

As with the passage from Graves above, there is a movement between a mimesis of sound in language and the naming of the sound emitters, "rifles and big guns," but the author also develops the metaphor of a "melancholy storm [that] never, never ends." Noise takes on an expanded temporality: it is endless and, though the rifles and guns are named, it becomes detached from its various causes and takes on a life of its own.

Many descriptions of the noise at the front use a complex of rhetorical effects that attempt to speak noise's contradictory presence and absence. In particular, comparisons to nature—storms, hurricanes—become a common trope. Ear-witnesses attest to the wild and topsy-turvy nature of storms. At times, this takes on a surreal, supernatural quality:

> And it did not move. It hung over us. … And the supernatural tumult did not pass in this direction or in that. It did not begin, intensify, decline and end. It was poised in the air, a stationary panorama of sound, a condition of the atmosphere, not the creation of man.
>
> (quoted in Ellis 1989: 63)

This anonymous NCO of the 22nd Manchester Rifles detaches noise from cause: the "supernatural tumult" exists on its own. The seeming stasis and inescapability of noise compares with a supreme nature perceived as a vast, unknowable, and random totality in which a body remains small, disoriented, and exposed.

Repeating

The endless, nameless, and autonomous "super-natural tumult" becomes deeply involved in the poetics of listening at the front. As the "roaring chaos of the barrage effected a kind of hypnotic condition that shattered any rational pattern of cause and effect," those at the front developed an improvisatory poetics of counteraction and even "magical reversals" (Leed 1979: 129). Where the listening membrane is in danger of rupture, it no longer focuses on particular identifications and narratives. Where listening for a particular sign gives way to the constant, overwhelming possibility of death, noise becomes an anti-figure or blank space to be filled in by little, irrational language acts that contend with such noise on the level of the individual psyche and an embodied sense of space.

Those under bombardment had to work to maintain the limits between meaningful sound and noise in order to maintain their sanity. A soldier reports: "Sometimes the terrible noise makes me nearly mad, and it requires a great effort to keep cool, calm and collected" (quoted in Ellis 1976: 64). Often, this "great effort" involved a return to memorized utterance—to little repetitive chants that could project a different acoustic space and time in the face of the seemingly interminable atmosphere of noise. The recitation of such incantations could act as a way of projecting oneself against (and protecting the self from) the onslaught of meaningless, unutterable noise. Prayers, mnemonics, even advertising slogans, acted as self-sustaining forms of voicing that pressed back against the terrifying sounds. Some soldiers repeated well-known Biblical verses ("I will fear no evil ... no evil ... I will fear no evil") or rote recitations like a "school mnemonic for Latin adverbs, beginning 'Ante, apud, ad, adversus ...'" (Fussell 1975: 169). Siegfried Sassoon unconsciously remembered and repeated an advertisement:

> They come as a boon and a blessing to men,
> The Something, The Owl, and the Waverly Pen.
>
> (Sassoon 1930: 46)

In his memoir, Sassoon emphasizes that he could not remember what that "something" was in the jingle. "Something" is nothing in particular, but it sustains the metrical movement of the couplet. It is this metrical movement that, in turn, sustains Sassoon: repeating this verse becomes for him one answer to noise's indifferent attack on the body and senses.

For bodies inhibited and inhabited by noise's dangers, these memorized rhythms—known by heart—enact the possibility for sound form and meter to produce, as Susan Stewart puts it, "volition towards mastery" (2002: 67). They also remake the grounds by which attention, will, and mastery function. And yet memorized and internalized rhythms also give themselves up to a "certain exteriority of the automaton, to the laws of mnemotechnics, to that liturgy that mimes mechanics of the surface" (Derrida 2014 [1988]: 289). In other words, these moments of incantation demarcate a fragile and contingent space in which language and noise simultaneously reject and interpenetrate one another. The autonomous, detached, unrepresentable totality of noise feeds the self-affecting power of memory, prayer, and song. It is not the magic of the speech act at work here, but rather the simple mechanics of the voice. The canons, codes, and wisdom of Western life are reduced to the rumbling of the throat. The body holds itself together with a vestige of a rhythm, and "mastery" is merely the "mystery" of repetition.

Gilles Deleuze and Félix Guattari write an allegory of the origins of rhythm through a situation that parallels this scene of terrified *poesis* in the war zone:

> A child in the dark, gripped with fear, comforts himself by singing under his breath. He walks and halts to his song. Lost, he takes shelter, or orients himself with his little song as best he can. The song is like a rough sketch of a calming and stabilizing, calm and stable, center in the heart of chaos. Perhaps the child skips as he sings, hastens or slows his pace. But the song itself is already a skip: it jumps from chaos to the beginnings of order in chaos and is in danger of breaking apart at any moment. There is always sonority in Ariadne's thread. Or the song of Orpheus.
>
> (1987: 311)

This "danger of breaking apart any moment" defines the re-versing of noise in these rhythms or skips of language fashioned out of chaos. The sonority traced in the thread out of the maze is a sonority already inhabited by the terror and fear of the unknown. The Latin grammar book, the unforgotten advertisement, the repeated prayer: these little, magical writings in the heart produce new origins and centers against a dissipated listening to noise. To re-verse is to trace a thread of old sound under new conditions—and to hear that trace fold into and out of the noise.

Counterattack

Rather than seeking a way to contain or represent a reality beyond reckoning, the poets of the Western Front reproduce both the microcosmic world-making effects of the remembered rhythm and the communicative gap—the nonce "something" or the silence—that reflects how old forms, rather than *mediating* noise, were mediated *by* noise. They reflect a poetry that, like the soldier that returns from the front in Walter Benjamin's "The Storyteller," is "not richer but poorer in communicable experience" (1968: 84). This reduction in experience was a product of violence, and many combatants and noncombatants experienced traumatic somatic, psychological, and linguistic reactions to the noise of war. As the historian Hillel Schwartz puts it, "the noise of the Great War was too great not to be visceral" (2011: 573). This visceral power directly contributed to the manifold psychological and somatic symptoms of shell shock. While the strategies of self-presencing mentioned above might have worked briefly for some soldiers, shell shock marked psychological and linguistic defenses that became "pathological." Temporary deafness, mutism, and paralysis were common symptoms. These psychological and physical effects denied the possibility of self-mastery or ordering—even through the microcosmic fictions of remembered rhythms.

To accept the therapeutic effects of poetry in the wake of war experience is also to emphasize its continuation and approximation of the trauma it seeks to heal. Siegfried Sassoon and Wilfred Owen, two of the most canonized soldier poets of the war, met in the Craiglockhart Military Hospital while convalescing from symptoms of shell shock. Their poetry was considered therapeutic by their doctors not only for its representational aspects but even more for its rhythmic entrainment. Through their poetic therapy, these officer-poets could recreate a "functional relation to time's movement through writing poetry" (Martin 2012: 171). They could reorient themselves within what Meredith Martin calls the "military metrical complex," a system that developed in the late nineteenth century, in which "military drill and metrical drill [were] established as counterparts" in order to discipline and nationalize English bodies (Martin 2012: 150). The meters of the soldier poets represent an ambivalence toward this metrical complex: meter may counteract the trauma of noise, but it becomes relativized and weakened through this mediation. Rhythms of self-mastery and temporal reorientation represent a form of sound sense working in the shadow of the haptic sounds of war. Approximation and digression—the fitful tactical magic of fragmented chant—work against the universalizing, strategic vision of metrical regularity.

Sassoon's "Repression of War Experience" from *Counter-Attack and Other Poems* (1918) produces a drama of neurasthenic passivity by enacting noise's violent rebuttal to the regularity of metrical movement. The mediation of sound in verse reproduces the soldier's dis-ease in the face of noise. A tension between the repressive regularity of traditional meter and a nerve-wracked listening plays out through the broken meters of the poem:

> You're quiet and peaceful, summering safe at home;
> You'd never think there was a bloody war on! …
> O yes, you would … why, you can hear the guns.
> Hark! Thud, thud, thud,—quite soft … they never cease
> Those whispering guns—O Christ, I want to go out
> And screech at them to stop—I'm going crazy;
> I'm going stark, staring mad because of the guns.
>
> (Sassoon 1918: 52–3)

These lines, though one can scan them for the five accents of iambic pentameter, are filled with exaggerated pauses—marked by ellipses, dashes, and exclamation points—that undercut any ostensible act of "repression." The timing of ordered speech is jolted and interrupted, and remaining "quiet and peaceful" is possible neither for the soldier speaker nor for his addressee. The "whispering guns" "never cease" for either, and as with the ear-witness accounts above, noise moves outside of time. It is not "something" to be encountered and repressed. Instead, even in the whispering distance, it becomes an endless source of distress and continually fragments both thought and verse. Each dash following the ominous four beats of "Hark! thud, thud, thud" acts not as a closed parenthetical statement but rather as a paratactic addition—and dramatic escalation. The transformation of the voice from sardonic quietude to the "screech" that announces "I'm going stark, staring mad" attempts to match the voice of the poem with the noise of the guns. But the "screech" emanates from the breaks in the lines, from the quick movements out of the time of versified regularity and into the displacing temporality of noise.

Though the freedom in versification attained here may be possible in traditional formal verse, the poem's counter-pattern of silence and its heaping up of paratactic intervention register—against the backdrop of the military metrical complex—a bodily and sonic revolt conditioned by the broken continuity of noise. This oxymoronic situation, in which "you only hear the noise when you listen" (Barbusse 1917: 6) and where it remains ever-present even in the "inaudible-audible," becomes the basis for the spastic movements of verse form as a figure of sound. By moving between the time of represented speech and the ceaselessness of noise, the poem indexes the instability of a figure of voice in relation to disfiguring noise. The fragmented, distraught figure of voice, situated in dramatic dialogue with a "you" that is and is not the "I," comes to figure noise as an effect, as reverberation within the verse. The listening—"Hark!"—that the poem demands remains simultaneously impossible and necessary.

Yopie Prins has called Victorian meters a kind of "acoustic device" for the mediation of a "voice inverse:" that is, "voice" imagined as a mobile metaphor indebted to material transformations in print, phonography, metrical form, and performance (Prins 2004: 47). The "voice inverse" that would "re-verse" noise calls into question the nature of this inverted voice. Verse sound forms that would produce a voice or a self against noise—as performed by soldiers in moments of critical fear and by poet-soldiers in moments of "tranquil" recollection—simply become one more noise among noises. Noise emerges in the negative space of a figure of voice torn between magical act, therapeutic protection, and public address. Patrick Deer suggests that these poets had to work through a poetic "double vision:" "the outrage that comes from being blinkered and trapped in the trenches, together with a desperate sense of speaking to, and for, a nation" (2009: 30). This double vision is also a double listening, a listening to a speech organized for and by a state-sanctioned version of self, and a listening to noise that undoes the measured rationales of time-keeping and sense-making.

Against Ritual

In remaking verse within noise, these poets simultaneously awaken and undo the ritual effects of the repetitive power of formal and metrical order. Wilfred Owen's sonnet, "Anthem for a Doomed Youth," ironizes the conventional acceptance of national sacrifice by systematically transforming funeral rites into the "the monstrous" sounds of war:

> What passing-bells for these who die as cattle?
> –Only the monstrous anger of the guns.
> Only the stuttering rifles' rapid rattle
> Can patter out their hasty orisons.
> No mockeries now for them; no prayers nor bells;
> Nor any voice of mourning save the choirs,
> The shrill, demented choirs of wailing shells;
> And bugles calling for them from sad shires.
>
> (Owen 1985: 76)

In the first eight lines, Owen transmits the anxiety around noise through various sonic orders: the displaced sounds of traditional funeral rites and the sonic disruptions embedded in the sonnet's form. The passing bells and choirs, ritual sounds that occupy the acoustic space of a mourning congregation, warn of human fragility and mortality, but in a purely formal, conventional way. This acoustic order becomes a "mockery," emptied of content by the power of noise. The "voice of mourning" transforms into the repeated "choirs," first presented as a possible collection of voices but then revealed as the "shrill, demented choirs of wailing shells."

These non-mourning non-voices are paralleled in the effects that register stutters and breaks, as in Sassoon's work. While Sassoon breaks open the pentameter line with pauses, Owen subtly uses foot substitutions and alliteration—as in "Only the stuttering rifles' rapid rattle"—in order to create, against the standard of iambic pentameter, a sense of reversal and stuttering movement forward. In addition to foot substitutions that transform the iambic norm, Owen also uses many sound figures—assonance and consonance along with rhyme—that create a counteracting excess in the lines. Three patterns in the first quatrain—the alliteration of "rifles's rapid rattle," the consonant "t" sounds in "cattle," "stuttering," "rattle," "patter," or the movement between "st" and "r" sounds in words like "monstrous," "stuttering," "rifles," "hasty orisons,"—create a movement of sound in the poem that resists the forward motion of narrative and the resolution of mourning. These sounds hold language in check and place it in the ironic shadow of noise.

The metaphoric displacement of funeral choirs and the cross-patterning of sound figures enact a general disfiguration of a "voice of mourning." The poem's "voice" remains distant. It does not speak an elegy per se but rather describes conditions of non-elegy. Resituating the funeral in the soundscape of the trenches places the sonnet into an antisocial rather than ameliorative sound world. Sound form does not order so much as disorder experience. This detachment of language sounds from their (proper) sense by imagining them within an environment of noise also functions at the level of grammar. Through a consistent use of substitution and restatement, Owen creates a stutter that affects even the descriptive powers of the poem. The poem begins with a question, and "—Only the monstrous anger of the guns" answers. The anaphora of the following line—"Only the stuttering rifles' rapid rattle"—ties it to that initial answer, even as it begins a new metaphoric statement: "Can patter out their hasty orisons." And "choirs" in the second quatrain, as we have already noticed, is presented as if it could be the choirs of funeral singing—only to be remade through a belliphonic substitution. These restatements shift the metaphoric register, but the repetition also delays any sense of forward movement or transformation in the poem.

All these figures—sound symbol and sonic excess, metaphoric displacement, the static movement of restatement—undergird the final sestet of the poem, which emphasizes the limited, belated, and ineffectual response of any would-be "voice of mourning" as well as of the poet himself. The predominant sense of a moving stasis parallels the complicated double movement of anthropomorphism in the text. As the mechanical sounds of war take on a life of their own, human life is made more mechanical:

> What candles may be held to speed them all?
> Not in the hands of boys, but in their eyes
> Shall shine the holy glimmers of goodbyes.
> The pallor of girls' brows shall be their pall;
> Their flowers the tenderness of patient minds,
> And each slow dusk a drawing-down of blinds.
>
> (Owen 1985: 76)

Though these lines do not register belliphonic sounds, they reproduce the effects of noise by cutting away the traditional movements and meanings of funerary ritual and replacing them with images that remain outside of the artifice of the funeral. Dead boys' eyes, girls' pallor, "patient minds," and the "drawing-down of blinds" become the new signifiers of a ritual goodbye. These images emphasize glassy stillness, a bodily reaction to sadness ("pallor"), patient or suffering minds, and the automatism of the "drawing-down of blinds." Bodies here respond only through flesh and habit, not through speech or symbol. This automatism also parallels the effects of silence at work in the poem. The contrast in the movement from funeral sounds to funeral objects—candles, palls, and flowers—emphasizes the poet's silence: rather than acting as elegist, he can only report these small acts of non-mourning. Seemingly untouched by the "mockeries" of social and conventionalized meaning, these images are fragments of human life left by the scouring effects of noise.

In this melancholic order of sound, noise forecloses the possibility of ritual narration through a mourning voice. In the midst of the "supernatural tumult," representation turns away toward the magical order of ritual only to find it demystified, a mockery, a collection of empty sounds. And yet the poet must go on telling, saying, writing, repeating, chanting. This is both for himself—as a form of survival and therapy—and for his ambivalent status as "war poet:" one who simultaneously represents and rejects "the nation." In both of these situations, words are not for communication. As a defense, words are reduced to a means of ordering experience against noise, and in a poetics of witness, words fail in the midst of an incommunicable experience. In the gap between communication and experience, only an affective, even automatic, response can emerge.

The "pity of war" depends, then, on breaks and silences. The artifice of fixed poetic forms emphasizes these gaps. While Owen and Sassoon (along with other combatant poets) use ordering conventions that should elide and naturalize the space between represented voice and listening audience, they also disintegrate convention by referring it to noise. In listening again to verse with ears affected by noise, they produce work that is suffused with the protective, world-making effects of rhythmic order and a formal irony that undercuts old forms of making sense by listening to and through the fixed order of verse. Their reduced language is at odds with the powers of unisonance, public cohesion, and rhetorical triumph associated with the nationalized poetic forms that dominated the early years of the war.

Other Verses

The representation of belliphonic sounds in poetry certainly did not originate with these poets—one thinks of Tennyson's "Charge of the Light Brigade" or even the *Iliad*—but the process of enfolding noise within language has changed. As poets working within the "military metrical complex" relativize its disciplinary grip—even as they use its ordering capacity for some therapeutic value—they are also expanding the range of the war zone and asking their audience to think within the "audible-inaudible" zone of listening. Because this zone demands either a cool desensitization—what Owen would call a "Dullness [that] best solves / the tease and doubt of shelling" (1985: 122)—or an ability to respond that can narrate the sound, transforming it into the sign of a threat, a warning, it becomes "one of the places where sound, listening, and ethics are most tightly intertwined" (Daughty 2015: 79). This responsibility of the listener/audience depends upon the noisy lack or absence written into the sound space of the poem. A story must be formed, and yet that story remains other, unassimilable— not only for the poet's audience but for the poet as well.

This projection of noise into the space between words is also at work in poetic sound forms that do not fit into the military metrical complex. The American writer and nurse Mary Borden—who had paid for and staffed a military hospital directly behind the trenches of the French army—wrote poems at the front, three of which were published in the *English Review* in 1917 under the title "At the Somme." They were subsequently republished along with her collection of prose stories, *The Forbidden Zone*, in 1929. These poems, indebted to the paratactic expansiveness of Walt Whitman, use a free verse form connected by anaphora and long lists. In "The Song of the Mud," the poet imagines an all-encompassing mud—as "the disguise of the war zone" and "mantle of battles" (192)—that can stop the war:

> This is the song of the mud that wriggles its way into battle.
> The impertinent, the intrusive, the ubiquitous, the unwelcome,
> The slimy inveterate nuisance,
> That fills the trenches,
> That mixes in with the food of the soldiers,
> That spoils the working of motors and crawls into their secret parts.
> That spreads itself over the guns,
> That sucks the guns down and holds them fast in its slimy voluminous lips,
> That has no respect for destruction and muzzles the bursting shells;
> And slowly, softly, easily,
> Soaks up the fire, the noise; soaks up the energy and the courage;
> Soaks up the power of armies;
> Soaks up the battle.
> Just soaks up and thus stops it.
>
> (Borden 1930: 191)

The dampening effects of mud—its power to soak up "energy," "fire," and "noise"—make it into a kind of magical double of noise. The long, unfolding lines maintain a sense of movement and energy, even of desperation, as the fantasy played out in the poem speaks—the mud "just soaks up [the battle] and thus stops it"—to the magical thinking of form. For the repeated incantation "this is the song of the mud" and the anaphoric repetitions weave together the disparate terrors of the battlefield. The front-loaded pulse of the anaphoric lines simultaneously tells of the expansive chaos of the war zone and draws it into the liquid, flowing artifice of the poem. Noise, fire, power, battle, all fall into the "slowly, softly, easily" moving mud. Mud remains ambivalent, is both "war and the cessation of war" (McLoughlin 2015: 233), and it contains an erotic, sensual undercurrent that contrasts with other poets' images of dead and mangled bodies on the front. The song of the mud—a song about mud, a song sung by mud, and a song to the mud—maintains a distance from noise. Mud—and this chanted song—defuses, undoes, and reverses noise. Even as it sucks noise into its formal embrace, it also pronounces the possibility of language to demand a stop: "Just soaks it up, and thus stops it."

In this relationship to noise—as a demand to stop—the lines contain not only an image of muddy, formless form but also a desperate sense of onrushing violence and unstoppability. In her stories, Borden uses "rhythmic and rhetorical repetition to convey the pulsing energy of her environment and the frantic logic of war" (Lambrecht 2017: n.p.), and this sense of repetition is magnified in the anaphoric lines of "The Song of the Mud." For in this constant movement and return between syntactic order and an excess of actions and adjectives, Borden attempts to make a form adequate to the ethical demands of the audible-inaudible figure of noise. She writes not only the mud she sees but also the noise she hears and wants, emphatically, to stop.

Borden is invested in translating the confusion and fragmentation of noise into a song that moves between the transparency of prose and the obscurity of verse. Influenced by Gertrude Stein and connected with avant-garde writers like Ford Madox Ford and Wyndham Lewis, Borden's clipped prose represents pain and death in ways that contemporary reviewers found excessive. In "Moonlight," she describes a soldier's death in the midst of noise:

> Now the monstrous mistress that he has taken to his bed has got him, but soon he will escape. He will go to sleep in her arms lulled by the lullaby of the pounding guns that he and I are used to, and then in his sleep the Angel will come and his soul will slip away. It will run lightly over the whispering grasses and murmuring trees. It will leap through the velvety dark that is tufted with the soft concussion of distant shells bursting from the mouths of cannon. It will fly up through the showery flares and shooting rockets past the moon into Heaven. I know this is true. I know it must be true.
>
> (Borden 1930: 60)

The "lullaby of the pounding guns that he and I are used to" undoes the gendered distinctions between combatants and non-combatants in the expansive "forbidden zone" of war. Here, all listening bodies feel themselves in relation to this otherworldly noise. As in the poem, the anaphoric repetition of "It will" weaves together the many individual belliphonic sounds into a "lullaby" of noise. Noise transforms into sublimated threat, but its effects create a stutter that aligns with Owen's repetitions and redescriptions. The stutter of the last two sentences emphasizes a hope that, in its need for desperate reaffirmation, seems all the more distant.

For an ear-witness like Borden, poetry's fantastic powers expanded just as the totality of the war—and the body's passivity in relation to it—became all the more overwhelming. Noise subtended every moment of utter waste, loss, and death. If "the Great War saw no consensus over how best to represent the 'reality of war', unleashing instead a symbolic battle over how to represent the totality of the conflict" (Deer 2009: 48), Borden and other poets could reimagine poetic sound in order to "un-represent" or undo the war. The work of translating the "sense-experience of the trenches" through the "sensuousness of poetic form" into the "tissue of language" (Das 2006: 30) depended not upon any single strategy of representation but rather upon a constantly shifting relationship between poetic artifice and testimonial naivety, which embedded an ambivalent relationship to the powers of poetry to address and affect a public outside of the trenches. And yet at the same time, these war poets use the mediated but visceral effects of poetic sound not so much to mirror reality as to work in a fantasy space opened up by noise, where the dream of a possible silence, a possible effect, translates into the momentary effects of organized language. These poets take part not in the transformation of noise into poetry but in the transmutation of poetry in contact with noise.

The work of the private soldier, Isaac Rosenberg, also finds its form outside of the disciplinary strictures of the "military metrical complex." Rosenberg, like Sassoon, was of Jewish descent, but—unlike the upper-class officer-poet—he grew up in the East End. With "little education," in which "[n]obody ever told me what to read, or ever put poetry in my way" (Rosenberg 1979: 52), Rosenberg became an artist and poet who moved between "the Jewish community with its radical politics and … English authoritarian structures" represented by the writer and politician Edward Marsh (Das 2006: 90). In his poetry, the link between poetic form and noise undergoes another variation, as he uses rhythms in a free verse that refuses either the regular metrical orders of Sassoon or Owen or the anaphoric repetitions of Borden's long lines. Rosenberg's "Break of Day in the Trenches" (from 1916) figures noise's disorientation of time by representing an encounter with a "queer sardonic rat" that interrupts and breaks up the "same old Druid Time:"

> The darkness crumbles away.
> It is the same old Druid Time as ever.
> Only a live thing leaps my hand,
> A queer sardonic rat,
> As I pull the parapet's poppy

> To stick behind my ear.
> Droll rat, they would shoot you if they knew
> Your cosmopolitan sympathies.
> Now you have touched this English hand
> You will do the same to a German
> Soon, no doubt, if it be your pleasure
> To cross the sleeping green between.
> …
> What do you see in our eyes
> At the shrieking iron and flame
> Hurl'd through still heavens?
> What quaver—what heart aghast?
> Poppies whose roots are in man's veins
> Drop, and are ever dropping,
> But mine in my ear is safe—
> Just a little white with the dust.
>
> (Rosenberg 1979: 103)

The rat, a parasite living in no-man's-land, was already a racist trope for Jewish cosmopolitanism and "rootlessness," and Rosenberg is playing with and against that modernist figure (Das 2006: 97). But the apostrophe to the "droll rat" also establishes the animal as a witness to the voicing of the poet. It is the condition for the poet's voice to take off despite his straitened and contained position behind the parapet. The parasite, the rat feeding off the wastage of war, grounds the lyric voice. The questions asked of the rat—"What do you see in our eyes / At the shrieking of iron and flame / Hurl'd through still heavens? / What quaver—what heart aghast?"—mark it as an element in a circuit of seeing that deflects what is actually seen or felt in the "quaver" or the "heart aghast." The rat—off to the side, a para-site—knows the effects of "shrieking iron and flame," but that reality remains unspoken. It is only initiated in a question with no response.

In its silence and indifference, the rat reflects the poet's own struggle to speak. The voice cannot tell the truth of the "hearts aghast" but rather indicates the absurd image of the poppy, "just a little white with the dust." The poppy—already by this time freighted with the symbolic power of the poppy fields in Robert Bridges's "Flanders Fields"—"is safe" only in a limited sense: its safety is in dramatic contrast to the dead bodies from which it grows. Rather than the poppy occupying the space of rebirth or perennial reminder, it becomes a way for the poet to turn away from the dead.

The poem's representation of this encounter with the rat does not simply function to lift up the poet's prophetic voice, as in the classic lyric apostrophe described by Jonathan Culler (Culler 1981: 139). If the Western wind grants an occasion for the flight of Shelley's voice, here the rat eats away at that poetic artifice. It inhabits and proliferates within the metaphor of voice. This identification of the poet and rat reflects the poem's interweaving of the non-language or silence of the rat with an attempt to speak the war's effects—to communicate the reality of noise. Figured as an anthropomorphic shriek, the guns here are not given over to representation but are merely facts or causes that then have effects on the faces, hearts, and bodies of those on the front. The rat, however, moves inside and outside of a space and time distorted by noise. It marks a reversal of the typical rhetorical flow of (imagined) addressee to addressor that defines the lyric as an event of voice. The rat appropriates this voice and marks its speech as absurd, invalid, and unauthoritative. Its "queer," "sardonic," and "droll" affects undo the language of the poem. In this sense, it becomes a counter-figure of noise. Like the mud in Borden's poem, the rat takes on the qualities of noise—its ubiquity and otherworldly "cosmopolitanism"—in order to show contact or contiguity with noise, not its description or representation.

As if to accentuate the usurpation of voice by noise, the varying free verse uses four-beat and three-beat lines that allude to but refrain from embodying a ballad form with its regular alternating movement of beats. Repetitions and irregular variations break up the communal rhythms of the ballad. Out of the collective, pluralized figure of a singing voice created by the metrical effects of the ballad tradition arises a sputtering temporality that moves between ritualistic incantation ("The darkness crumbles away") and chatty dialogue ("Droll rat, they would shoot you if they knew"). The play of rhythmic effects displays neither a mastery over contingency nor a safe continuation of poetic tradition. These rhythms accentuate the fiction of a control over time that poetic repetition pretends to enact. The gaps in rhythmic continuity suggest that the voice of the poem is only itself a fragmentary collection of movements, images, and statements. It cannot overwrite noise. Each rhythmic event refuses to congeal into song. The voice goes nowhere, undoes its own narrative, and looks out at the blankness and ubiquity of death.

In this poem, as in all the poems of witness discussed here, the rhetorical and metrical figuration of voice cannot simply "record" the blast of contemporary warfare. It can only produce—through its visceral encounter with noise—a warning that sounds both alarm and retreat. In Rosenberg's case, the poet questions the status of poetry to document, record, and narrate history, or even the historicity of its own speaking. Noise—as a shrieking index of danger and as a visceral excess—presented sense perception with an unaccountable and inhibiting encounter so that the "missives" of soldier-poets were neither a definitive report nor "mere verse." They register a dis- and re-membering of language in an attempt to translate the anxieties of ear-witnesses encountering a world of noise.

Reversing Noise

The reversals of noise that I have described in this chapter show the ways in which poets attempt to reimagine the stakes of poetic form in relation to a "noise" that is more than just the belliphonic sounds of war. Noise represents, for these writers and for those at the front more broadly, an audible-inaudible totality that breaks up continuities of time and space. The otherworldly, supernatural sound of noise demands a listening that is constituted not within the movements of rationalized time and the smooth order of cause and effect but rather in fragmentary breaks, where sound loses its epistemological value and becomes, rather, a violence filled with a preconscious threat. Paradoxically, noise represents death and violence and yet the very possibility of hearing it confirms life. Bringing the sensory disfiguration of noise into the timed space of the poem amplifies this disorientation and disjunction while simultaneously using verse— in its most basic repetitive, even automatic sense—to suture the familiar and yet desperately uncanny sounds of noise.

Jacques Attali defines noise as a violence, in particular a violation of a given acoustic order: an irruption of other sound in a given communal or conventional auditory situation (Attali 1985: 6). It is a simulacrum of murder. Noise marks the limits of social space and exists outside of acoustic order as such. For Attali—as well as for the Italian Futurists who were contemporaneous with the First World War poets—the catastrophe of noise makes the possibility of new social and semiotic orders possible. For the Futurists, war noise in particular promised new orders of human experience that could expand the human ear beyond the norms of the past. The trench poets, however, heard the collapse of a social world and an inhuman distance within noise. In this way, the implicit sonic epistemologies of these poets fit into a trend in early twentieth-century philosophy, psychology, and physiology, by which the rhythmic movement of music or poetry "ceases to be a medium through which the listening individual constitutes itself as a substantive subject, [rather] the listener takes on the intermediary qualities of a medium" (Erlmann 2010: 283). Rather than making an "Art of Noises" that celebrated the triumph of the individual subject to take in, regulate, and mimic noise, they became lost in a way that carried into their work what was therapeutic, traumatized, and resistant. To take up the terms from Veit Erlmann's work on acoustic epistemology *Reason and Resonance*, these poets violently resonate with noise as a percussive, concussive excess that stands against reason and its implications of distance, ordered time, substance, and clarity (2010: 342). The atmosphere of noise conditioned by a world of random and futile death preceded and exceeded any warning that a soldier might hear or that a poet might give in verse. And yet these poets persisted in translating this futile "truth." They continued to listen to the noise and to make this listening known.

2

Dada Bruitism and the Body

The English war poets made verse with patterns and rhythms that self-consciously failed to figure the sonic experience of noise. Dadaist poets and performers, in contrast, figured noise as a possibility and a necessity: they sought to make poetic sound in excess of language. And yet, for the Dadaists I take up in this chapter, noise is not an inexpressible "outside" that language can only attempt to represent. It is rather a negating flow of sound emerging from processes of representation, performance, and life. In this way, Dadaist noise explicitly critiques language convention as a form of power linked to rampant nationalism and total war. Hugo Ball, one of the founders and central figures in Dadaism in Zurich, Switzerland, succinctly phrases this critique in a diary entry from 1915: "If language really makes us kings of our nation, then without doubt it is we, the poets and thinkers, who are to blame for this blood bath and who have to atone for it" (Ball 1996 [1927]: 29). Noise becomes the means of this atonement.

In this chapter, I will describe the work of the central members of the Dadaist movement in Zurich—Ball, Emmy Hennings, Tristan Tzara, Richard Huelsenbeck, Marcel Janco, and Hans Arp—in relation to their figuration of noise as sound that responds to and corresponds with a reality outside of language, a life outside of art. Tzara, writing on Huelsenbeck's book of poetry *Fantastic Prayers*, describes the power of noise to emerge out of its representation: "The representation of noise sometimes really, objectively becomes noise, and the grotesque takes on the proportions of disconnected, chaotic phrases" (Tzara 1977: 73). The avant-garde desire to collapse art and life—to distend the "inside" of art with different unprocessed materials "outside" of its expected practices and genres—manifests in the act of making noise. Noise begins to undo the divisions between beauty and "the grotesque" and between order and chaos.

This collapse primarily figures in the Dadaist reduction of language to "disconnected, chaotic phrases" and an expansion of sound poetry. They organized mouth sounds in opposition to conventional signification. Newly constructed forms like Ball's "verse without words" and Tzara's simultaneous poetry effect a transformation of words into sound. These radical formal experiments spring from Zurich Dada's emphasis upon performance in the Cabaret Voltaire, where Hennings sang protest songs in an enervating and aggressive style and where a theatrical bruitism (or "noise-ism") reigned. For Huelsenbeck, "bruitism is life itself, it cannot be judged like a book, but rather it is a part of our personality, which attacks us, pursues us and tears us to pieces" (Huelsenbeck 1951 [1920a]: 26). This connection of bruitism and life suggests an ambivalent relation between "personality" and noise. Noise is both inside of and violently in opposition to personality.

In this way, subjectivity is consistently made other to itself, and the human figure is abstracted, negated, and masked:

> The image of the human form is gradually disappearing from the painting of these times and all objects appear only in fragments. This is one more proof of how ugly and worn the human countenance has become, and of how all the objects of our environment have become repulsive to us. The next step is for poetry to decide to do away with language for similar reasons. These are things that have probably never happened before.
>
> (Ball 1996 [1927]: 55)

To "do away with language" suggests that Ball's sense of Dadaist abstraction is not the ordering abstraction of numbers and music but rather a form of erasure and subtraction. In a variety of performances, printed poems, and manifestoes, the Dada bruitists erase or over-perform language in a way that emphasizes embodiment, chance, and interruption in order to create "a temporary relief" from "the ugly and worn human countenance." They sought to "[o]ppose world systems and acts of state by transforming them into a phrase or a brush stroke" (Ball 1996 [1927]: 56).

The sonic abstraction in Dada performance typifies the wider Dadaist critique of and in language. Noise emerges as a "simulacrum of a semiosis" (McCaffery 1998: 164), the negative image of meaning-making. Such a simulating—which is also a dissimulating—distorts the social force of language by undoing its signifying conventions. The power of statement is reduced to mere sound and chance. In this way, the noise of Dada inserts a kind of nothing—a nothing filled with other sounds, the sonorousness of life—into meaning, rationality, and beauty. As Ball alludes to in his search for "atonement," the Dadaists take to task the Shelleyean cliché that poets are "legislators of the world." Poetry fails when it meets with destructive modernity. A causal connection between "rational" language and total war provides Ball and other Dadaists with the impetus for a total revaluation of language as such. In the act of negating meaning and rationality, they also reveal them to be versions of noise: mere nothing sounds. Tristan Tzara in 1918 sums up this movement of language into noise:

> If I cry out:
> *Ideal, ideal, ideal,*
> *Knowledge, knowledge, knowledge,*
> *Boomboom, boomboom, boomboom,*
>
> I have given a pretty faithful vision of progress, law, morality, and all other fine qualities that various highly intelligent men have discussed in so many books, only to conclude that after all everyone dances to his own personal boomboom.
> ("Dada Manifesto" [1918] in Motherwell 1951)

The desire to escape such language of the "ideal" and of "knowledge" by refiguring it as a resounding "boomboom" drives the bruitist poetics of Dada.

"The Thought Is Made in the Mouth"

This oppositional urge marked the Dadaist synthesis of other European avant-garde movements, in particular Italian Futurism and German Expressionism, with forms of popular cabaret, American mass culture, and (secondhand) African and Oceanic poetry. Dadaist internationalism and eclecticism strongly informed their critical stance toward modernity. Its initial milieu was the bars, galleries, and theaters frequented by an international set who were in neutral Zurich to avoid military service, work in the black market, or simply escape from the nationalism and jingoism in their home countries. Other famous residents at the time included Vladimir Lenin and James Joyce. During and after the war, the Dadaists—in particular Tzara—began to construct an international network of associates by sharing journals and pamphlets through the mail. Many artists took up the challenge of Dada in Europe, America, Japan, and across the globe.

But before this networked spread of a globalized Dada—aided, as we will see in the next chapter, by the word-sound "dada" itself—the Dadaists in Zurich synthesized a new noise. The "boomboom" that obliterates idealism and exchanges it for rhythmic movement characterizes the performance aesthetics of the Dadaist cabaret in Zurich. Rhythm and performance emphasized the body and the event over the seeming permanence of text. Tzara placed thought thoroughly in the realm of the body: "The thought is made in the mouth" (1977: 87). Hugo Ball made rhythm an oppositional aesthetic project: "Adopt symmetries and rhythms instead of principles. Oppose world systems and acts of state by transforming them into a phrase or a brush stroke" (1996 [1927]: 57). The site of this initial emphasis upon performance was the Cabaret Voltaire, where the "the ideals of culture and art [became] a program for a variety show;" this was the Zurich group's "*Candide* against the times" (Ball 1996 [1927]: 67).

Dada, then, did not begin with a manifesto but rather a public announcement for "artistic entertainment:"

> Cabaret Voltaire. Under this name a group of young artists and writers has been formed whose aim is to create a center for artistic entertainment. The idea of the cabaret will be that guest artists will come and give musical performances and readings at the daily meetings. The young artists of Zurich, whatever their orientation, are invited to come along with suggestions and contributions of all kinds.
>
> (Ball 1996 [1927]: 325)

Inside this "center for artistic entertainment" where anyone "whatever their orientation" could be heard, a Russian balalaika orchestra would play one moment and a poet would recite the next. Hennings would sing folk songs or Ball would play ragtime music on the piano. This eclecticism already differentiated the Zurich cabaret from the cabarets like the Café Simplicissimus in Munich, where Ball and Hennings met. And it came to define the movement even beyond Zurich. Roman Jakobson (disapprovingly) observes this impulse toward mixing registers: "[T]he Dadaists are also eclectics, though theirs is not the museum-bound eclecticism of respectful veneration, but a motley *café chantant* program" (Jakobson 1987: 39).

Certainly, "respectful veneration" was far from the minds of the Dadaists, who were happy to exchange "ideals" for the "boomboom" of the variety show. This work of contrast and juxtaposition worked through the active collaboration of what Hans Richter called a "six-piece band," Ball, Hennings, Tzara, Huelsenbeck, the painter-performer Marcel Janco, and the painter-poet Hans Arp (Richter 1964: 27). Of this "band" retrospectively modeled on a jazz ensemble, Richter goes on: "Each played his instrument, i.e. himself, passionately and with all his soul" (Richter 1964: 27). This collective but individualized system allowed for frictions and tensions to develop between different genres, traditions, forms, and languages (as well as between personalities). The reduction of the self to an "instrument" valued a form of experiment outside of traditional instrumentality, in which a self is exalted by its mastery over an external tool. Rather, here, the instrumental self is produced through its friction with others and within itself, thus emphasizing the unsettling and the unreadable over the traditional and familiar. As Tzara reports, "It is only contrast that connects us with the past" (1951 [1918]: 78)—and, perhaps, to each other.

With contrast—and incoherence—already built into the programming, individual performances offered extremes of Tzara's "boomboom." Here is where Dada made its strongest claims as "a principle of pure energy which simply *is* rather than *means*" (Nicholls 1995: 228). Forms of sonic reduction and interruption—noise—enacted a desire for an "anti-philosophy of *spontaneous* acrobatics" (Tzara 1951 [1919]: 82). Huelsenbeck "reads, accompanied by the big drum, shouts, whistles, laughter" (Ball 1996 [1927]: 56). He would also drum and chant "umba" in a parodic fantasy of "Negro" song. Tzara's "Zurich Chronicle" notes some of the sonic intensity: " ... DADA! Latest novelty!!! Bourgeois syncope, BRUITIST music, latest rage, song Tzara dance protests— the big drum—red light, policemen—songs ... " (1951 [1920]: 235). As Tzara's paratactic list of people, events, and objects shows, the song and dance of a variety show seamlessly weaves with the noise of "pure energy" or "spontaneous acrobatics."

In this way, the Dadaists worked to undo any distinction between the embodied mouths emitting songs and poems and the noise of bruitist sound, drums, and life. The body becomes another source of the noise "outside" art. The performance work of Hennings particularly focused this abstraction of mouth sound through the transfiguration of thought into mouth, word into noise. As the most well-known performer of the group, and as the acknowledged "star of the cabaret" (Ball 1996 [1927]: 63), Hennings "provided a distinctive contribution, one that constituted a vital bridge between the experimental artistic forum and the more popular cabaret forum, between writer and audience" (Hemus 2009: 34). She sang and recited her own poetry, popular songs, folk songs, and protest songs composed by Ball. It was as a performer— as an embodied interpreter of songs, music, poetry, and performance—that Hennings created a mediating position between language and noise.

Though her voice and her body were on display and at the center of the cabaret, Hennings also performed with an intensity that could "affront" an audience:

> As the only woman in this cabaret manned by poets and painters, Emmy supplied a very necessary note to the proceedings, although (or even because) her performances were not artistic in the traditional sense, either vocally or as interpretations. Their unaccustomed shrillness was an affront to the audience, and perturbed it quite as much as did the provocations of her male colleagues.
>
> (Richter 1964: 27)

Hennings's "shrillness" and seeming lack of art "in a traditional sense" show her realizing a new performance aesthetic in the midst of Dada. Other comments on her voice (by male observers) emphasize a quality of childishness and weakness: it as "thin, anti-diva-ish," "unrefined, youthful," and so "meager and boyish that we sometimes had the feeling it might break at any moment" (Richter 1964: 20; Huelsenbeck 1991 [1969]: 16). At the same time the Zurich newspaper that described Hennings as a star also described her performing her songs with "a body only slightly ravaged by grief" (quoted in Ball 1996 [1927]: 63).

The clear sexism in these subordinating descriptions of her performances—and in the general lack of attention to her contributions in the many Dada memoirs written by male participants—may be counteracted by recognizing in these descriptions a dialectic between weak and strong, song and noise, which Hennings manifested in her performances. In gathering together the traces of her performance style, we can imagine the ways in which she put this dialectic to work in the cabaret—and how she subverted the cabaret tradition from which she came. If she created a persona that seemed at risk and unprotected—on the very edge of silence, or of an overwhelming noise that could overtake her at any moment—she also could attack, disturb, and activate the audience:

> Emmy recited [a poem against war and murderous insanity], Hugo accompanied her on the piano, and the audience chimed in, with a growl, murdering the poem[s].
>
> ...
>
> [Emmy's] songs created the "intimate" atmosphere of the cabaret. The audience liked listening to them, the distance between us and the enemy grew smaller, and finally everyone joined in.
>
> ...
>
> She sang Hugo Ball's aggressive songs with an anger we had to credit her with although we scarcely thought her capable of it. Was this a child disseminating anti-war propaganda?
>
> (Huelsenbeck 1969: 10, 16)

These effects of Hennings's singing reveal a relationship of call and response, in which the singer's performance simultaneously draws in and alienates her audience. This alienation was particularly heightened by the fact that she was a well-known female performer:

> Hennings accompanied her singing with bizarre gestures and body movements, the combination of aural and visual effects heightening the audience's uneasiness. It may be that her approach was not only as perturbing as that of her male colleagues but even more so, given her status as an admired, female performer who subverted expectations of popular accomplished performance.
>
> (Hemus 2009: 28)

Hennings, then, broke away from a tradition of cabaret singing in which the singer was to occupy her theatrical role in the song and seduce her audience.

However, this was a complex rejection of tradition. For Hennings's work seems to adhere to an "atmospheric" tradition of singing made popular by other well-known performers like Yvette Guilbert. In a singing manual from 1918 Guilbert describes this tradition as the "supreme act of coloring" by which the singer employs different vocal techniques to create a "series of voices" (Guilbert 1918: 4–7). The singer must have "multiple powers, multiple colors, multiple voices" (Guilbert 1918: 4). In addition, Guilbert describes how "the words are nothing but an accessory" to a total performative effect (1918: 22). For the cabaret singer or *diseuse*, language's construction in the body—as a total visual and auditory emitter—becomes primary because the singer combines heterogenous techniques from opera, theater, and popular song to express the text of each song or poem performed. For Guilbert, who had no formal training, the singer's technique must not be "uniform" like an operatic artist, but multiply voiced. It must give a total "atmospheric" effect.

This emphasis upon reception and adaptation rather than normative technique is an important principle that Hennings brought to the Zurich cabaret and Dada, but at the same time, Hennings's "shrill" performances did not emphasize a theatrical fiction or escape from reality. The mask of performance was hardened and abstracted, disconnected. In a poem entitled "Maybe the Last Flight" printed in *Cabaret Voltaire*, the first collection of Dadaist poems and visual art, Hennings creates a dialogue between a man and woman in which the dynamics of seeing, being seen and performing come to the fore. As the man speaks of a desire "to look at you. Keep looking at you," the woman (with the parenthetical performance directions "slowly and with drawn out voice") replies, "I think one / should never look closely" (Hennings 2006 [1916]: 26).

After the couple consummate their strange, narratively incoherent relationship and leave each other, the poem ends with a later chance encounter where "she died because she felt watched" (Hennings 2006 ([1916]): 26). Hennings's performances parallel this questioning of the male gaze—and the male listening ear. She challenged the dramatic transparency and relations of desire that seemed part of the escapist fiction of traditional cabaret. Hennings intensified the mask of the performer and the figure of a body as a form for her own escape rather than that of her audience. Her "shrill" or "thin" voice pushed the boundaries of language and of the limits of her body. She demanded an active response from her listeners rather than a passive consumption of her image. In this way she sought to activate in her voice a "concept of grasping life in art without any detour via the intellect" (Hennings, quoted in Hemus 2009: 27).

This "grasping for life in art" involved the amplification of noises in life. Peter Middleton describes the typical poetry recital as a site where "[m]eaning arises out of the noise of the lifeworld, both as sign and other materially intelligible forms of order and significance" (Middleton 2005: 31). Here, rather than meaning rising out of the lifeworld, the alienating recitation amplifies and focuses the noisy, bodily emanations of a lifeworld turned upside down. Hennings's performances provided a way of abstracting the female body out of a social world of desire and into a floating and random world of insignificance and disorder. In this way, the body connects with noise as another noise emitter among noises, an assemblage of purely accidental causes. Hennings, a maker of puppets, describes automatism in these terms:

> When man lives, acts, he is an automaton, a doll, yet how sensitive he is as a doll. We were puppets and God was like a child who held us by the strings, making us play according to his whims. It was difficult, not being allowed to disappear from the scene.
>
> (quoted in Hemus 2009: 51)

Caught between machinic automatization and its enabling language, the body emits mouth sounds in the grain of the lifeworld rather than as meanings and orders that separate from it.

Bruitism and the Simultaneous Poem

In the alliance of noise with the automaton body, however, the Dadaists were not simply naive vitalists. Life was inextricably caught up with an apocalyptic sense of modernity. Ball read Marcel Janco's abstract masks—inspired by African and Oceanic models—as a way to make "the horror of our time, the paralyzing background of events ... visible" (Ball 1996 [1927]: 65). The mask of the performing voice makes audible this same background. Huelsenbeck, perhaps the most exuberant performer and theorist of bruitism in Dada, wanted to bring life "unmodified" directly into art. He describes life as "a simultaneous muddle of noises, colors and spiritual rhythms, which is taken unmodified into Dadaist art, with all the sensational screams and fevers of its reckless everyday psyche and with all its brutal reality" (Huelsenbeck 1951 [1920b], 244). The bruitist poem carries the noise of life—its "brutal reality"—into the artwork.

The symbolic violence of the Dadaists came to the fore in their bruitist tactics. Huelsenbeck hears "the streetcar" as the quintessential subject of the bruitist poem:

THE BRUITIST POEM
represents a streetcar as it is, the essence of the streetcar with the yawning of Schulze the coupon clipper and screeching of the brakes.

(Huelsenbeck 1951 [1920b]: 244)

The streetcar calls to mind the screeching of metal on metal, but the noise poetics of Dada does not aspire to an "accurate" transport of the sound of the streetcar to the poem but rather attempts to capture the "essence" (an abstracting figure) of the streetcar: a kind of surprising, interruptive, loud, and modern sound.

Many Dadaist performances paralleled this "essence" of noise through sound acts that masked or overpowered reciting voices. Huelsenbeck famously wanted to "drum literature into the ground" (Ball 1996 [1927]: 51), and his performances in Zurich combined poetic declamation with the percussive "boom" of the big drum. He would also whip a cane through the air during performances of his poems (Ball 1996 [1927]: 56). This provocative gesture was only one among many, but it invited audience disruption in a way that (even if retrospectively exaggerated by the Dada memoirists) added to a sense of a breakdown between the expected sonic relations between audience and performer and between recitation and distraction. Similarly, Tzara's first performance in Paris, in January of 1920, involved him ironically reading a right wing parliamentarian's final speech while two co-conspirators (Andre Breton and Louis Aragon) rang bells loudly, drowning out his recitation (Sanouillet 2012: 105). Dadaist performances depended upon the discontinuity of purposeless, centrifugal sounds—misplaced bells and drums—to break the frames between song, poem, political speech, and the generalized, confused simultaneity of background sound.

The texts from Huelsenbeck and Tzara also trace this sense of bruitism as an interruptive flow or rhythm in the midst of recognizable (if still syntactically off-kilter) words. As printed, Huelsenbeck's *Phantastiche Gebete* (*Fantastic Prayers*) included nonsense sounds like "umbaliska" and "bumm Dadai" that interpose themselves in the midst of lists, declamations, and "fantastic" sentences (Huelsenbeck 1969: 62). Huelsenbeck was also well known for including his primitivist "umba umba" in the poems as printed and in the performances. These interpolations of drum beat and rhythmic nonsense work against any fixed, communicative value in language but they also have an "abstract, talismanic quality: as a manifestation of rhythm [that] is both irreducibly elemental and indefinitely polysemic in its significance, provisionally structuring through its pulses of energy the passage of time, but expressing nothing definable" (Gascoigne 2010: 199). Tzara also participates in this reduction of language to rhythm and noise in performances and texts like *La première aventure céléste de Mr. Antipyrine* (*The First Celestial Adventures of Mr. Fire-Extinguisher*) (1916). In this dramatic performance, characters like "Mr. Cricri" or "Pipi" often include nonsense syllables like "dzïn aha dzïn aha bobobo" or "zoumbaï zoumbaï," and at points in the play, the characters come together to perform these kinds of phonetic sounds simultaneously (Tzara 1916: 2–3).

These various sound tactics—words nonsensically associated interposed with pulses of phonetic energy—highlight the precarity and instability of the body and its speaking voice. As we have seen in the case of Hennings's performance style, abstraction sets the movements of the body within a lifeworld exterior to it. Huelsenbeck emphasizes that Dadaist culture is "above all of the body," a body filled by intuitions and instincts that do not follow from rational thought or ideological programming (Huelsenbeck 1951 [1920a]: 44). Dada's automatism (as opposed to its Surrealist successors) worked less in the uninhibited psychic realm and more in the body imagined as a material substrate for poetry, language, and thought. This animated material emits irrational noise as much as communicative speech. For Tzara, this body lived in "a tottering world in flight, betrothed to the glockenspiel of hell" (1951 [1918]: 78). Dada bruitism, then, follows from a scatological, irrational, spontaneous body, disconnected from the "human" as humanist, idealist enterprise but also "betrothed" to the "glockenspiel of hell"—a figure for the destructive sounds of modernity and the inherent noise of a language that "betroths" a subject to that destruction.

Tzara echoes Ball's desire to undo the relationship between language and the "bloodbath" of total war (Ball 1996 [1927]: 27). For the Dadaists, language and industrial warfare collapse into each other through a relationship of contiguity and causality. Implicit in every language act is a "yes" or "I'm here" that accedes to the situation of communication. Roman Jackobson calls this the "phatic" element in communication, a "physical channel and psychological connection between addressor and addressee" (Jakobson 1987: 66). Dadaist noise is the figure of a break in this "psychological connection" in favor of the "physical channel" alone. By not only disarticulating signifier from signified but by disarticulating language from sound, Dadaist poetry and performance reject the implicit "yes" of communication—which is imagined as a "yes" to the totality of modernity.

An important part of the mythology Dada created for itself and that grew up around it is a sense of the world historical forces that an individual mediates as both a representative of those forces and an anarchic actor against them. In his diaries, Ball imagines the artist as a medium for "the times:" "To confess their crimes, the times need a medium" (1996 [1927]: 78). What this medium does is not only caught up in the act of *doing* but also in *listening*: "perhaps it depends less on what one does than on where one has one's ears while doing it" (Ball 1996 [1927]: 78-9). Frequently, then, Dadaist activities are generalized and abstracted in order to challenge a generalizing and abstracting modernity. Of Huelsenbeck's poetry, Ball writes, "His poetry is an attempt to capture in a clear melody the totality of this unutterable age, with all its cracks and fissures, with all its wicked and lunatic genialities, with all its noise and hollow din" (1996 [1927]: 57). To locate one's ears away from language and toward sonorous life is also to remediate language as if from an "outside" of that language. If Dadaist sound poetry engages in a "simulacrum of a semiosis" (McCaffery 1998: 164), it both reduces language to mere sound and mirrors the sounds that move meaning from one place to another, from one speaker to one listener, from one nation to another, from the city to the front, from the ideologue's voice to the general's command to the gun's explosion. Noise emerges as the sonic effect of these conflicting and simultaneous movements of meaning and communication. Dada tries to hear this totality as if from the outside—even as it remains deeply embedded in its workings.

This is perhaps the most important contrast of Dadaist bruitism with the noise music and "words-in-freedom" of the Futurists. While the Dadaist use of bruitism is indebted to Italian Futurist experiments in noise music, it also implicitly critiques the Futurist aesthetic and uses different techniques for producing noise. For the Italian Futurists, noise is almost purely figured as the sounds of machines and urbanity, and Futurist noise music seeks a mimesis of these new sounds that will both destroy traditional music and renew music as a tradition. In the "Art of Noises," Russolo isolates and incorporates the sounds of modernity through classical musical systems (the staff and notation) and through new technologies—in particular the *intonorumori*, machines made specifically to create particular sounds: the gurgler, the whistler, etc. (Russolo 1986 [1913]: 75). Russolo claims that "noise is triumphant and reigns over the sensibility of men" (10), and the Futurist harnesses that power because machines "everywhere collaborate with man" (11). Noise, in the Futurist imaginary, is ultimately the very sound of modernity, and the Futurist attempts to harness such noise as auditory progress.

In contrast, Dadaist bruitism comes out of a sense of the subject's lack of control over modernity and of a sense of noise as a sonic figure for violence, interruption, irrationality, and destruction. As Richard Sheppard suggests, the Dadaist "experiments with various forms of bruitism were a simultaneous conjuration and critique of the violence of modernity, attempts not to imitate and celebrate but to enact discordant, chaotic, heteroglossic reality" (2000: 216). Figuring noise as part of a chaotic lifeworld rejects an auditory fantasy of transformation and renewal. Rather, it sounds out an inability to progress outside of sheer sonorousness, of the simultaneous muddle of a fractured totality. Rather than a temporality that looks to the future for the possible enfolding of noise into music, Dadaism refuses to look or listen ahead: "Dada; abolition of the future" (Tzara 1951(1918)). Its bruitism erupts within the simultaneity of a present moment, an enfolding and excessive totality of sound. Noise exists in the sheer weight of separate actions and objects happening together. It happens in the violent confrontation between the subject and its overwhelming inability to differentiate meaning from a muddled layering of organic, inorganic, machinic, linguistic, embodied, human, and non-human sounds (and more) that coincide at any particular moment.

Tristan Tzara's simultaneous poem, "L'Amiral cherche une maison a louer" ("The Admiral Is Looking for a House to Rent"), first performed on March 30, 1916 in the Cabaret Voltaire, inaugurated this negative form of bruitist experiment. Whereas previous versions of simultaneity (by poets like Apollinaire) figured poems in the context of radical visual practices like the multiplied perspective of cubist painting, Tzara's simultaneous poem employed a specific performance context. He literalizes the figure of simultaneity. As reprinted in *Cabaret Voltaire*, the poem is musically notated for three performers, each speaking a different language (Tzara in French, Marcel Janco in English, and Huelsenbeck in German), making different nonsense sounds ("shai," "uro," "hihi"), playing percussion (Huelsenbeck's "big drum" is there), or variously whistling and making other sounds. While each performer spoke or chanted in a recognizable tongue, their combined output results in a conflicting mass of sounds. The "accompaniment" of mouth sounds, crashes, sirens, and whistles limits content and overwhelms the human voice.

Ball, impressed by the performance, reads it as an allegory of voice and noise:

> [The simultaneous poem is] a contrapuntal recitative in which three or more voices speak, sing, whistle, etc., at the same time in such a way that the elegiac, humorous, or bizarre content of the piece is brought out by these combinations. In such a simultaneous poem, the willful quality of an organic work is given powerful expression, and so is its limitation by the accompaniment. Noises (an rrrrr drawn out for minutes, or crashes, or sirens, etc.) are superior to the human voice in energy.
>
> (Ball 1996 [1927]: 57)

The conflict in Ball's telling between the willful quality of an organic work and its limitation by the "accompaniment" becomes the basis for reimagining the relationship between a sonic figure (the voice) and ground (background noise):

> The "simultaneous poem" has to do with the value of the voice. The human organ represents the soul, the individuality in its wanderings with its demonic companions. The noises represent the background—the inarticulate, the disastrous, the decisive. The poem tries to elucidate the fact that man is swallowed up in the mechanistic process. In a typically compressed way it shows the conflict of the vox humana with a world that threatens, ensnares, and destroys it, a world whose rhythm and noise are ineluctable.
>
> (Ball 1996 [1927]: 57)

This allegory of voice and noise emphasizes in particular the undoing of the relationship between figure and ground taken for granted in poetic performance. The organic, abstract, and spiritualized voice is lost in two ways: it is lost in the "ineluctable" rhythm and noise, and it is lost to humans as a home or guide in the midst of noise.

In the performance, however, Tzara radically materializes the voice. It remains just "the human organ," an emitter of sounds on the blurry edge of meaning. It collapses into sheer physicality and is incorporated into noise. A mirror of the many languages spoken in Zurich at this time—as refugees from all over Europe escaped the war—"L'Amiral cherche pour un maison a louer" works against the differentiation of figure and ground, soul and body, content and form as well as between national languages. The poem enacts a kind of international cooperation while at the same time parodying it through the decay of meaning in simultaneity. The failure of language and of voice in the midst of noise remains ambivalent. Rather than a limited utterance in a single language for a single audience—and rather than a univocal utterance at the center of an auditory situation—the poem figures the social fact of language's circulation and dispersal within a sonorousness that threatens to destroy it and expand it at the same time. Or, to reverse these terms, the poem figures noise as both Ball's threatening background of mechanistic systems and as a force for life in the face of the overwhelming abstractions of convention, order, and rationality. Noise remains both threat and cure, a homeopathic remedy for undoing language's mad hold on human life.

Abstraction, Sound Poetry, and Noise

This ambivalence about the significance or use of noise is played out through the division between Ball and his younger comrades. Ball quit Dada early on in its history (in 1917) despite the fact that he was the driving force behind the group in its first year. Noise began to tire him. At first, Ball participated in the joys of noise. He wrote a bruitist "Nativity Play" with animal sounds, bells, and gongs playing alongside (and over) the recitation of the biblical text. After a few months of the cabaret, however, he was already growing tired of the eclectic performances: "For the first time I was ashamed of the noise of the performance, the mixture of styles and moods, things I have not physically endured for weeks" (Ball 1996 [1927]: 65). Ultimately, bruitism demanded a certain kind of physical, enervated endurance that Ball left behind when he left Zurich for the Swiss countryside. Even this move, however, reflects on the figurative ambivalence of noise as sign both of life and of death.

Ball's influential legacy as a maker of "sound poetry" or "verse without words" places him at the forefront of a poetics of noise, but the transformation of language into noise depended, for him, on a different form of abstraction than that of the simultaneous poem: he sought the reconstitution of a mystical logos, "the 'word' (logos) as a magical complex image" (Ball 1969 [1927]: 68). In the diary entry quoted at the beginning of this chapter, Ball speaks of abstracting or "doing away with" language in order to reveal its relationship to an "environment" that renders human life "ugly," "repulsive," and meaningless:

> The image of the human form is gradually disappearing from the painting of these times and all objects appear only in fragments. This is one more proof of how ugly and worn the human countenance has become, and of how all the objects of our environment have become repulsive to us. The next step is for poetry to decide to do away with language for similar reasons. These are things that have probably never happened before.
>
> (Ball 1969 [1927]: 55)

In imagining the translation of painterly abstraction to poetry, Ball describes an anti-humanism that sees fragmentation in aesthetic and cultural terms. An anthropomorphic world in which "all the objects of our environment have become repulsive" presents exhaustion and decay as the underside of narratives of industrial progress and modernization. As we have seen, this rejection of language by poetry doubles noise: it occupies the negative side of language (a background to representation's foreground) while at the same time reducing language to another contingent product within a repulsive modernity.

Ball's thinking behind verse without words is notably and literally logocentric: the sound poem releases the plenitude of "the word" (logos) behind a fallen language, a language that can only be heard as noise. Ball reports a conversation he overhears in Zurich:

> What will you do if Russia makes a separate peace?
> I would not believe in divine providence anymore. There would be nothing left but the most brutal class struggle.
> It is just a noise. It makes no big difference if it is with cannons or debates.
>
> (Ball 1969 [1927]: 85)

The reduction of "cannons" and "debates" to noise mirrors the negative image of noise in Dada: as the ineluctable auditory outside, a nothing in which cannons and debates simply collapse into each other. Yet earlier in the diary, Ball celebrates Marinetti's "parole in liberta" as a form of freedom in the rejection of language:

> Marinetti sends me *parole in liberta* ... They are just letters of the alphabet on a page; you can roll up such a poem like a map. The syntax has come apart. The letters are scattered and assembled again in a rough-and-ready way. There is no language any more, the literary astrologers and leaders proclaim; it has to be invented all over again. Disintegration right in the innermost process of creation.
>
> (Ball 1996 [1927]: 25)

Here, he sees the destruction of language as an opportunity for reinvention. As Ball works through words in freedom, bruitism, and sound poetry, he finds in the "innermost process of creation" a purity that goes beyond the mimetic desire of Marinetti's words in freedom. Ball searches for an immediacy that would seem to reject the antinomies of language and noise (figure and ground, inside and outside). Ultimately, sound poetry, a poetry of nonsense syllables, is the answer:

> gadji beri bimba
> glandridi laula lonni cadori …
>
> (Ball 1996 [1927]: 70)

The contrast between extra-poetic sound effects and recognizable words typical of bruitism collapses in this turn toward autonomous phonemes, disconnected from referentiality and linguistic category. Ball's first performance of sound poetry, in June of 1916, has become a mythological touchstone: "a single evening's ten or fifteen-minute performance," in which "Ball became the century's poster boy for the avant-garde" (Rasula 2015: 27). Before this performance he read a short text:

> In these phonetic poems we totally renounce the language that journalism has abused and corrupted. We must return to the innermost alchemy of the word, we must even give up the word too, to keep for poetry its last and holiest refuge. We must give up writing secondhand; that is, accepting words (to say nothing of sentences) that are not newly invented for our own use. Poetic effects can no longer be obtained in ways that are merely reflected ideas or arrangement of furtively offered witticism and images.
>
> (Ball 1996 [1927]: 71)

The "innermost alchemy of the word," a "last and holiest refuge," shows the religious intensity around Ball's performance, and, as if to amplify this mysticism, in his recitation he took on an "ancient cadence of priestly lamentation" (71), only to collapse on stage, a "magical bishop" (71).

But this "innermost alchemy of the word," just as with the "*vox humana*" in Ball's reading of simultaneous poetry is a transcendent abstraction built out of a sense of the world as fallen and corrupt. Paradoxically, however, the move toward the "innermost" and "pure" elements in the word can only be made through the transformation of language into noise. A language of "just noise," a fallen materiality, is opposed to the purifying nonsense of sound poetry—another kind of noise, in its emphasis upon the phonetic and rhythmic values of mouth sounds alone. The turn toward the "pure" poetry of verse without words, and

Ball's act of linguistic destruction, was also a recomposition that dramatized the dedifferentiated listening highlighted by Hennings's, Tzara's, and Huelsenbeck's performances. As in those actions, sound texture and rhythm come to the fore, connecting language to an embodiment in the diffuse matrix of noise.

In another sound poem, "Karawane" (or "Elephant Caravan"), these textures and rhythms have some mimetic potential:

> jolifanto bambla o falli bambla
> großiga m'pfa habla horem
> egiga goramen
> higo bloiko russula huju
> hollaka hollala
> anlogo bung
> blago bung blago bung
> bosso fataka
> ü üü ü
> schampa wulla wussa olobo
> hej tatta gorem
> eschige zunbada
> wulubu ssubudu uluwu ssubudu
> –umf
> kusa gauma
> ba–umf

(adapted from text in Green 1993: 61)

But even if Ball evokes the march of elephants through "o" and "u" vowels and through the heavy rhythmic "-umf" at the end of the poem, the vowels and consonant clusters remain self-referential as the sounds of Ball's phonemes repeat with an interweaving excess that belies a specific evocation.[1] Poetry becomes a figure of noise music that does not use language as a code but rather as a sound-source to be manipulated and refigured. These quasi-musical qualities—in the context of an almost recognizable language—redefine these sounds as noise, as language abstracted from a matrix of differences that would give it meaning.

As the contemporaneous Swiss linguist Ferdinand de Saussure relates in the *General Course in Linguistics*, the arbitrary and conventional nature of language means that the particular sounds of any language are not as important as the

---

[1] It may be worth mentioning, however, that in Ball's diary months after he performed this poem, he reports a letter from Hennings that describes men in gas masks at the front as "elephant-like." This poem may be closer to war poetry than usually allowed.

differentiation of those sounds within a matrix of grammatical categories and functions (Saussure 1959: 67–78). In this way, the Dadaists—and in particular Ball's sound poems—upset the phonological element in language and replace it with a pure phonetics with only localized, formal differences, not structural or grammatical ones. These formal differences—differences from linguistic difference—seem to skip over language in order to rupture "the stability of signifying practices that are anchored socially, the conventions of language and literature and of the speakable and thinkable, the entire conception of the world within language" (Jones 2014: 35). In the abstraction of sound from these categories, the world falls apart and voice becomes, rather than a sound shape signifying a person, a depersonalizing force of purity without reference or rationality. This might be read as a reversal of the movement from babble to speech, where the "integrating power of voice (babble) is cast aside while its disintegrating efficacy (speech) is cultivated" (Appelbaum 1990: 78). But voice is thrown into a disintegrating context that renders it noise. While Ball turns toward the figure of the "magical bishop" in his chanting, he also loses himself in a noise beyond reckoning, a totality that subjects the person—already abstracted in a ridiculous metallic blue lobster costume—to a radicalized version of the older dedifferentiating forces of the religious and sublime.

Othering Noise

There is a dramatic reversal in this Dadaist critique of language and subjectivity: language and the self are alienated—pushed outside and made other—through the forces of war and violence that define modernity. This reversal parallels the European avant-gardes search for images of otherness that might locate this reimagined outside and its noise. As we have seen with Ball's analysis of the mask, the abstract masks of African and Oceanic peoples became ciphers for channeling a totalizing sense of the otherness of modernity. These images—transformed into idealized signifiers of absolute difference and attention to substance itself— took on mythological, oppositional force. In this primitivist aesthetic, the languages and culture of colonized subjects of European imperialism become figures of noise, embodiment, and primal life. Huelsenbeck's "big drum" was the vehicle for an imagined "negro rhythm" (Ball 1996 [1927]: 51), a kind of rhythm that precedes and exceeds—and yet parallels—modern life. In thrall to this idea, he created fantasy "*Negerlieder*" (many with the refrain: "umba umba") that may have been influenced by African place names like the Umba River between Tanzania and Kenya (Huelsenbeck 1969: 20; White 2016: 165). Douglas Kahn suggests that the "trivializing appropriation" of non-European cultures emphasizes how the figure of noise contains the other in two senses: as those who are "outside any representation of social harmony" and as way of limiting others through the ears of the dominant listening culture (Kahn 1999: 47). In this way, "avant-garde noise ... both marshals and mutes the noise of the other: power is attacked at the expense of the less powerful, and society itself is both attacked and reinforced" (Kahn 1999: 48).

In the case of Dada, primitivist fantasy revolved around a search for a primal otherness that could disorient audiences through this containing noise. This search, however, involved an active removal of the trace of the other as a way of emphasizing and amplifying noise in the face of Western bourgeois values. Given an ignorant bourgeois public's sense of "primitive" languages as unintelligible noise, the Dadaists ambivalently mirrored this sensibility back to the public. As creators of noise, Dadaists reproduced an ethnocentrism that simply heard colonized subjects as "noisy" others. At the same time, however, they sought out images of otherness as a forcible decentering of Western consciousness—not as a simple trivialization of the lifeworld of colonized others. The appropriated sounds of otherness depended on an active undoing of language's ability to signify.

In this way, fantasy "primitive" languages became radicalized versions of Dada heteroglossia and xenoglossia. Poets used languages they did not know and could not really speak. The polyglot environment of Zurich and the multinational origins of Dadaists associated with Dada created an atmosphere in which languages and language barriers proliferated. At the Cabaret Voltaire, the Dadaists and their audiences spoke and heard many different languages: French, German, English, but also Russian, Turkish, and Chinese (Ball 1996 [1927]: 65). For the Dadaists, the noise of others is not merely the limited non-understanding that manifests in a situation where one does not know another's language; it is rather the noise inherent in the active effacement of understanding. The rejection of language's movement by difference—as seen in Ball's sound poetry and in Tzara's and Huelsenbeck's bruitist experiments—has a parallel in the critical use of blackness against language. Blackness here signifies against what Tzara describes as a "dark, grinding whiteness" (Tzara 1977: 58). Blackness also signifies a generalized otherness that for Tzara was embodied in the word "*nègre*" which he used in relation to African, Oceanic and Australian languages and cultures. Even to the fascinated researcher (which Tzara was), reading and hearing a highly mediated *chant négre* does not reinforce the Western ear's sense of itself. The rhythms and defamiliarizing sounds of *chant négre* embodied the Dadaist desire to unhear or undo language and to decenter the imperialist, German idealist subject that knows itself only through manifesting and casting out an Other. In this way, the "othered" noise of Dada does not only think of the contained and containing noise of others but also of ways to loosen that containment through an emphasis upon the desubjectivizing possibilities for decontextualized and reappropriated sounds. The desire to reimagine language as if from a primal, uncomprehending position connects with a fascination with the sounds of non-Western others because the Dadaists sought to hear not the social conventions embedded in language—its proper contextualization within a place and a culture—but rather a sonic trace of language's materials: rhythms, intonations, and mouth sounds.

One route toward this decontextualizing expansion is through fantasy: Huelsenbeck claims to care little for an "authentic" reproduction of his "African" chants. When the landlord of the Cabaret Voltaire, Jan Ephraim, tells him that his poems were fictions and that he had spent time as a trader in Africa, Huelsenbeck dutifully uses some of Ephraim's remembered sounds in a performance—"trabadja bono"—but ultimately he dismisses the effort, contrasting himself with Ephraim who "wanted everything to be 'authentic,' literal, factual, just as he had heard it in Africa and the South Seas" (Huelsenbeck 1969: 9). Operating with only the simulacra of other languages, Huelsenbeck consciously performs his misappropriations and fantasy formations. What these sounds do, as sounds, is emphasize another side to European languages—syllables gone awry—that abstracts those languages. In this sense, Huelsenbeck's sound forms simultaneously project "an extended, disconnected, bewildering world of phenomena" and simplified, regularized sound sequences that, in the language of the contemporary aesthetic theorist Wilhelm Worringer, took joy "in the possibility of taking the individual thing of the external world out of its arbitrariness and seeming fortuitousness ... of finding a point of tranquility and a refuge from appearances" (Worringer 1997 [1908]: 16).

Tzara moves toward a decontextualizing abstraction not by fantasy but by appropriation. He goes to the Zurich library, finds "*poem négres*" in ethnographic texts, and retranslates them for early Dada periodicals. These texts in *Dada 2* (from 1917) are given only tribal sources—the Aranda and the Loritja peoples from Australia (Stephen 2009: 155). Tzara simultaneously gestures toward an idealized otherness *and* reframes that otherness through its multiple mediations.

From oral performance, transcription, translation (first into a "line-by-line" German translation), and then into a fragmented French, these songs take on layers of mediating significance (Veit 2009: 59–77). One song, "Toto Vaca," was presented by Tzara, in the *Dada Almanach* of 1920, as a Maori work song, but subsequently was reprinted as an abstract sound poem (White 2016: 166). Though Tzara worked on a translation of the song, he never published it in his lifetime. Pierre Joris translated Tzara's notes in the second edition of Jerome Rothenberg's *Technicians of the Sacred*:

Ka tangi te kivi	Kiwi cries the bird
Kivi	Kiwi
Ka tangi te moho	Moho cries the bird
Moho …	Moho …

(Rothenberg 1985: 414)

Like the other songs appropriated by Tzara, this one is multiply translated and circulated through oral performance, manuscript, and print. The routes of this circulation are figured in the seeming referential confusion and break from reality that these simplified words and phrases create. Tzara rejects a multiply layered philology by removing the ethnographic apparatus and instead taking only the trace of an "original" song. In this way, he emphasizes these words as a kind of nonsense: "what is 'said' … points to a vast and rich domain of the 'unsaid'" (Stewart 1979: 87). The "unsaid" includes here the processes of translation and transcription, not only between languages but also between (oral, written, and printed) mediums that render the original song and context unknowable. The song, like the reductive abstraction of painters like Hans Arp, becomes "first and foremost concentration" (Tzara 1977: 57).

This concentration of layered mediations reflects back on what Tzara would have his readers learn from "Negro Art:" "From blackness let us extract light. Simple, rich luminous naivety. Different materials, the scales of form" (Tzara 1977: 57). The "different materials" and "scales of form" involve an unsaying that simultaneously reflects the arbitrary totality of modernity (and its imperialism) while also concentrating that totality into a figure of nonsense, distance, and difference. Tzara performs an operation that removes the poems from their environment (cultural or textual) and reimagines their place within the material mediums and substances that carry them over (translate them) from one place to another. The noise of the untranslated sounds of "Toto Vaca" or of the translated but unassimilable songs of the Aranda and the Loritja depends upon a sense of abstraction in which "the invisible radiation of substance" emerges in a "relationship, naively, without explanation" (Tzara 1977: 69). The radiating substance of noise—in its inexplicable relation to life—does not simply mimic a bourgeois hearing of colonial subjects as noisy. It rather employs a sense of abstraction—as subtraction from, as a cutting out of, as the reversal of figure and ground—to "primitivist" materials that allows noise to irradiate from the substance of language and culture.

This taking on of otherness not as an ethnographic knowability but as the energizing difference from an ethnocentric white European gaze remains limited by its inaccuracies and thus is open to critiques of trivialization and racism. Dadaist primitivism, then, sustains only an empty coalitional desire lost in its own noise. Later conscious and unconscious reprises of certain Dadaist techniques by black writers and performers, such as the use of "dada" I will describe in the next chapter, suggest ways in which the critical work of black art—particularly in a transatlantic context—writes difference in ways that refuse the mask-like abstraction of Dada and instead embrace a blackness that is, in the words of Ashon Crawley, "an ongoing, anoriginal assault on desire for normative beauty, normative form" (Crawley 2017: 141). The parallel assaults between Dada and black art—made even more apparent in poems like Amiri Baraka's "Black Dada Nihilismus" (from 1964)—begin to show a possible alliance based not in a reproduction of a particular avant-garde techniques but rather in the resilient power of black bodies to create new rhythms and new forms of space that are not organized by white demands for homogeneity (or its abstract negation in Dada).

Everybody's Doing It: Ragtime

The power of a decontextualizing and abstracting mediation of materials to create a noise is also present in the Dadaist reappropriation of American ragtime music, a music that, in its relationship with African-American musical sources and American mass culture, connoted both primitive and modern life. If the international impulse of the Dadaists stemmed from an anti-humanist disidentification with the nation-state and Western culture, then the invading and infecting rhythms of ragtime produced this movement in parallel. While many writers have commented on Dada's obsession with the African primitive, the Dadaist debt to ragtime—an African-American popular music that presaged the appearance of jazz in the late 1910s—often goes unnoticed despite a definite transatlantic sensibility among the Dadaists. Ball celebrated "any Americanism that art can include" because "otherwise art will remain sentimentally romantic" (quoted in Huelsenbeck 1969: 51). Tzara characteristically turned this sentiment into a pithy equation: "transatlantic art = the people rejoice" (1951 [1920]: 235). Meanwhile, Huelsenbeck directly invokes the music of ragtime and its relation to the noise of the Dadaists: "the same initiative which in America made ragtime a national music, led to the convulsion of *bruitism*" (Huelsenbeck 1951 [1920a]: 26).

Ragtime developed in the late nineteenth century as a black rhythmic and harmonic tradition in relation to "barrelhouse" piano entertainment, march music, parlor music, banjo accompaniment, and minstrelsy. Though it emerged in conversation with other popular song and dance forms like "coon songs" and "cakewalks," ragtime as developed by African-American composers like Scott Joplin was a written piano style with heavily syncopated rhythms (Southern 1997: 317). Ragtime's use of syncopation quickly passed into popular song, in particular the work of the Jewish-American composer Irving Berlin and other composers of Tin Pan Alley. Berlin's huge hits like "Alexander's Ragtime Band" (1911) and "Everybody's Doing It Now" (1911) came to define "ragtime" in the popular imagination, and this music drove a nascent mass culture dependent upon an almost factory-like production of new but familiar cultural material and globalized forms of production and distribution (Baxendale 1995: 140).

Ragtime was well known in Europe. It had been popularized and played by military marching bands, minstrel troupes, club orchestras, and touring dancers in the years before the war (Lotz 1984: 217). In the Cabaret Voltaire, ragtime would have been the dance music of choice. Richard Huelsenbeck described the dancing scene at the cabaret:

> That first evening, as I entered the cabaret ... Hugo was sitting at the piano, playing classical music, Brahms and Bach. Then he switched over to dance music. The drunken students pushed their chairs aside and began spinning around. There were almost no women in the cabaret. It was too wild, too smoky, too way out.
>
> (Huelsenbeck 1969: 10)

Dada's "wild" and "way out" strain—its revolt as a "variety show" to recall Ball's words—took much of its energy from the syncopated rhythms of ragtime. In contrast to the tradition of Bach, ragtime gets bodies moving. Huelsenbeck presents an image of Dada's embrace of mass culture against official culture.

The central feature of ragtime—and the central cause of its enchanting and enervating effects—was the "ragging" of a common march beat through pervasive syncopation. Against a simple eight-beats-to-a-bar rhythm, ragtime composers and performers would accent off beats so that different rhythmic profiles played simultaneously against each other. By emphasizing beats in the right hand against the regularity of beats in the left hand, early piano ragtime would create polyrhythmic figures that "obliterated the bar line" and broke away from a fixed, metrically regular melody (Peress 2004: 110). Gunther Schuller calls this a "democratization" of the beat (1968: 16). Wilfrid Mellers hears in ragtime music a structure of feeling in opposition to the blues: "Perhaps it is better to be a merry machine, the music says, than to be human but blue" (1987: 278). The music presents a kind of precise, machinic depersonalization, literalized in its adaptation for pianola rolls (Mellers 1987: 278).

This sense of ragtime's machinic regularity, polyrhythmic simultaneity, and invigorating ebullience was widespread in the years before and during the First World War, when ragtime was imagined—in both Europe and America—as the singular sound of modernity and modern America. Ragtime's precise irregularity—even in the water-down form of Tin Pan Alley popular song—matched the modernist turn toward abstraction, depersonalization, and mechanization. As a reflection of global capitalism and the mass culture it produced, the music resisted state-based nationalism and romantic ideas of "the folk." In the midst of this ambivalent relationship to a changing culture of modernity, ragtime—like other popular musics before and after—also came to signify the "noise" of the new and the unfamiliar. Dada's appropriation of ragtime music in its bruitist figures does not simply take up this conservative, bourgeois view of ragtime as a kind of noise but rather listens to ragtime against the grain, thus amplifying the noise within the music. That ragtime and "the convulsion of bruitism" could be in parallel depended upon reformatting ragtime—already standardized and at the end of its fad—for a different and appropriately bewildering context: the simultaneous poem.

In "L'Amiral Cherche a Maison Louer," Tzara interpolated Berlin's ragtime hit "Everybody's Doing It Now" into the texture of the multivoiced recitative along with two other popular ragtime-inflected tunes, "Rebecca of Sunnybrook Farm" (1914) and "I Love the Ladies" (1914):

where the honny suckle wine twines itself around the door a sweetheart mine is waiting patiently for me I can hear the weopur wil around around the hill / my great room is mine admirably comfortably Grandmother said / I love the ladies I love the ladies I love to be among the girls / And when its five o'clock and tea is set I like to have my tea with some brunet shai shai shai shai shai shai shai shai Everybody is doing it doing doing it Everybody is doing it doing it see that ragtime couple over there see that throw there shoulders in the air She said the raising her heart oh dwelling / oh / oh yes yes yes yes yes yes yes yes yes yes oh yes oh yes oh yes oh yes oh yes sir ... (adapted from text in *Cabaret Voltaire* 1916)[2]

Tzara fragments these words from these popular tunes and so feeds back to his audience the culture of the Cabaret Voltaire, the variety show in general, and modernity at large. Broken up by nonsense sounds ("shai shai"), a few cross-language puns ("my great room is mine admirably" and "raising her heart oh dwelling"), and an ecstatic and erotic repetition of "yes oh yes," this concatenation of references concentrates modernity's madness, chaos, and desperate eroticism into the microcosm of a vocalized line in counterpoint with the other performers' lines.

In this performance, the machinic simultaneity of ragtime gives way to the messy simultaneity of multiple voices speaking at once. Whereas ragtime demands a kind of bodily response—"Everybody is doing it doing it doing it"—the kind of rhythmic response expected in a poem or song is dissipated and undone. *L'Amiral..* creates a sense of moving stasis. Unlike the songs referenced (and other lyric effusions), one is not "in" the piece as a speaker or dramatic participant but rather simply watching an inexplicable, nonsensical, chaotic surface of movement, like leaves blowing in the wind or the flow of traffic in a city. Rather than presenting the possibility for an empathetic "feeling into" a song or situation, there is instead an incalculable mess of sound. This radicalizes the simultaneous—polyrhythmic— elements in ragtime that make it seem machinic and automatic.

Tzara's—and Dada's—refiguration of ragtime noise, then, is dependent upon a sense of time without narrative, a modernity without progress that is also subterraneously embedded within ragtime form. Irving Berlin's "Everybody's

---

[2] From "where" to "hill" the words come from "Rebecca of Sunnybrook Farm," lyrics by Seymour Brown and music by Albert Grumble. This sentimental tune from 1914 was based upon a popular children's book of the same title written by Kate Douglas Wiggin and published in 1904. "I love" to "brunet" is "I Love the Ladies" by Grant Clark, music by Jean Schwartz. And "Everybody is doing it" through "shoulders" comes from Irving Berlin's major ragtime hit from 1911 (in addition to the even more famous "Alexander's Ragtime Band"), "Everybody's Doing It Now."

Doing It Now"—perhaps the most well-known song in Tzara's remix—begins with a call to music's intoxicating effects:

> Honey, honey, can't you hear?
> Funny, funny music, dear
> Ain't the funny strain goin' to your brain?
> Like a bottle of wine. Fine!
>
> (Berlin 1914: 1)

Berlin's compositional style in this work emphasizes rhythmic and vocal effects common in African-American musical practice: a kind of rhythmic complexity and eclecticism is matched with a play on the permeable boundary between speech and song. The rhyming stutter-stop at the end of each quatrain of the verse, as in "wine. Fine!" above, as well as the use of measured speech in the chorus, creates rhythmic and textural disruptions that become more important than the relatively simple harmonic, melodic, and thematic basis of the song. Rhythmic ground overtakes figures of voice. The song self-reflexively imagines this movement: the "funny strain" invades its listeners' brains and breaks down any sense of their resistance to the dance. Subjectivity disappears in favor of the collective "it" that "everybody's doing"—the speaker-listeners must move to the beat and keep up with the "mob… on the job" (Berlin 1914: 2). This loss of self within movement—also projected in the stutters, breakdowns, and spoken intonations of the song—imbues the music with the potential for a dissipation: "Hear that trombone bustin' apart?" (Berlin 1914: 5).

Tzara effectively busts apart the trombone to extract the qualities of ragtime that make it work in parallel with bruitism. Its insistence on rhythm, its refusal of national limits, its emphasis upon the dancing, out-of-control automatic body, its rejection of language as the driving force of the song: all these elements parallel the bruitist critiques of language, experiments in interruption, reversal of figure and ground, and celebration of an abstracted embodiment. The noise of Dada, however, remains rebarbative in a way that ragtime is not. The Dadaists intensify and skew the qualities present within the song's form that can be figured as noise. This Dada figuration of noise incorporates the movement of social life outside of language.

In this way, Dada also suffuses ragtime form with negativity. Noise arises out of a language reduced to sound through its relation to totalizing and destructive sounds of modernity. Ragtime, even in its happy-go-lucky way, remains a source of such sounds. For the Dadaists, ragtime models a way for thought to be made—

but also pulverized—in the mouth. This loosening of the grip of language upon the body allows ragtime—along with the other performance-based elements of the Dadaist synthesis—to precede and influence the creation of a poetry of noise. This poetics of noise emerges through the production of sonic effects that emphasize language as sounds in a mouth, and, even more generally, as a sonorousness in contact with all other sounds. By erasing the filters controlling the transition of noise into meaning, the Dadaists recast rational subjects and their aesthetic autonomy as situated sound-emitters, unfit for the transcendental aesthetic of musicality, unfit for normative use, and, ultimately, unfit for battle. By de-instrumentalizing language, Dada noise worked to undo the insanity of administered or so-called normative rationality. In doing so, the Dadaists critically opened up aesthetics and politics to the body and its precarity.

3

The Persistence of "That Da-Da Strain": The Modernist Travels of "Da"

> *That makes a sound that gently sings that gently sounds but sounds as sounds. It sounds as sounds of course as words but it sounds as sounds. It sounds as sounds that is to say as birds as well as words.*
> —Gertrude Stein, "What Is English Literature" (1957 [1935]: 30)

In this chapter, I will take up a language fragment—"da"—that not only "sounds as sounds" but also sounds as noise within a language that "sounds of course as words but it sounds as sounds" as well. In a variety of modernist texts, "da" emerges as an itinerant phoneme that holds together both the sonic material of language ("sounds as sounds") and the channels of reference and repetition that would carry that material ("sounds as words"). Noise emerges when these elements of language cross: when "da" as sound infests and interrupts the systems of communication that would carry it. These systems work at different levels—as words functioning in the language system of difference and deferral, as mass media like newspapers and phonograph recordings, or simply as speaking and moving human bodies. "Da" moves within these channels not as a token or sign but as a "free radical," ready to attach itself to any word, medium, or body that hears it. As such, this radical plays on a linguistic sense of a "root" word and a sense of a reduction or destruction of language. It works as what Michel Serres calls a "parasite" in mediation: a static noise that threatens communication while also creating new complexities and new orders of significance (Serres 2007 [1982]: 14). The poets in this chapter take up different media forms—early twentieth-century print media, nineteenth-century comparative philology, popular song, and poetic text—as "hosts" for the parasite of the nonsense syllable "da." The process of citing and reciting "da" exposes channels of poetry and song to the communicability of the "strain" or "germ" of noise. As "DA" and "da, da, da" this nonsense sound resists efforts to order, define, and delimit its meanings and effects. It opposes homogenizing systems that would attempt to uproot and banish noise by continuously showing forth as complexity and possibility outside of radical fixity.

The array of texts in this chapter fashion this mere "sound as sound" into a noise that materializes disruptions and gaps within established orders of meaning-making. While the performance work of the Dadaists and the verse of the First World War poets both figure noise as an exteriority that carries over into the poetic and lyrical text, "da"—in its automatism and autonomy—spreads through modernist texts and turns language inside out and outside in upon itself. "Da" moves across the soundscape of literary and musical modernism, simultaneously over- and under-determined, because it is not so much incorporated into the body but continuously exteriorizing what would seem internal or systemic in the work of language. In this way, "da" is a reverse image of how techniques and technologies mediate language: as they reproduce various "interiors"—of thought, of speech, of writing—they not only transfer but transform them. "Da" moves and changes language from within it—and exposes the very sense of being "within" a language—even as it emerges in a variety of phonographic remediations from around 1916 to 1926: in the "dada" of Dadaist manifestos, posters, and other print materials; in the "da-da" of Mamie Medina and Edgar Dowell's 1922 hit, "That Da-Da Strain;" in the quasi-scat "da, da, da" of Langston Hughes's poem "Negro Dancers," and in the "DA" of T. S. Eliot's *The Waste Land*. Of course, "da" has been written and spoken in countless other contexts both before and after this moment in high modernism, and I do not want to claim that "da" itself is particular only to the modernist moment. Rather, I want to show how different modernists arranged this pervasive "da" within systems of public address in order to imagine a reproducibility against powers of containment. These various iterations of "da," then, do not simply represent "pure" vocality or singsong. This fragmentary syllable figures the noise of sound-writing gone astray, of a murmuring multiplicity possessing and undoing the forms that would contain, define, and limit voice and communication.

"Da"—as sonic material, a tool for erasure, and a vessel for citation—focuses and amplifies the sounds of the environments in which language events happen. It recedes into its setting and thus foregrounds the ways in which media frame representations. Allen Weiss defines the parasite as the "outcome of citation, that unavoidable and ludic condition of speech" (Weiss 2005: 29), and "da" in its various guises produces such an "unavoidable and ludic" condition. A citation effects a movement beyond its particular use: it also enfolds a whole system of discourse and mediation. Saussurean linguistics defines language through this movement. In this account, a language is not a static series of objects but a collection of differences: sequences of words and sounds signify by virtue of the fact that they are not some other sequence of words or sounds. The play of "da"—through media systems, dance music, modernist mytho-poetic epic—forces an interruption in this passage of citation as it draws attention to the identity of words with what they are not. "Da" presents a kind of stoppage—a percussive sound that gets in the way of the smooth flow of meaning. But "da" also disappears into the system of difference or citation that it occupies. It becomes mere sound and, as such, it resists attachment to any particular meaning.

This parallels the media parasitism of noise discussed by Michel Serres in *The Parasite* (1982). The parasite—the noise and static that works "next to" the site of a message or productive energy in a system—takes sustenance from but does not kill its host. Rather, the parasite complicates things: because "noise temporarily stops the system, makes it oscillate indefinitely," it can "give rise to a new system, an order that is more complex than the simple chain" (Serres 1982: 14). The purveyors of "da" play off the urge within discourse and communication to create definition and clarity, counteracting the movement toward meaning with the dissipative force of a noise. Even the seeming immediacy of a "pure" sound is lost in "da," because its many cross-cultural determinations—and even its connection with the very roots of language—place it within a condition of mediateness, embeddedness, and possible order. The parasite could also be the host.

In using Serres's terminology, I do not want to suggest that the writers and performers I take up in this chapter are information theorists *avant la lettre* but rather that they are experimenting with the parasitical effects of language sounds on language. Occurring simultaneously inside and outside of established systems for making meaning, "da" in these experiments becomes a sound-written glossolalic fragment that emphasizes the fragility of communication. It produces relationships of destabilization through a "scriptural economy" that denies the fixity of origins and their smooth flow from place to place, site to site, or body to body: "The origin is no longer what is narrated, but rather the multiform and murmuring activity of producing and producing society as a text" (de Certeau 1984: 134). "Da" telescopes this murmuring multiplicity in language. It draws attention to the sounds that seemingly disappear from language when it becomes written in discourse and dialogue.

In taking up the poetic uses of "da," then, I also take up the sense-making systems that would differently carry and structure "da." The poet-performers in this chapter figure the noise of "da" into these systems as ways of revaluing their use in a changing modern world. The rumor production of the "news," the sonic color line that defined early jazz's reception, and nineteenth-century philological fantasies all distribute and define noise in different ways. "Da" intervenes in these noise regimes because it cites the babble of linguistic free play without resolution or meaning. It conjures an irrational infinity and so remains unsettled by the systems that would structure it. Through the specter of continual repetition, it threatens language with the possibility of receding into the background—into a nothing. But this is a nothing charged with the possibility of new events. This "magical word" becomes a paradigmatic noise in modernism because its eruptions in text and song figure new relations between bodies and languages, between automatism and autonomy.

Dada Media Parasite

For the Dadaists, the negating work of bruitism—as the over-writing and debasement of language—was matched by the plenitude of the word "dada" itself. While Dadaist performances created noise to interrupt declamation in particular theatricalized events, their use of "dada" also spread beyond these spectacles of noise. "Dada" became a tool for reimagining public discourse and lines of communication—in mass markets and in political speech. While bruitism invited listeners to hear outside sounds with and against language, the spread of "dada"—as name and as irritating nonsense—invited its reading and listening audience not only to hear a defamiliarized language anew but also to place language within its mediated forms—in particular, the print culture of publicity and journalism.

Though the history remains mired in *ex post facto* mystification, the poet-performers Ball, Tzara, and Huelsenbeck each claimed to have first hit upon the verbal sound "dada" as the name for their collective artistic activities in Zurich in the years 1916–18. Given the many disparate forms, works, concepts, and people who laid claim to some part of the Dadaist movement, the word (or anti-word) "dada" was often the only connective tissue holding the group together. Huelsenbeck even went so far as to claim that this "mere word actually conquered a large part of the world, even without association with any personality. This was an almost magical event" (1951 [1920a]: 33). This mere word—simultaneously meaningless and overflowing with meanings in a variety of languages—stands at the crux of the Dadaist relationship to noise. These two "reduplicated phonemes ... could be substituted into any slogan" (Sieburth 1984: 46). This exasperated Roman Jakobson in 1921:

> It is simply a meaningless little word thrown into circulation in Europe, a little word with which one can juggle *à l'aise*, thinking up meanings, adjoining suffixes, coining complex words which create the illusion that they refer to objects: dadasopher, dadapit.
>
> (Jakobson 1987: 37)

"Dada" acts as an anti-word that refuses denotation and fuses with the words and structures around it. This "illusion" of reference threatens all statements with infection by repetitive stutter. In its reduplicative excess the noise of "dada" is not figured as a particular quality of sound—striking loudness, irregularities, or timbres—but rather as a rhythmic supplement to language, a dedifferentiating force that weakens the referential use of words, leaving only the bare registration of their movement. The word "dada" registers the contact zone between materials, rhetorics, techniques, and bodies. In this sense, it marks the beginnings of a poetics of noise not based upon a physics of sound but rather upon an inchoate theory of media publicity.

The first uses of "dada" in print were Tristan Tzara's performance piece, "La premiere Aventure celeste de Mr. Antipyrine" ["The First Celestial Adventure of Mr. Antipyrine"], and Ball's "editorial" manifesto in the first and only issue of *Cabaret Voltaire*, both published in the summer of 1916. Ball's manifesto ends with a barrage of "dada"—"DADA ('Dada') Dada Dada Dada Dada" (*Cabaret Voltaire* 1916: n.p.)—while Tzara's speech for the "fire extinguisher," Mr. Antipyrine, continually (and unhelpfully for the "bourgeois" he directs the speech toward) defines and redefines the utterance: "Dada is our intensity ... Dada is life without carpet-slippers or parallels; it is for and against unity and definitely against the future ... Dada is not madness—or wisdom—or irony ... " (Tzara 1977: 75). For Tzara, "dada" is an anthropomorphized entity, an abstract quality, a thing that can be "ours," and the name of a group (later in the speech, he makes this explicit with a reference to "we Dada"). This excess becomes the model for Tzara's manifestos. "Dada" remains a mobile term, unfixed, linked too many times and in too many ways. At the same time, it seems pushed by Ball toward a nonstop self-replication: "Dada Dada Dada Dada ...." "Dada" rests in a space between word and non-word. It is simultaneously overdetermined and under-determined.

This play between recalcitrant blankness and mobile possibility is made even more apparent by the various definitions of "dada" referenced by its founders. It is, in various contexts: just nonsense; in French, "hobbyhorse;" in German, an indication of an "idiot naivety and … a preoccupation with procreation and the baby-carriage" (Ball 1996 [1927]: 64); in Romanian (the nationality of Tzara), "da, da" for "yes, yes;" and (according to Tzara) the African Kru's name for the tail of a cow; "baby talk, jungle noise, parrot chatter" (Huelsenbeck 1991: 56); a joke; and, even, "nothing, nothing, nothing" (Tzara 1951 [1918]: 77). Ball described "dada" as a brand in his first manifesto: "Dada is the world's best lily-milk soap" (Ball 1996 [1927]: 221). And "dada" was in fact the name of a popular hair tonic on sale in Zurich at the time, marketed by the same company that made a "lily-milk" soap (Dickerman 2005: 43). The reappropriation of "dada" as a brand for an artistic movement self-consciously plays with the contradiction between "dada" as name and as nonsense. "Dada," then, could become a powerful anti-slogan, "the signboard of abstraction," because, after all, "advertising and business are also elements of poetry" (Tzara 1951 [1918]: 78).

In taking up the seemingly "unpoetic" realms of advertising and business—and in actively taking on the publicity work of a brand name, the Dadaists "brought journalists to the gates of a world unforeseen" (Tzara 1951 [1918]: 76). In this sense, the (non)word "dada" came to work within modernist media ecologies as a kind of "parasite that had the power to irritate and occupy public communication" (Niebisch 2012: 31). This uninvited guest that could expand and complicate forms of communication depended on remaining everywhere and nowhere at once, and in this way, it played mass communication against itself, simultaneously providing content and evacuating that content. Huelsenbeck discusses the word's "aggressive power and propagandistic force" in his 1920 *En Avant Dada: A History of Dadaism*. Dada became "an immense sensation in Europe" because "men who were no Dadaists" reproduced the word:

> Dada has operated—not as mild suasion but like a thunderbolt, not like a system set down in a book, which through the channel of superior minds, after years of chewing and rechewing, becomes the universal possession of nations, but like a watchword passed on by heralds on horseback. The immense effect of Dadaism on the great mass of the artistically indifferent lay in the senseless and comic character of the word Dada, and it would seem that this effect, in turn,

must derive from some profound psychological cause, connected with the whole structure of "humanity" today and its present social organization.

(Huelsenbeck 1951 [1920a]: 29–33)

Dada could act as a "watchword passed on by heralds on horseback," or a kind of rumor, because of its "senseless and comic character."

If the word could be passed through different mediums—newspaper publications as well as an international print culture of letters, little magazines, and advertising posters—its "magic" might lie in its nonsensical, stuttering form. The form of "dada's" nonsense matters: in the meta-communicative playfulness of the word, or non-word, "the work of nonsense is reflection and self-perpetuation" (Susan Stewart 1979: 119). Within this sound unit closed off to reference and utility, a kind of infinity "is realized" (Stewart 1979: 119) in which an implicit infinite regression in signification holds open the possibility of overflowing and undoing any discourse with which it makes contact. So while "dada" maintains a "senseless and comic" veneer, it also possesses the implicit threat of an origin-less upheaval of the ordering, useful effects of language.

Dada's direct attack on media ecology stems from this capacity to present the reader, the reporter, and even the Dadaist as both Dada and not Dada at the same time. This confusion is necessary to present Dada as simultaneously nothing and a world historical force (Niebisch 2012: 40). A constant nonsensical paradox is established by the word, which *matters* in each singular production and reconstitution of its image and sound because it calls for its audience to form a relationship with it not merely as meaning or lack of meaning but as a difficulty that demands a response: a question, a repetition, a denial, a show of support, a purchase, an essay, an explanation, a re-explanation, etc. In this way, it interrupts early twentieth-century media interconnectivity by presenting, within that space and time, a trace of a fundamental instability in difference and deferral. Dada figures the Derridean "arche-trace" through its demand for definition and reference within a chain of significance that is also a set of mediations. "Dada" sounds noise as the fragment of an infinite regress and an infinite substitutability. It destabilizes its material channel, and it thus makes apparent—through its constitutive indeterminacy—the systems of reproduction and retransmission within which it flowed. The ontological question of "what is it?" falls back upon mediation itself—to the noise arising in the transfer of language across time and space.

That Da-Da Strain

As the international presence of "dada" expanded in the postwar years, another similarly over- and under-determined word seemed to match it: "jazz." Just after the war, the association of jazz and Dada became such that the two seemed "interchangeable" (Rasula 2015: 144). The 1922 song "That Da-Da Strain," by Mamie Medina (lyrics) and Edgar Dowell (music), emerges at a moment when jazz was becoming intimately connected with ideas of modernism, modernity, and global cosmopolitanism (Rasula 2006: 66). While I have not been able to track down a scene of direct contact between Dada and the work of the little-known songwriter Mamie Medina, I follow Jerome Rothenberg in hearing the nonsense "da" in this song in relation to the media parasitism of "dada" (Rothenberg 1982: ix). Certainly "dada" was in the air in postwar New York. The "dada" in "That Da-Da Strain," rather than merely marking a coincidence, suggests the close continuity between the production of noise in black popular music and modernist poetics. As we have already seen in the case of ragtime's early influence on Dada, in a modernism redefined as "jazzbandism" (Rasula 2006: 61), African-American experiments with the boundaries of poesis—with the play between constraint and freedom in rhythm, sound, lyric, and voice—could produce new forms in a variety of cultural spaces. As a form, the modernist popular song, inflected by black popular forms like ragtime and jazz, changed in relation to its various mediations. The short duration, verse-chorus-verse structure, and syncopated rhythms of popular songs accommodated their reproduction in theatrical productions, in dance halls, in sheet music, and on phonograph record. While modernist critics like Theodor Adorno see jazz as purely expressive of these "external" elements and so, therefore, hear jazz music as merely the delusional "freedom" of a stereotyped commodity form (2002: 478), I hear "That Da-Da Strain" as the poetic product of a transitional moment in jazz music and as a lyrical and performative figuration of noise that celebrates embodiment, irrationality, and blackness as creative and destructive powers.

In this, I am following Paul Hegarty's suggestion that we read Adorno against the grain and seek out jazz's "weak" figurations of noise within what Adorno calls "the subject of weakness" (Adorno 2002: 490). For Hegarty, "weakness, in the form of the refusal of dogmatic supremacy or assertion of rules, will remain a central part of noise, and like much that constitutes noise, it arrives through negativity" (Hegarty 2007: 48). It is important to note, however, that the "subject of weakness"—the "weak" listener who cannot help but be "caught" by the tune and the "weak" performer breaking up or ornamenting "simple" rhythms and melodies—is also, explicitly, the subject marked by a racialized blackness. Though Adorno critiques the prevailing primitivist fantasy of jazz as "a confusing parody of colonial imperialism," he also imagines the "primal structure of jazz" as "the spontaneous singing of servant girls" (Adorno 2002: 478). For him, this represents a damning aspect of jazz: that it emerges from the "domesticated body in bondage" only reproduces such bondage (Adorno 2002: 478). But in addition to critiquing the obvious racist inadequacies of such an origin story, we might also make an effort to listen carefully to the music made by black women in jazz, in particular, "That Da-Da Strain," a song written by a woman and made famous by women performers. Rather than training our ear to a self-replicating pattern that merely reenacts dominant narratives of race, we can reimagine blackness outside of primitivist fantasy by attending to the production of writing and music from the standpoint of what Fred Moten hears as the "interarticulation of the resistance of the object" with the Marx's illustration of the commodity fetish, the "subjunctive figure of the commodity who speaks" (Moten 2003: 5). That is, what might otherwise be perceived as the "weakness" of the object can be understood instead as part of a particular resistance and resilience that embeds itself inside and outside literary, musical, and commodity forms.

"That Da-Da Strain" takes up a demotic, everyday experimentalism and performs a kind of "waywardness" that Saidiya Hartman reconstructs and reimagines in the lives of black women at the turn of the twentieth century. In *Wayward Lives, Beautiful Experiments*, she narrates the "open rebellion" of black women as they "struggled to create autonomous and beautiful lives, to escape the new forms of servitude awaiting them, and to live as if they were free" (Hartman 2019: xiii). The writing of Mamie Medina and the performances of the song by Mamie Smith, Ethel Waters, and other early blues singers amplifies the noise of this waywardness. This writing and performing of "dada" works to disarticulate autonomy from idealist forms of individual agency and to promote instead a free but embodied sense of movement and transformation.

It is nothing new to note that the sound of jazz was represented as a racialized and sexualized waywardness by white critics. Typical of conservative ire against jazz's possible unruly nonnormativity was the opinion of an American rector who called jazz the "national anthem" and drew up his attack along sonic and racist lines:

> Jazz is retrogression. It is going to the African jungle for our music. It is a savage crash and bang. It rings the bell for full steam astern. Its effect is to make you clatter. ... There is no pathos or no idealism about jazz music. It is for sensation. In the dance, instead of symbolism, it becomes sensuality.
>
> ("Rector Calls Jazz National Anthem" 1922: 9)

Simultaneously from the "African jungle" and the "bell for full steam astern" (that is, both "primitive" and a product of industrial modernity), the "crash and bang" of jazz has no "pathos" or "idealism." Accounts like this combine a horror of the (black) body and a nostalgia for old tunes that had "symbolism" rather than "sensuality."

The metaphysical, culturally embedded sense of "noise" as a material "crash and bang" outside of idealism meets with its counter-figuration in jazz music. With their singing and performance work already imagined as "noise" within the racialized economy of listening that Jennifer Stoever calls the "sonic color line," the jazz artists who popularized "That Da-Da Strain" used the nonsense of "da da… " to reverse and break through a barrier—impenetrable to dominant, "rational" discourse—in which the "white listening ear determined which sounds to amplify… and which sounds to ignore, suppress, and drown out" (Stoever 2016: 108). In the midst of a culture that determines who gets to speak and whose voices amount to mere noise, a self-conscious mirroring of this racialized (non)sense works to reverse its power. Purposeful representations of voices, bodies, and objects as figures of noise can resist and negate the metaphysical and social divisions of the embodied sensuousness and messiness of sound. In this way, a song like "That Da-Da Strain" embeds a critique of the racist conservative, the primitivist fan, and the skeptical cultural critic. While Adorno is right to find fault with certain forms of jazz built on the myth of the primitive, the form and the performances of this song materialize a noise that is different from a projected Otherness. Rather than producing a difference that conditions an "ideal" or normative principle, in this work noise can emerge within the repetitive, embodied "stuff" of language without a telos or meaning.

It is important to note that "That Da-Da Strain" emerges at a transitional moment in jazz when what constitutes "commercial" jazz is shifting away from "novelty" music and toward the music of blues singers like Mamie Smith and, later, Bessie Smith. Gunther Schuller emphasizes that "the blues craze, following on the heels of the novelty-jazz fad, served to clarify the distinctions between the musical expression of a certain ethnic group and a rather superficial, derived commercial commodity" (1968: 252). When the sheet music for "That Da-Da Strain" was published in 1922, Mamie Smith had recently performed and recorded 1920's "Crazy Blues," a song written by the black composer and entrepreneur Perry Bradford. Bradford tirelessly argued to executives at the Okeh label that the song could be a hit with both black and white audiences, and he was right. This first commercial recording by a black woman became a huge success, and it inaugurated the sale of what became known as "race records" marketed specifically to African-American audiences (Kenney 1999: 117). It also started off the 1920s "blues craze" that would make the careers of "Classic Blues" singers like Ma Rainey and Bessie Smith.

"That Da-Da Strain" was written, then, at a moment when black musicians, business people, publishers, theater producers, and performers were taking a greater part in the production and dissemination of their music. The song was published by Clarence Williams, one of the central figures of the New Orleans-style jazz music that found its way to the commercial center of New York City. The cover to the sheet music of "That Da-Da Strain" also advertises the network of black performance in which the music was first received. The actress and singer Gertrude Saunders is pictured, along with the information that she was "formerly of *Shuffle Along*." *Shuffle Along* had been a Broadway hit for Eubie Blake and Noble Sissle, and the all African-American production attracted a broad and mixed audience. Though Saunders never recorded the song, connecting her with the music spoke to the aspirations of the songwriters and publisher. The cover for "That Da-Da Strain" also includes references to productions like "Up and Down" and "Oh Joy." The latter was a revue produced by the black vaudevillians the Tutt Brothers, and singer and actor Ethel Waters had been a star in that show (only to leave when the Tutts wanted the revue to perform in a tent pitched in an empty lot on Broadway) (Waters 1992: 179). The urbanity of jazz was built upon just these sorts of contacts within the business world of popular music, where theatrical production, songwriting, and sheet music sales had long gone hand in hand.

"That Da-Da Strain," despite following upon the "blues" of Mamie Smith's "Crazy Blues," is not a blues song. It does, however, "cure all kind of blues you've got" (Medina and Dowell 1922: 3–4) and asks both the singer and listener to hum the catchy, sinuous verse tune that comprises the song's signature effect. This tune supports a dance song rhetoric of abandonment, and the lyrics announce the melodic strain's affective and infecting powers:

Have you heard it, have you heard it, that new da-da strain?
It will shake you, it will make you really go insane.

(Medina and Dowell 1922: 3)

The repeating motive of the verse melody (with its half-step drop and larger interval of a fourth) twists around the initial tone. The listener is invited to hear the insanity, to listen again to the "da-da strain." The chorus incites the singer not only to report upon the effects of this strain but to embody them fully:

I go crazy as a loon
When everybody hums the tune:
da-da-da-da, da-da-da-da ...
When everybody starts to da-da-da-da
I want to do it once again
I'm simply wild about that da-da-da-da strain (5)

The song turns around these moments of loss of control, and "strain" simultaneously connotes the music, the stress of its effects, and the strenuousness of the dancing. In a series of self-references, the song seems to belittle its lyrical and harmonic value:

Da-Da-Da-Da-Da-Da-Da-Da is a freaky strain,
Not much wording, just the writing of a freaky brain.
But it's such a pleasing trot,
cures all kind of blues you got;
It's so snappy, makes you happy, and its harmony
Ain't no corker but it's full of 'riginality
You can't resist its melody,
For you are surely bound to say:
Da-Da-Da-Da ... (3–4)

Despite the claim that the song "ain't no corker," the lyricist presents the music's rhythmic, melodic, and harmonic power. Our inability to resist this "writing of a freaky brain" emphasizes its weird mechanical energy: a bodily, material "brain" produces a "freaky"—capricious, even tricky—"writing." In the context of the song, the word "freaky" connects with its Old English cognate, *frícian*, to dance (OED, "freak"), but it also valorizes and reverses a racialized conception of "freakiness" centered around black female bodies in which a person is "reduced to a pure body through representation" (Garland-Thomas [2017]: 60). Rather than the spectacularization of the "freakish" body, the listener—in listening at all—joins in freakiness. Unlike Irving Berlin's "Everybody's Doin' It," in which the singing couple looks on and yearns to join the action, this song demands the co-presence of "I" and "you," a collective experience that also provides a release from "the blues" and the self. Unlike classic blues songs (but in conversation with them), it refuses to narrate a story or represent a fictional scene. Instead, it places you in the here and now of the song: "Have you heard it?" is answered before the question ends.

This "freaky" portrayal of sonic immediacy creates a strange temporal effect because it precedes and exceeds itself. We are in this sound before we have the chance to know where we are or what is happening. Similarly, the spatial coordinates of the song are playful. "That" strain is over there, away, seemingly a fact already known and outside the framework of the song—and yet it is, also, this song, this moment. The flood of "Da-Da-Da-Da-Da-Da-Da-Da" emerges out of a "that" that already is and that must yet still come into being. The nonsense sounds, then, while seemingly referencing immediate embodiment, also remain self-referential, as if they emerge out of a timeless and formless past into a present split both by the announcement of its coming and the performance of an arrival. This figuration of sound out of bounds—not as the support for a linear narrative but as a confused performance of a "freaky brain"—violates the expectations of the "I-you" relationship in love songs, ballads, and even other dance tunes.

"That Da-Da Strain" thus bridges the transition from the "novelty" song to the blues stage of early jazz. It does so because it combines its comic and dance song elements with a figuration of itself with and against the blues. It aligns itself as an extreme, "freaky" version of the psychological portraits created by blues singers that constituted a nascent black feminist tradition and "a patchwork social history of black Americans during the decades following emancipation" (Davis 1998: 92). Adam Gussow specifies the social appeal and power of Mamie Smith's version of "Crazy Blues" as "partly the result of the complex symbolic rebellion it enacted" (Gussow 2002: 163). When the singer in that song fantasizes that she might "shoot myself a cop," the "black feminist subject's 'crazy' blues response to such a situation is to avenge herself on violence with a fantasized violence of her own" (Gussow 2002: 189). "That Da-Da Strain" enacts such a "crazy" response in the movement of language.

Mamie Smith, along with Ethel Waters, made "That Da-Da Strain" famous in black theaters throughout the United States, and what a listener might have heard in "That Da-Da Strain" is not only an embodied, irrational, temporally shifting, nonsensical, and joyfully alluring escape but also a "freaky" or "crazy" inhabitation of a world of violence, a world in which bodies are fragile, under threat, and displaced. This "da-da" reflects and refracts the white world's socially constructed noise of blackness, transforming black noise into a form of rhythmic power.

The invasion of the "strain" of "da-da" emphasizes the body as a medium that breaks up and breaks away from the containments of (white) language. This mediating effect on the body—and the pleasures embedded within it—also grounds what Mark Gobel calls a "feedback loop between race and technology" in US modernism:

> [R]ace was already so inscribed in the language surrounding new technologies that communicated the immediacy of music like never before, that it was difficult for the musical aesthetic of modernism to register its appeal without recourse to a whole network of racial meanings and iconographies that projected fantasies of blackness onto the medium of recorded sound—making U.S. modernism itself into a kind of feedback loop between race and technology.
>
> (Gobel 2010: 158)

In "That Da-Da Strain," however, this appeal becomes excessive in a way that works against such a "network of racial meanings and iconographies." The song asks its singers and listeners to sound out an objectivity—and a subjectivity—that remains amorphous and actively unformed. It is an objectivity without the stabilizing figure of an object. Language and sound become provisional—weak but irresistible, embodied but outside of the (racialized) body, identity-based but self-consuming, improvisational but notated. These wayward sounds refuse to be merely an expression "of."

This vibrating and unstable objectivity parallels jazz's confusion of noise and music through percussion, particularly in its new attitude toward the ambiguous resonance of everyday objects. An oft-reported aspect of jazz's initial novelty was the inclusion of more percussion sounds—for both sonic and comic effect. Many early descriptions of jazz make a point to emphasize the jazz drummer and the range of sound-making objects they would have arranged around them. Gilbert Seldes, in an article titled "American Noise," mentioned the many "accessories" bands would use: "hardware capable of producing noise, hollow and resonant hardware, frying pans and cowbells" (Seldes 1924: 59). The Belgian jazz critic Robert Goffin described the drummer of early jazz in similar terms:

> No mere skin-beater, the drummer vented his ire on a whole battery of cymbals and other percussive instruments, to the delight of the audience. There were

any number of grotesque utensils to replace the drums of Congo Square. The noisemaker had made its appearance.

(Goffin 1944: 52)

A critical report in *The London Times* also lists the many sound-making objects at hand for the jazz drummer, the "chief conspirator" in the production of noise:

> The object of a jazz band, apparently, is to produce as much noise as possible; the method of doing so is immaterial, and if music happens to be the result occasionally so the better for all concerned. The chief conspirator is the drummer ... Grouped round him are as many things as he can possibly need, motor horns, bells, sheets of tin, anything from which noise can be extracted.
>
> ("The Art of Jazz. Drummer as Chief Conspirator." 1919: 11)

This focus on the noise of the drummer suggests a disorienting effect by which every object becomes a possible noise emitter. Similarly, instruments could become stand-ins for objects; in a recording like the Original Dixieland Jazz Band's "Livery Stable Blues" (1917), instrumental sound becomes comically imitative. The search for strange sounds had a decidedly "corny" quality, but the urge to extend instrumental technique beyond a "well-formed" sound—the trombone glissandos of many early jazz recordings or the intense "blowing" tone of early trumpeters like Louis Armstrong—also emphasized the objective limits and properties of the instruments and the bodies playing them.

Likewise, the intensely repeated "Da-Da" in "That Da-Da Strain" asks the body to resonate as an object, not merely a speaking subject. Even more, "da" with its percussive dental phoneme transforms the voice into the noise-making drum of earlier jazz novelty acts. At the same time, however, "da-da" is a kind of proto-scat that opens up the performance styles of the individual singers who sing the song. Both Mamie Smith and Ethel Waters are not considered "Classic Blues" singers like Bessie Smith and Ma Rainey because their training and sensibility emerged out of vaudeville and theatrical production. Their voices and performances do not emphasize a psychological, expressive interiority but rather a personified mask in character. They use the song to emphasize the belting and "wide-open shouting style" honed through the medium of theatrical performance (Schuller 1968: 226 n.34). This clear style does not emphasize the throaty, microtonal, and sliding aspects of the voice for which Bessie Smith and other blues singers were famous. Instead, this vaudevillian way of singing demands a strong projection with a distinct, consonant-heavy enunciation. These performances might be thought of as ways of writing the song in sound. The voice is on display as a medium for the language of the song, even when that language—as in "That Da-Da Strain"—is unmoored from any representational order. Mamie Smith and Ethel Waters sing with all of their bodies, but those bodies also become the substrate for a language disconnected from any communicative, narrative, or character function. Their bodies are possessed, and they resonate with the noise of "da" as their voices shape its percussive figure. This sounding out also transforms them into "mute" or "mere" objects, noise emitters within channels of communication that mediate the social, political, and material relations between bodies and their sounds.

Noise, then, becomes the amplification of a sound underneath and yet within language. Noise's object for singers like Mamie Smith and Ethel Waters is not only to undo language but also to reimagine the dancing body as a node in a new collective outside the bounds of sound and sense, an insanity of melody. The flood of "da-da-da-da …." is a figure of noise based upon neither a totalizing ideal nor an overwhelming sonic density but rather the headlong and "freaky" production of an undersound within the social fact of difference. By this term "undersound," I mean the sounds that surround, invest, and move through the voices of reason, poetics, tradition, and culture. These inchoate sonic elements become noise when the context shifts, when listening suddenly or surprisingly opens up from an encounter on the page or the phonograph. The noise of "da-da-da-da … " emerges in the sudden shift in context that the song demands: a movement out of "the blues" of everyday life and into the joyful compulsion to become an empty, resonant object communicating by sound.

Eliot's DA DA DA: What the Thunder Said

If Mamie Medina's strain of "da-da" enacts a joyful—if anxious—repetition as a form of communal noise-making, the well-known repetitions of "DA" at the conclusion of T. S. Eliot's *The Waste Land* produce an all-together different tone. Though Eliot's work was deeply associated with "jazz" imagined as a cultural movement, was indebted to the popular song traditions of musical hall and ragtime, and, later, was received by Caribbean writers like Edward Kamau Brathwaite as an expression of "the riddims of St. Louis" in parallel with "the dislocations of Bird, Dizzy, and Klook" (Brathwaite 1984: 41), the way in which the ambiguous call of "DA" reimagines noise through collectivity is very different from the communal movement of bodies in space. Eliot is captivated by the possibility of a radical return to a primitive collective. He reframes Dadaist primitivism to suit his own purpose and, in place of a de-contextualized return of a repressed Other, seeks out origins: "Poetry begins ... with a savage beating a drum in a jungle, and it retains that essential of percussion and rhythm ... " (Eliot 1964: 155). "DA" mimics this percussive origin of poetry.

Its use, however, also shows Eliot's ear caught between a parasitical strain of "da"—"da" as nonsense and deracinated percussion—and a philological listening that produces roots and revelation. Eliot explicitly references the *Brihadaranyaka Upanishad*, in which "DA", the voice of the thunder, is heard as three Sanskrit words. These words—"Datta," "Dayadhvam," and "Damyata" (give, sympathize, control)—follow each iteration of "DA" along with lines of illustration by Eliot. As a sound in excess of and yet caught within the poem's—and language's—mediating system of citation and recitation, the syllable condenses within itself an irrational materiality that Eliot seeks to translate and order. However, this sound also remains, as Mladen Dolar has said of the sound of shofar (a ram's horn instrument blown in Jewish ritual), "a stand-in for an impossible presence, enveloping a central void" (Dolar 2006: 53). In turning to this "DA" and its explicit rendering as "What the Thunder Said" Eliot opens up language to a receding sonorousness that is both the condition for the possibility of a meaning-bearing voice and an active force in such a voice's undoing.

In taking up "DA," then, I want to tie together two disparate readings of the syllable by connecting it with Eliot's philological education. Though *The Waste Land* has been called a "score for a Dada performance piece" (Albright 2004: 51), Eliot described Dada as "mythopoetic nihilism" and a "disease of the French mind" (Eliot 2005 [1921]: 141, 144). On the one hand, against Dada, "DA" foregrounds the "fantasy of a single word that, starting from the same material base as dada, means everything" (McGee 2001: 507). On the other hand, "DA" parallels Dada as it "represents a radical challenge to the primacy of conventional European culture" through the "reduction of language to its barest elements, especially when these are associated with cultures outside of Europe" (North 1998: 89). "DA" holds language and noise in negative dialectical tension. The synchronic spread of "da" as a free radical attaching itself to words and bodies meets the diachronic trace of syllabic radicals in language's history. Eliot's philological citation of "DA" enacts the counter-production of noise embedded within a listening that searches for the roots of language.

Comparative philology, as it developed through the nineteenth century in Germany, England, and America, depended upon methods of listening that drew conclusions by comparing sounds across languages and through the grid of grammar. A root like *Da*—or perhaps more accurately *Dâ*—was literally exemplary because its phonetic and etymological traces could be mapped from ancient- to modern-day languages. Max Müller, an Oxford professor who brought German philological techniques to England, imagined roots as the "germs of human speech:"

> The Aryan root DÂ, to give, appears in Sanskrit dâ-nam, Latin *do-num*, gift, as a substantive; in Latin *do*, Sanskrit da-dâ-mi, Greek *di-dō-mi*, I give, as a verb; but the root DÂ can never be used by itself. ... Roots ... are not, as is commonly maintained, merely scientific abstractions, but they were used originally as real words. What we want to find out is this, What inward mental phase is it that corresponds to these roots, as the germs of human speech?
>
> (Müller 1885: 407)

And yet despite their importance, roots like "DA" also manifested a strangely irrational, ungrammatical character. In books like *The Science of Language*, Müller claims that "[we] have learned what language is made of; we have found that everything in language, except the roots, is intelligible, and can be accounted for" (1885: 316). The roots represent the radical of speech: at what point does a meaningless sound become speech, and when does an "inward mental phase" map onto a mouth sound? Answering these questions usually meant abstracting language sounds through a movement of spatialization that "derives from the imposition of a conceptual grid that enables every phenomenon to be compared, differentiated, and measured by the same yardstick" (Poovey 1995: 9). The list, the grid, and print enabled a mode of comparative listening where grammatical and phonetic rules could be revealed.

This philological sound writing—a phonography *avant la lettre*—also opened up broad questions about the nature of sensation and representation. These questions formed the core "riddle" in the nineteenth-century science of language, particularly as espoused by Müller's comparative method:

> If we were asked the riddle how images of the eye and all the sensations of our senses could be represented by sounds, nay, could be so embodied in sounds as to express thought and excite thought, we should probably give it up as the question of a madman, who, mixing up the most heterogeneous subjects, attempted to change colour into sound and sound into thought. Yet this is the riddle which we have now to solve.
>
> (Müller 1885: 392)

The question of embodiment highlighted here is a question of mediation. Sensory perception parallels the relationship of raw, non-signifying sound to sense: "What is antecedent to the production of roots is the work of nature; what follows after is the work of man" (Müller 1885: 445).

Eliot's "DA" troubles these sensory and media transformations because it states not only the abstract origins of language in prelinguistic perception but also creates a counter-figure of noise—an irrational radical, a linguistic "nature"—that is carried along the signal chain from root to word, sonic value to moral value. For Josh Epstein, Eliot's "DA" reproduces a "'natural' sound as a hybrid palimpsest of media" (Epstein 2014: 97). Eliot thickens the texture of "DA" by rewriting the possibilities for hearing and understanding in *The Waste Land*. Hearing as a form of understanding is the subject of the "Great Forest Upanishad" from which Eliot derives the fable of "What the Thunder Said." This fable, translated into English in 1913 by Eliot's Sanskrit teacher at Harvard, Charles Rockwell Lanman, is based upon listening as an interpretive act (Eliot 2015: 699). The god Praja-pati, "Lord of Children," speaks the syllable "Da" three times and asks three classes of his children (gods, humans, and demons): "Have ye understood?" Each hears the syllable differently: the gods hear "dámyata"—control yourself; the humans, "dattá"—give; and the demons, "dáyadhvam"—be compassionate. At the conclusion of the fable, the narrator aligns god's voice with the voice of the thunder: "This it is which the voice of god repeats, the thunder, when it rolls 'Da Da Da,' that is damyatta, datta, dayadhvam" (quoted in Eliot 2015: 699). In this narrative of hearing and understanding, the voice of the god already speaks before it becomes the voice of thunder. Rather than enchanting nature with a voice, nature supplements what has already been given: the god's syllable.

Eliot's "DA" plays with this movement between hearing and understanding, and between vocalism and thunder. "DA" produces a doubled listening. It reenacts the voice of the thunder—and places the reader in the position of interpreting this percussive and disruptive materiality—while also acting as a citation of the story in the *Brihadaranyaka Upanishad*. In signaling the story as a retelling (done even without the apparatus of the notes), Eliot purposefully distances the "given" exterior moral code that would provide an interpretive frame for the sound. He instead allusively illustrates each word with ambiguous instances of giving, compassion, and control. This provides a mechanism by which Eliot can embody and yet undermine what Jed Rasula calls "Understanding the Sound of Not Understanding" (Rasula 1998: 252). In his estimation, Eliot compensates for the "signifying seditiousness of language" by finding solace in the values of myth: "Language might be slippery, but the enduring values are pre- or extra-linguistic" (Rasula 1998: 252). In this way, for Eliot and other writers working to make up for the play of sound in language, "[t]he work of literature is ... to master unruly dependent classes of signifying particles" (Rasula 1998: 252). The "signifying particle" of "DA" acquires a voice in the anthropomorphic speaking of the thunder. This is also a philological moment: the crossover when "those typical sounds [that are] the residuum of all human speech" become proper "roots," not mere phonation (Müller 1885: 441). However, this "outside" (nature, thunder) is already embedded within language (the voice of god, "typical sounds"). Language carries within itself an excess sonorousness—in the words of Foucault, a "murmur" composed of "continuities, resemblances, repetitions, and natural criss-crossings" (Foucault 1994: 120)—that both demands interpretation and must be pushed aside as a remainder.

It seems that a pre-given moral understanding might guide interpretation: after all, how do the gods, humans, and demons so readily know the right answer? But Eliot's form wrenches the syllable away from its context in the *Brihadaranyaka Upanishad* and with the cut-up texture of surprise and hiatus in the poem before and after it. If poetry must be "more and more comprehensive, more allusive, more indirect, in order to force, to dislocate if necessary, language into ... meaning" (Eliot 2005: 65), the sudden irruption of "DA" in the text produces not only a dislocation but a material that refuses to be made inaudible through the mediation of the fable, its translation, and its explanatory moral. Eliot emphasizes the unintelligibility of "DA," an unconscious randomness at the core of language. This is a strategic element in his "auditory imagination:"

> What I call the "auditory imagination" is the feeling for syllable and rhythm, penetrating far below the conscious levels of thought and feeling, invigorating every word; sinking to the most primitive and forgotten, returning to the origin and bringing something back, seeking the beginning and the end.
>
> (Eliot 1964: 118–19)

In its stark replication on the page and subsequent elucidations, Eliot models this return to the "primitive and forgotten," by which an unconscious sonic particle could invigorate language by charging it with a "feeling for syllable and rhythm."

Eliot, however, does not so much reinforce an essential root of language as relativize and displace its originality. "DA" in each of its iterations remains interjective and interruptive in a way that resists a simple incorporation into the body of the poem or the narrative of "What the Thunder Said." The syllable draws attention to language as an index of citations, a mediating system that changes through time, like a giant game of telephone. Noise exists as a shadowy countercurrent to the figure of voice at the roots of language because the nonsense of "DA" remains a threat to rational discourse. That threat—of breakdown, of instability, of dis-ease, and of strain on the language—moves with the syllable so that the sonic specificity of "DA" matters only so much as it also fills a negative space in an infinite chain of possible sounds. Its arbitrariness is catching. Eliot amplifies "da" into "DA" in a way that emphasizes the "drift" in languages, the "cumulative changes in the articulation of sounds [that] can be related in turn to the interferences that distort any audible communication" (Kubler 1962: 54). Noise resides as a destabilizing effect in the syllable's perceptual, historical, vocal, linguistic, written, and mytho-poetic circulation. Its noise is the arbitrary sound emerging from a *mise en abyme*.

In this way, "DA" gathers together the dissonant acoustic field of *The Waste Land* and reflects the representation and arrangement of noise in the rest of the poem. Juan Suarez hears this arrangement of "abrupt, seemingly haphazard transitions" as "a way to encode the noise in the circuits" of the new media of modernity, in particular the gramophone (Suarez 2007: 134). All the rattling, chuckling, shouting, whining, sighing, crying, twittering, "jug jug jug-ing," "DA"-ing, and grunting, do not represent a return to mythological or primordial origins so much as the distortions of a world mediated by the mechanical—gramophone, film, typewriter, telephone, radio, even the internal combustion engine. The gaps in the poem's structure allow for the noise of mechanical mediation to flow into the space of language. Eliot models an undifferentiated listening that works like a gramophone (or phonograph) because it "does not hear as do ears that have been trained immediately to filter voices, words, and sounds out of the noise" (Kittler 1999: 23). Such a phonographic listening reduces "articulateness" to "a second order exception in a spectrum of noise" (Kittler 1999: 23). As Eliot listens through a dedifferentiating sonic environment, voices only arise as so much sonic wreckage shored against the ruins of subjectivity. In this soundscape of modernity, "sounds became indistinguishable from the circuits that produced them" (Thompson 2002: 3). Meaningful sound gives way to the spaces and channels in which it is produced. The multiple interruptions of modern urban life—the specific noises that overwhelm communication, like internal combustion engines, and a generic level or saturation in noise (newly measurable by "decibels")—reduce the listener's ability to spatialize and organize sound in a field. Eliot's poem diagnoses—and symptomizes—this larger shift in auditory culture.

As a critic, Eliot ambiguously positioned the work of the artist in relation to such control. He describes a version of this phonographic listening in his famous essay, "Tradition and the Individual Talent," in which he claims that the poet has not a "'personality' to express but a particular medium, which is only a medium and not a personality, in which impressions and experiences combine in peculiar and unexpected ways" (Eliot 1950: 9). The poet becomes a "receptacle for seizing and storing up numberless feelings, phrases, images" (Eliot 1950: 6). In closing the gap between a personality and a medium, between the subject and the data it receives, Eliot reimagines the poem as a place for calling forth and recombining what has already been written upon the body and memory. In writing the final section of *The Waste Land*, Eliot described an experience of possession akin to surrealist automatic writing, but he framed it in terms of a feeling of a mediation, as though he were merely a "vehicle and not a maker" of the materials (Eliot 2015: 687). This experience of automatism puts Eliot within a Dadaist and surrealist poetics that questions the relationship between self-possession and being-possessed-by, autonomy and automatism, the perceiving self and modernist writing machines like the phonograph or Freud's unconscious modeled on a mystic writing pad.

Eliot's desire to return to an abstract, purifying, and originary moment in language reflects what Emily Thompson hears as a reactive culture of control in modernity. This is a culture of noise control, mechanical efficiency, and, as we have seen with Adorno, anxiety about musical commodities (Thompson 2002: 3). Eliot is an orchestrator who uses musical culture—in particular Wagner and Stravinsky—to mediate noise (Epstein 2014: 50). His 1921 review of Igor Stravinsky's *Rite of Spring* provides a model for this kind of outside-in transformation of noise into music. Eliot claimed that Stravinsky "transforms the rhythm of the steppes into the scream of the motorhorn, the rattle of machinery, the grind of wheels, the beating of iron and steel, the roar of the underground railway, and the other barbaric cries of modern life; and ... transform[s] these despairing noises into music" (Eliot 2005: 189). *The Waste Land* similarly translates the "despairing noises" of modern life into the space of the poem—not only through motor horns and engines ("But at my back from time to time I hear / The sound of horns and motors" [lines 196–7]) or ragtime ("O O O O that Shakespeherian Rag" [line 128]) but also through the gaps in the text. These elements parallel Tristan Tzara's instructions to write a poem by simply cutting up a newspaper and transcribing results that "will be like you" (1951 [1921]: 92). In this way, the poem "can be heard not only to put the noises of modernity to a beat, but to have an internal grating among its dissonant component parts" (Epstein 2014: 49). As much as Eliot attempts to control his materials, they also necessarily break free of such control, producing an unresolved crisis in representation and listening.

In radicalizing a culture of automatic sound-writing—through the many clanging voices of the poem and in the figure of the linguistic radical "DA"—Eliot exposes the textual voices reproduced in the poem to violence and decay. As they move through their citational circuits, they gather and dissipate their meanings. They become porous. Maud Ellman has discussed how an anxiety over sound, control, and order in *The Waste Land* stems from imagining noise as a kind of abjection:

> In fact, the "horror" of *The Waste Land* lurks in the osmoses, exhalations and porosities, in the dread of epidemic rather than the filth itself, for it is this miasma that bespeaks dissolving limits. The corpses signify the "utmost of abjection" in Kristeva's phrase, because they represent "a border that has encroached upon everything:" an outside that irrupts into the inside, and erodes the parameters of life.
>
> (Ellmann 1987: 94)

The abject—which is neither subject nor object but between them—is waste, excess. *The Waste Land* "repeats the horror that it is trying to expiate. In particular, it desecrates tradition" (Ellmann 1987: 95). Eliot's very cure includes the disease.

In positing a model of philological listening that informs Eliot's "DA," I am drawing on the dis-ease of Dada and—just—"da" as elements that undo the ostensible cure of "roots." The methods of philology—along with Wagnerian sound form, Stravinskyean neo-classicism, and gramophone records—produce another proto-phonographic culture of sonic abstraction. But within this abstraction of sounds—the recording, rewriting, gridding, and comparing of languages—the process of remediation, citation, and circulation reproduces the irrational, erratic transformation of phonetic babble into representative speech, of noise into voice. In implicating philological reproduction in his poem of abjection, Eliot emphasizes the "mediumicity" of language. This is not only what Roman Jakobson would identify as a "set toward the message"—an emphasis upon the code of language itself—but also a phatic checking of the channel of communication (Jakobson 1987: 68). That is, Eliot's poem creates a context in which "the medium can be disturbed or manipulated in such a way as to heighten its reflexivity, resulting either in noise or poetry" (Guillory 2010: 352). "DA" manifests the failure of a poetic myth of wholeness when a disturbance in the channel between gods and mortals interrupts the voice of the thunder. Eliot figures noise—the parasite within citation, the sonic movement of difference and deferral—at the very roots of language, and an imagined "primordial" listening collapses into the dispersal and fragmentation of modernity.

Langston Hughes's "Da, Da, Da": "Negro Dancers"

To conclude this chapter, I would like to turn to a short poem by Langston Hughes, "Negro Dancers," first published in the NAACP's periodical *Crisis* in 1925 and printed again in Hughes's first book, *The Weary Blues* (1926). In this poem, the dance of "da" is evident in another iteration of the syllable's movement through a black modernist literary tradition. If Eliot's poem is epic in scope and spectacular in its failure at coherence, "Negro Dancers" represents a modest fragment of modern life: a scene of black dancers in a cabaret. Written during or just after Hughes's year working at a nightclub in Paris (in 1924), the poem begins with the voice of a "brown-skin stepper:"

> "Me an' ma baby's
> Got two mo' ways,
> Two mo' ways to do de buck
> Da, da,
> Da, da, da!
> Two mo' ways to do de buck!"
> Soft light on the tables,
> Music gay,
> Brown-skin steppers
> In a cabaret. ...

(*Crisis* [March 1925]: 221)

Here, the dance of "da" works doubly, as both the reported voice of the dancer and the sound of the music mediated through that speaking voice. As a representation of the music, "da" marks a beat—one, two/one, two, three!—that grounds the dance of "de buck" (which was changed to the couples dance of "Charleston" after its printing in *The Weary Blues* in 1926).

Hughes shows the dancers caught in another "da-da strain," but he also shows the embeddedness of this "da, da" within an economy of reproduction. Spoken or sung by the voice of the dancer, "da" marks the intrusion of music and rhythm into the speaking voice. And this voice is itself represented as a quoted statement within the poem. "Da, da / da, da, da" functions as the rhythmic "hook" of the poem, and yet discursively it works as an aside or an intrusion, a momentary break from the repetition of "two mo' ways" and the abstract consciousness reporting the scene. The dancer speaks to a kind of phonographic void. The poem records his speech but there is not a univocal "voice" or "speaker" holding the poem together. This is because this recorded speech breaks off for a textual and tonal shift to the generic scene of this encounter. In two-beat, alternately rhyming lines, Hughes calls up the "soft light" of the cabaret. This space, with its tables and rhetorically inflected "music gay," suggests a marginal zone of stillness and spectatorship outside of the dancers' movement and possession. Poetry and writing work within this marginal zone: as technologies for recording, they hold rhythmic possession in place in order to open up its potential for witness.

This marginal zone is a medial and a racialized space. There is an audience of onlookers for the "brown-skin steppers," and they are white. The poem addresses them: "White folks, laugh! / White folks, pray!" The acknowledgment of this particular audience produces a command to parallel the possession witnessed in the dancers' "da, da" movement. In a letter to Countee Cullen, Hughes explicitly sets up black dance against the white world's self-destruction: "We'll dance! Let the white world tear itself to pieces. Let the white folks worry. We know two more joyous steps—two more ways to do de buck! C'est vrai?" (Quoted in Hughes [1995]: 44).

In describing this scene of black joy, Hughes also reveals a question implicit in the act of hearing noise. The violation of "da, da"—a violation that can be spectacularized, transformed into a scene—also functions as a test of hearing. Mamie Medina's "That Da-Da Strain" asks, "Have you heard it"? The voice of the thunder asks its listeners to hear and understand its commands. The Dadaists refuse hearings—as sites of judgment or accounting. In "Negro Dancers" Hughes implicitly asks what he explicitly asks in later poems like "Montage of a Dream Deferred:" "Ain't you heard ... ?" (Hughes 1995: 387). What noise is heard in "da, da"? Is it the noise of a reduction or a rejection—simply nonsense? Or is it the noise of an undersound—something previously unhearable—rising to the surface?

The poem represents the possibility of hearing the otherness of sounds anew. Noise—the parasite—combines with speech, language, rhythmic verse, and song in order to create new complexities, new ways of stepping together. For the poem, as Hughes hints at in his letter to Cullen, embraces blackness not as an escapism but as another way of adapting to a world falling apart—not through a fretful desire for purity but through the coming together of bodies in dance. The noise of collapse is inscribed—and reversed—in "da." Noise arises not only out of the reduction of words to sounds but also in the deferral of expression, the starting again and again with a differently repeated movement. Brent Edwards Hayes describes how "scat aesthetics distends an expressive medium through a proliferation of index" (Hayes 2017: 56). The quasi-scat of "da"—to give way to Louis Armstrong's first recorded scat singing in 1927's "Heebie Jeebies"—proliferates noise as a multiplicity at the crossing point between language and sound, text and speech, performing and recording.

Hughes's textual portrait of "da," then, participates in resignifying what Henry Louis Gates calls the master trope of the black literary tradition—the paradoxical "talking book" (Gates 1988: 130). He does this in the context of an actual sound-writing, a phonographic mediation for texts that makes possible new forms of performative power. For Hughes creates kind of chiasmatic reversal in his rewriting of "da." By embedding the syllable's performance within text constructed as reported and recorded speech, he is also placing writing within the production of an orality that is also an aurality: a sound in the mouth that attempts to translate a movement that exists both inside and outside of the body. Noise emanates from a chaotic, wayward, even freaky citational space, where "da" is all "da's", where rhythmic short circuits can be constructed within and between Dada, jazz, scat, and modernist poetry—and between speech and world. This noise of "da"—in its proliferation of indexes, its deferral to further points of contact—reverses, dissipates, and negates the violence that would demand automatic responses and homogenous results.

4

Projective Versification, Sound Recording, and Technologizing the Body

At Goddard College in 1962, a student asked the poet Charles Olson for permission to tape his reading. In response, Olson contemplates the recording apparatus:

> No, as a matter of fact, I'm just going to watch it, like a fire, let's sit here and watch that tape. [Laughter from Olson] What happens if it just goes on and I don't say anything? See, that's the problem with reading, it gets to be kind of a bore, because it—it's become a performing art, you feel as though you have an audience, and as if you're supposed to do a concert or something, and uh, I don't think I believe in verse in this respect at all. As a matter of fact, I know I don't. [A long pause, followed by the shuffling of papers]
>
> (Olson 1962: 0:33-1:50)

To watch the tape like a "fire" is to transform it from a mute, invisible mechanism into a primordial spectacle. Time flickers and passes. Nothing (or nothing-in-particular) happens "if it just goes on." For this brief moment, Olson embraces the moving tape for the possibility of refusal that it offers. Against the obvious use of tape as a means of preservation, he offers his silence and, with it, the specter of noise. This specter arrives in unbidden fragments—in the shuffling of papers, the incidental sounds of others in the room, and the recorded static on tape. Olson's call to attention (or, rather, to *in*attention) folds these marginal sounds into the reading and recording—not through an active search for those sounds but rather through their resonance within the evacuated space of Olson's oral performance. These sounds—unvoiced, barely there, and, in the moment, even impossible to hear (as in the case of the tape hiss)—counter the use of verse as a "performing art" while also emerging out of and in contact with the speaker's voice.

In this chapter, I follow this counteracting trace of noise as a refusal *of* performance *within* performance. Such a figure of noise emerges within a projectivist impulse that binds together two radically different and yet intimately related poetic projects at mid-century: rock 'n' roll and experimental verse influenced by and in conversation with Charles Olson's influential essay, "Projective Verse." These two different forms of verse intertwine in complementary ways. Both begin in the mediated production of voices as recorded or textual artifacts. In what would seem to be exactly the opposite of the import of the Goddard College recording, each art emphasizes a specifically oral performance of voice through the mediation of print and audio recording. "Projective Verse" is thick with references to the spoken, embodied condition of poetry, and many historians of rock 'n' roll make much of the fact that the mid-fifties were not only the years in which Elvis Presley first topped the charts but also the first years in which phonographic recordings outsold sheet music in the United States.[1] In other words, both poetic forms might be read as evidence of Walter Ong's concept of "secondary orality," "a more deliberate and self-conscious orality" produced through and by writing, in which new forms of inscription—in particular the sound-writing of audio recordings—emphasize the presence of the spoken word through mediations that distance it in time and space (Ong 1982: 133). But both of these arts defamiliarize this "secondary" experience in the midst of a vast expansion of mediated sound after the Second World War. The proliferation of voices in sound media paralleled the use of "voice" as the ideal of communication that could mask the noises of public life. By opening a space for—and even amplifying—the outside, incongruous, grainy, and disruptive sounds within speech and song, projectivist work pushes against the masking and domesticating effects of voice.

In doing so, both of these forms of organizing voice, speech, and sound implicitly and explicitly critiqued an expanded sound culture of vocalization by turning the mediation of orality away from itself and toward noise. They seek out the distortions available through mouth sounds and what Charles Olson calls "mu-sick." Literally to "twist in different ways," distortion combines the actions of rending apart and folding in ("Distortion," OED). It creates breaks where other sounds can emerge in accidental ways. Poets like Olson, Robert Creeley, and Amiri Baraka as well as musicians like Little Richard, Fats Domino, and Elvis Presley performed methods of distortion that not only

---

[1] For references to rock as a return to an oral condition, see David Hatch and Stephen Millward, *From Blues to Rock: An Analytical History of Pop Music* (1989); Richard Peterson, "Why 1955? Explaining the Advent of Rock Music" (1990); and Robert B. Ray, *How a Film Theory Got Lost and Other Mysteries in Culture Studies* (2001).

deformed the voice as a metaphorical and a sonic figure but also arranged the sounds of a voice within a wider matrix of spatial and temporal transformation at work at mid-century. As social and technological change reorganized the presence of sound for performers and audience-members as well as workers and consumers, the manipulations of voice in rock 'n' roll and projectivist verse actively refused and reframed "voice" in order to amplify energies outside of but contiguous with a classic scene of poetic communication. This amplification explicitly distorts by feeding an outside of voice—a continuous sounding against but also within performance or communication—into the vocal projection of a body. Through their emphatic performances, voice becomes a destabilized conduit for noise rather than a reified index of a personality, character, subject, or institution.

Voices

The specter of noise that emerges through the mask of voice is the materialized sound of mishearing: sounds out of place in both space and time, sounds that break up sequences and articulations. After the Second World War, decentralized networks of communication and new portable technologies for playback and recording meant that not only were there more sounds, they were also available to more people. As Douglas Kahn succinctly states, "there were more sounds and people could hear them more quickly" (1999: 12). A diverse array of sound designers—phone company engineers, military researchers, psycho-acousticians, city designers, and Muzak operators, not to mention record producers and avant-garde musicians—reshaped this expanded sound world through what Jonathan Sterne calls the "domestication of noise" (2012: 117). This "domestication" stemmed from a more robust definition of noise in the nascent field of information theory. Claude Shannon and Warren Weaver's *Mathematical Theory of Communication* (1949), contrary to earlier formulations of communications theory, included noise as a necessary element *within* an information system (Sterne 2012: 87). In their theory, "[t]he significant aspect is that the actual message is one *selected from a set* of possible messages," and so any information not preselected as the message to be moved from one point over to another point is, simply, noise (Shannon and Weaver 1949: 1). This abstraction effectively relativizes the distinction between noise and not-noise: noise is reduced to an effect on (as well as a condition of) the passing of a message. In this figuration, it emerges not as an outside or "other" sound but rather as the effect of an internal framing, a given obstacle for successful communication. Paradoxically, just as noise is figured as an "objective" mathematical generalization it also emerges in its most "subjective" form. It is simply what is not "selected from a set of possible messages." In a world of constant communication, noise is everywhere and nowhere.

This theoretical flattening conditioned the ways in which sounds were heard. A practice emerged of masking rather than attempting to eliminate unwanted sounds. The "easy" and "productive" sounds of Muzak expanded their reach into factories, stores, mass transit, and public spaces. Though the practice of piping in music in factories and workspaces began in the 1920s, it was only in the 1940s that the amplification of music became powerful enough for factory managers to use it to mask mechanical sounds (Bjisterveld 2008: 86). Masking sounds with other sounds also became a domestic possibility. With the expansion in the number of local radio stations following the war, the growth in transistor radio ownership, and the segmentation of radio programs, portable sound became highly individualized. People listened to their radios as a way of defining themselves within social spaces—and shutting out the contrary "noises" of others (Douglas 2004: 221). Listeners could territorialize space in new ways (Deleuze and Guattari 1987: 312). Similarly, within the milieu of communications technology, rather than attempting to refine away unwanted sound, "communication engineers began to articulate a paradigm where noise no longer needed to be eliminated or reduced if it could simply be rendered imperceptible to the ear" by the masking of "unnecessary" frequencies (Sterne 2012: 124). From the suburban mall to the city street and from powerful amplified speakers to tiny telephone receivers, newly developed forms of electro-acoustic mediation could cover over or overpower the sounds that did not produce coded messages.[2]

The metaphor of "volume" works here at the confluence between space and energy or power. In all these diverse spaces and mediations, coded sounds had more volume. They literally took up more space in order to saturate channels of communication and public places. As social space at the micro- and macro-cosmic level split into a variety of "acoustic territories" that each masked and domesticated a different noise, it also manifested a "relational geography" that

---

[2] For more on the design of audio spaces: Karin Bjisterveld, *Mechanical Sound*; Brandon LaBelle, *Acoustic Territories*; Michael Bull, "Soundscapes of the Car;" Barry Blesser and Linda-Ruth Salter, *Spaces Speak, Are You Listening? Experiencing Aural Architecture*; Jonathan Sterne, "Sounds Like the Mall of America;" Joseph Lanza, *Elevator Music: A Surreal History of Muzak, Easy Listening and Other Moodsong*.

created new demands for reaction, response, and attention (LaBelle 2010: xxv). For instance, as radio stations proliferated, they also reduced the variety of their programming to include a single format or musical genre. Radio stations attempted to appeal to particular demographics and to develop loyalty, but at the same time, listeners had the freedom to choose among various stations and therefore between different moods and identities (Douglas 2004: 221). Thus, greater technological and commercial refinements in the mediation of sound expanded the number of *significant* sounds—sounds calling listeners to attention—and, at the same time, increased the amount of noise by creating more interstices between stations. The well-known sonic cliché of "dialing in" to a radio station—with its uncertain blast of static giving way to voice or song— figures noise within an overlapping and pluralized sound world.

In the midst of such din, "voice" took on a newly expanded role. Voice, or rather the "mechanical semblance of voice," becomes "the signal in a medium whose material base is sonic, not vocal" (Bernstein 2011: 110). The voice—as the sonic bearer of a code and message through the mediation of sound—becomes a mechanism for the production of presence through the medium. It is the means by which the strange process of disembodiment becomes naturalized through the anthropomorphic figure of personification (Prins 2004: 47). Commodified and recognizable "voices" emerged from radios and records—think "The Voice," Frank Sinatra. The production of voice was explicit in radio, as "listeners developed personal bonds with the personification of postwar radio, the disc jockey" (Douglas 2004: 225). DJs' voices created the means for identification and consumption through the anthropomorphism of agency and the mask of a persona.

Voice as a mechanical semblance of intention also describes the effects of Muzak and other background sounds. Even as it hides a specific "vocalic" agent, Muzak sets the tone for a space. It creates ambience and masks noise. As it covers over the incidental sounds of conversation, work, and movement in a store it also sets the conditions of possibility for a participant listener to feel and "know" a space. Hence, "volume and tempo come to impress themselves upon the shopping body, as a contouring intervention onto the energy flows and expenditures, continually modulated so as to structure or contort the movements of spending" (LaBelle 2010: 179). This "contouring intervention" works as an agency suturing bodies to movements and spaces. Such sound masks—as in those of radio and records—function like poetic masks or personas. These (ambient) voices are mechanically reconstructed sonic surfaces projecting personality and authority.

The constant emergence of vocalic agency defines what Olson calls in his "Songs of Maximus" the "musickracket / of all ownership... " (*The Maximus Poems* I.14). It is also the condition for an increase in noise imagined as sound working against sounds that are coded as voices in a particular time, space, and situation. "Musickracket" holds "music," "sick," and "racket" together as an indication of the ways in which vocalic sounds continuously vie for attention and obedience from listeners. A dense sound world of mediated and remediated electro-acoustic signals made more demands upon listeners to recognize not only the address within such sounds but also themselves as "the addressed" within such calls. The increased presence of mediated sounds in everyday life demanded an increase in listeners' awareness *of* sounds and presence *to* sounds. Listeners had to navigate new forms of mediated agency and ownership that expanded the meaning and range of voices in order to mask noises.

Sound in Projective Verse

It is in the midst of such an extension in vocalic recognition and listening—fronting an ideology of domestic order and self-determination—that Olson first used the pun "mu-sick" in his 1946 "ABC" poems. Throughout his long, unfinished epic, *The Maximus Poems*, "mu-sick" denotes the encroaching sounds of a new culture industry. The implicit etymology in "mu-sick"—the Greek root *mu* is mouth, hence "mouth-sickness"—denotes a larger social disease in which language separates from action and myth ("muthos" for Olson). The word invokes the sounds of "the pejoracracy," the culture that would "advertise us out" (*The Maximus Poems* I.4). The sick mouth—the sick myth—undergirds a fantasy of regulation, rationalization, and coercive enjoyment, a domesticity in which "a house these days / [is] so much somebody else's" (*The Maximus Poems* I.14).

Olson's reaction—the reaction that defined projective verse—was to produce a kind of "illiteracy:" "In our post-pre-literate period you must get close to illiterate to be a human being" (quoted in Boer 1991: 26). In "The Songs of Maximus," an early poem in the series, the poet commands the listener to sing—and also "sings" alone—in order to turn language against the "post-pre-literate period," a period in which the eye and ear are "invaded, appropriated, outraged" (*The Maximus Poems* I.13). The "mu-sick" that puts "words, words, words/all over everything" and makes it so that "no eyes or ears [are] left to do their own doings" defines a sound world in which "no moving thing moves / without that song I'd void my ear of ... " (I.14). Olson experienced such domination over the senses in the Washington, DC, transit system in the late 1940s and 1950s. The Muzak corporation created a "Radio Transit" program for the streetcars. Protests against this "compulsory listening" resulted in a legal battle that went to the Supreme Court in 1951 (Lanza 1995: 51). As if in response to this music meant to muffle the noise of the cars and other passengers, Olson asks rhetorically, "how can we go anywhere, / even cross-town // how get out of anywhere" (*The Maximus Poems* I.13)? There are no opportunities to escape the already given. Olson's "Songs" figure singing against the compulsion of mu-sick. They counter it with an exhortation to "go / contrary, go // sing." They command a movement against what one is "in:"

> In the midst of plenty, walk
> as close to
> bare
>   In the face of sweetness,
> piss
>   in the time of goodness,
> go side, go
> smashing, beat them, go as
> (as near as you can
> tear
>
>   (*The Maximus Poems* I.14)

To sing is to push language away from the kind of sound that "public conveyances / sing" (I.13). To sing is to piss, to beat, to tear, to "go side, go"—that is, to rip apart, to move "as close to / bare" as possible, and, even more, to listen against the grain. Rhythmically, the lines emphasize a rending movement, as the prepositional phrase and nouns ("in the midst of plenty") give way to dramatic monosyllabic commands separated by pauses (a comma and then line breaks).

In this way, Olson contests one version of an addressing song with the song of "you" in "Song 6:"

> you sing, you
> who also
> wants
>
>   (*The Maximus Poems* I.16)

This singing calls up an "illiterate" vocality against the "street-cars['] / song." Such an oral resistance becomes generalized in the essay "Projective Verse," written by Olson in correspondence with Frances Bolderoff and Creeley and first published in *Poetry New York* in 1950. It celebrates a poetics of presence and energy based upon breath and speech: "[B]reath allows all the speech-force of language back in (speech is the 'solid' of verse, is the secret of a poem's energy)" (Olson 1997b [1950]: 244). In this way, Olson imagines a poetic language that actively pushes against both the "closed" "verse which print bred" and the piped-in communication of Muzakified voice by the embodied movements of breath and speech (Olson 1997b [1950]: 239). He imagines verse as the possibility of moving away from a univocal model in which a message is simply reported to passively listening ears.

As a media theorist of verse, Olson in "Projective Verse" imagines a form of communication, of "energy transfer" in "composition by field" that hears the poem at work within an oral culture made available through the typewritten page. Many of Olson's early assumptions about the mediation of print and orality are built upon the work of Albert Lord and Milman Parry. Their studies examined the compositional methods of a Balkan singer who rhapsodized by memory and by ear, and they theorized the distinct poetic elements of Homeric epic and oral cultures—in particular metrical repetition and rhyme schemes—as mnemonic devices (see Lord 2000 [1960]). In "Projective Verse," Olson hears an immediacy and spontaneity in such speech-based oral poetics, but he also sees the typewriter and page as materials that can open the ear to new sound values in speech. As "a script to ... vocalization," "the intervals of [the ear's] composition," as in the work of William Carlos Williams and Ezra Pound, "could be so carefully put down as to be precisely the intervals of its registration" (Olson 1997b [1950]: 245). Phonographic precision, Olson suggests, directly "registers" oral performance.

Even more, this direct registration is already a recording of the ear's movement at "the mind's speed." For Olson, writing begins with the "minimum of speech," the syllable, and so it begins with a relation to "the ear, the ear which has collected, which has listened, the ear, which is so close to the mind that it is the mind's, that it has the mind's speed ... " (Olson 1997b [1950]: 242). In this way, his work precedes the idealization of orality in the media theories of Marshall McLuhan and Walter Ong. Ong describes "secondary orality" as "deliberate and self-conscious orality, based permanently on the use of writing and print" (Ong 1982: 133). In this belated orality, the speed of speech is conflated with the speed of electronic mediation. As Olson's ear listens to speech at the "mind's speed," it is moving at what Marshall McLuhan, in *Understanding Media* (1964), called the "quick and implicit" speed of "the spoken word" (1964: 89). Olson's celebration of a speech-based energy in "composition by field" parallels McLuhan's sense of a radiophonic, "electric age" that gives humans "the means of instant, total field-awareness" (McLuhan 1964: 58). Sound, particularly the sound of speech in Olson's and McLuhan's formulations, is figured as "a unified field of instant relationships" (McLuhan 1964: 304). For Olson, as for Ong and McLuhan, the fugitivity of sound conditions an instantaneity that can, paradoxically, be captured through the "secondary" mechanism of recording.

This field of instant relationships is the material of McLuhan's famous figure of the "global village" (1964: 106). It is also the stuff of Olson's vision for the "polis," a politics in which word and thing, speech and action, are not separated but rather consubstantial (*The Maximus Poems* II.15). To begin the poem at the level of the syllable, to organize the poem in the "field" of the typewritten page, to use the typescript as a score for performance—all of these parts of Olson's program sought to replace and dismantle centralized aesthetic autonomy with a spontaneous transference of energy. The instant, idealized feedback between hearing, speaking, and writing/recording imagines an unmediated presence that can, as Ong describes, produce a "participatory mystique, [and foster] a communal sense" that emphasizes "the present moment" (Ong 1982: 133). The instantaneous, improvised "sound" of the poet rethinks the relationship between sound and sense. Language becomes reenergized and reintegrated as a physical, even physiological, emanation of a body.

Sound against Voice

The projectivist turn toward orality, breath, and "the ear" participates in a wider cultural turn toward "sound" as a category separate from music and poetry at mid-century. "Sound in itself" became a contested philosophical and sensory locus that challenged the anodyne soundscapes produced by acoustic territorialization, commodity culture, and urban and suburban isolation.[3] In addition to advances in sound recording and transmission, the theories of writers and composers as well as, importantly, the *uses* of sound by composers

---

[3] A split presaged by the science of acoustics, urban planning, and architectural design, in addition to new aesthetic experiments like sound poetry and the burgeoning creation of a spatialized "sound art" separate from the other arts of sound. See Kate Bjisterveld, *Mechanical Sound: Technology, Culture, and Public Problems of Noise in the Twentieth Century* (Cambridge: MIT Press, 2008); Brandon LaBelle, *Background Noise: Perspectives on Sound Art* (New York: Bloomsbury, 2006); and Emily Thompson, *The Soundscape of Modernity* (Cambridge: MIT Press, 2002).

and poets of all sorts (from popular musicians to avant-garde poets), shifted away from a sense of music as ineffable spirit (an organizing metaphor in high modernism) toward a self-conscious concretization of acts of listening that could trouble the lines between index and representation, rhythm and duration, sound and noise.

Thinking with the music of John Cage and Edgard Varèse, Jean-Francois Lyotard argues that "what we call music never stops becoming, or becoming again, an art of sound, a competence *to* sound" (Lyotard 1991: 178). Though Lyotard is making a general comment about music as a totality, he shows how this "competence to sound" is a historical artifact, a "discovery" built into the radical means by which composers emphasized *listening* over the act of producing sound. John Cage's 1952 silent piece 4'33" spectacularizes such acts of listening, but it is one example in a generalized shift in "the production of music from the site of utterance to that of audition" (Kahn 1999: 158). This turn toward listening aligned with a radical attention to the construction of sound as an object, material, or sensation separate from its referential or signifying effect. Different avant-garde composers created theorizations for a "purified" or absolute sound: in Cage's indeterminacy and silences, "sound in itself;" in Pierre Schaefer's *musique concrete*, "sound objects;" and in early electronic music, the pure synthesized periodicities of sine waves. Many of the experimenters in these fields were working with the same tools and paradigms of telecommunications engineers, though for seemingly opposed ends.

In this version of music's "marriage ... with techno-science" (Lyotard 1991: 178), composers who worked closely with technologies of recording and production could produce a critique of vocality in music and communication. While communication engineers worried over trade-offs between bandwidth and clarity, these composers critically reevaluated the domination of acoustic space and asked how to produce new modes of listening outside of reified or ideological frames. Douglas Kahn describes Cage's project to cleanse music of all referentiality: "communication, ideas, and intention were ... to be expunged so all that was left was a *sound in itself*" (1999: 165). Similarly, Pierre Schaefer's theorization and use of "acousmatic sound"—sound in which the source is hidden or undetermined—emphasized a mode of listening that bracketed the recognition or ascription of a sound in order to hear sound objects as distinct phenomenological forms (Kane 2014: 121). The turn against the intention-bearing utterance of the voice is a reaction to the constant call of various social, institutional, and political uses for sound.

Perhaps the most famous instance of this deinstrumentalization of sound through its conditions of technological mediation is John Cage's storied visit to Harvard's anechoic chamber in 1948 (1961: 4). Built to muffle all reverberation, these rooms, specialized for studies in acoustics, make it possible to listen to another form of "pure" sounds, i.e., sounds unmuddied by the infinitesimal echo returning from a space's walls and crevices. There, Cage realized "there is no such thing as silence," a radical discovery that continues to influence thinking on the relationship between sound, life, and noise (Cage 1961: 8). Cage's simple act of listening does not necessarily contradict the space's purpose. An instrument of measurement and analysis, the chamber becomes a means of negation as Cage performs a techno-scientific *reductio ad absurdum*. In this technologically mediated phenomenological reduction, what the listener hears is the body listening to itself—heartbeat and tinnitus, rhythm and ringing ears.

This zero degree of listening allows Cage to produce an ontology of sound that would reduce relationships of power—the projection of messages, the domination of acoustic territory—to an anarchic flux. Cage called for the "demilitarization of language; no government" (Cage 2004: 224). His project was built on Zen-inspired philosophy of being that sought not only to overturn logic and statement but also to make "the being of sound ... a metonym for (ideal) being in general" (Dyson 1992: 384). Sound's phenomenal qualities—its nondirectionality, its filling up of space, its inability to be "silenced," its ephemerality, its seeming "immediacy," its constant movement—become important openings into being in general. This projected anarchic, paratactic listening dedifferentiates self and world. The "nothing" that is the subject can possess the nothing that is sound—"no one loses nothing because nothing can be securely possessed"—and every body and every object becomes equivalent (quoted in Dyson 1992: 385). Rather than a symbolism in which "a particular thing is a symbol of a particular other thing," Cage's music shows how "each thing in the world can be seen as a symbol of every other thing in the world" (quoted in Nyman 1999: 36).

What is removed in this philosophical armature that rejects intentionalized sound is the continued contestation of difference: of the unstable movement between ways of clear listening and ways of creating productive mishearing. Voice and noise collapse into an abstract, all-over sound. *Imaginary Landscape No. 4* (1951), a piece that calls for twelve radios, twenty-four performers, and one conductor, produces a cacophony of overlapping acoustic territories.

The score, constructed with the use of chance operations from the *I Ching*, consists of indications for radio tuning, volume, and tone color. The imaginary landscape of musics, voices, and static directly indexes how radiophonic expansion shifted postwar acoustic space into a fragmented register of competing auralities. This is the underside of McLuhan's "global village." But the piece also asks us to imagine this cacophony of sounds as a new "landscape," a composition of a space that is neither here nor there, produced neither inside nor outside of the room, and that says "nothing." In Cage's music sound is "liberated from traditional representational devices," and so listeners' ideal, zero degree relationship to these liberated sounds becomes most important (LaBelle 2015: 25). *Imaginary Landscape No. 4*, however, also explicitly "devoices" the radio and shows how Cage's "emblematic silence was founded on a silencing of communications technologies" (Kahn 1999: 199). Cage's "silence" is not a neutral void but rather an act of silencing in order to discover or find sound in itself.

Sound in Rock 'n' Roll

In contrast to the search for a sound in itself, the studio art of rock 'n' roll produced a spectacularized figuration of sound. A record's "sound" became a malleable sound form, untethered from both an essential sonorousness and an indexical realism. Rock 'n' roll's particular amalgamation of styles and initial popularity was connected to expanded markets for listening to and buying records. As an exemplary case, Elvis Presley's admitted sources were "his radio, his phonograph, and religious 'camp meetings'" (Gracyk 1996: 192). The range of styles that Elvis used—the rhythm and blues of Arthur Crudup, the country of Bill Monroe, the pop of Dean Martin—resulted from a musical education via the disembodied voice of the radio. Rock 'n' roll was produced in a radiophonic world, and its first practitioners were privy to an unprecedented variety of broadcast music. Thanks to the "secondary orality" of the radio and the record, they were able to select their own auditory environments and listen to songs over and over again. The hybrid genealogy of rock 'n' roll reflects these multiple sources of tradition.

Even more, these pure products of America—or rather, American secondary orality—made *records* first:

What distinguishes rock & roll from all the music that precedes it—especially classical, Tin Pan Alley, and jazz—is its elevation of the record to primary status. While classical and jazz recordings for the most part aimed only at approximating live performances, regarded as the significant event, many of rock's most important musicians, beginning with Elvis, made records before ever appearing in public.

(Ray 2001: 72)

This attention to records also helped create a sea change in commercial music sales:

The commercial success of rock & roll promoted the gramophone record to the position of being the most successful medium for the dissemination of music in the United States: overtaking, after more than thirty years of competition, the medium of sheet music. This change in the balance of marketing power resulted from the location of rock & roll within the oral/aural tradition. Thus the music was learned by its established musicians and novices, and appreciated by its fans, by means of gramophone records alone, sheet music exposition being a redundant medium in the dissemination of rock & roll.

(Hatch and Millward 1989: 8)

As recordings of rock 'n' roll sold more than sheet music, record labels as opposed to music publishers took on more economic power. An economy of phonography, of "written sound," overturned an economy of print.

This economy was reflected in a formal shift, as well: it was "the sound" that became a central element in the emerging genre of rock 'n' roll. Rock 'n' roll artists experimented with phonographic inscription by playing with different ways of documenting the sound of an ensemble performing:

Recording musicians are well aware that as they sing and play they also perform acts of inscription, they leave something behind. Or better, they pass something on. Although their performances originate as activities, they become textual content.

(Zak 2001: 51)

Such "textual content" combined the techno-science of recording with the human production of sound through voice and instrument. In this way, they produced a form of written song invested with both the force of performance and the self-conscious creation of a "sound." David Byrne describes his own interest in this manifestation of sound, imagined, in particular, as a "texture:"

> When I grew up and first started hearing rock music, pop, and soul, it was the sound that really struck me. The words were, for the most part, pretty stupid. But it was the sound, the texture of the guitar and drums, the way one song sounded so completely different than another. The texture a group of musicians arrives at, in support of melody or lyrics, can be at least as important as the melody line or lyrics or whatever.
>
> (quoted in Gracyk 1996: 64)

Such a differentiated and varied texture is based not only upon the performance of a group of musicians but also upon the manipulation of recorded sound through studio engineering, collage, and electronic effects. Rock 'n' roll, as "a music of very specific sound qualities and their textural combination" (Gracyk 1996: 161), also depends upon a demotic techno-science of sound, a cheaper version of the experimental electro-acoustic laboratories found in Ivy League colleges and telecommunications companies.

Even as a recorded inscription of sound texture, rock 'n' roll poetics still depended on the voice as a suturing, expressive figure. Just as the voices of DJs connected audience members and radio stations, the "voice" of the singer became an object of fascination and fetishization. There is an insistence on not only sound texture but also the sound of the voice. In the words of The Rolling Stones (channeling Wordsworth), it is "the singer not the song." The generalized expansion of aurality that defines this moment in sound culture and audio technology was, as we have seen, given shape by a renewed orality. But the sound values changed. The textural emphasis in rock 'n' roll emphasized the distortions made possible by the doubled mediation of the singer: a mediation by the mouth within and in relation to the mediation of electro-acoustic transmission. Artists—with the help of producer-engineers who negotiated the technological demands of recording with the psychological urgency of performance—created a style for and by the recording medium. Sam Phillips saw his work as a producer in terms of another figure of embodied listening, the psychologist:

> I went into the studio to draw out a person's innate, possibly unknown talents, present them to the public, and let the public be the judge. I had to be a psychologist and know how to handle each artist and how to enable him to be at his best. I went with the idea that an artist should have something not just good, but totally unique. When I found someone like that, I did everything in my power to bring it out.
>
> (quoted in Marcus 1975: 145)

What this means in material terms is the manipulation of the sound of the voice for the recording apparatus. Phillips at Sun Studios in Memphis and other producers recorded artists with an ear to their recorded output—to the sound of voices heard through the electroacoustic medium. The "voice" of the performer thus became the site of a multiplicity of transformations, of listenings overlaid by more listenings. For the performer's voice emerged not only as an imitation of other voices but also as a configuration of multiple technologies of recording, filtration, and transformation.

The transformation of mediated aurality into a vocalized orality connects this moment in communications technology, projective verse, and rock 'n' roll. The avant-garde turn toward sound in itself or sound alone reacted to this trend to subsume sound under the figure of voice. However, rather than merely masking noise through an overpowering and territorializing vocality or, alternatively, imagining a purifying eradication of the trace of causality in sound, rock 'n' roll and projective verse staged a conflict between voice and noise by folding speech and electronically mediated sounds into each other through forms of distortion. In this way, these mixed and hybrid forms of song open up a space between the articulate and the inarticulate, rhythms and spasms, person and instrument that let noise in to the figure of voice, that figured noise in the silencing and breaking up of voice.

From Voice to Noise

Even as technological mediation spectacularized the production of sound and voice in rock 'n' roll, this spectacle was also built upon extremes in which the failures of embodiment and the distortions of an objectified voice came to the fore. In this way, a poetics of noise becomes available within the technoscientific and verse genre of rock 'n' roll. Noise in this instance is not the simple nominalism of critical misprision (as in the many instances of the reduction of the newest popular music to a belittled "noise") nor is it a fixed sound object— an identifiable acoustic "irregularity." Rather, noise remains a spectral figure written in relationships between the sounds of voices and instruments as well as the relationships between embodied performances and the recording apparatus. Performers and producers could open up new possibilities of distortion in which acts of twisting and rending could destabilize the boundary between the textual and textural elements of a recording and its marginal and excessive ones. Rock 'n' roll made possible the discovery and amplification of the sonic remnants of communication, a broken and "transistorized" orality that bracketed the resistance of objects to the theoretical dreams of the smooth flow of information in a "global village."

The treatment of voice in rock 'n' roll performance directly manifests this search for and amplification of noise. The new techniques of listening that emerged from rock 'n' roll not only emphasized a new performance of voice, but also positioned that voice in (and *as*) an abstract, free-floating sonic space composed of textures and accidents. New techniques in capturing sound—particularly through tape machines—allowed for voices to be written as sound in ways that opened them to disorder and excess. Three different sound-shaping methods emerge: an emphasis upon vocal grain, nonsense language, and para-linguistic sounds; the over-performance or "overdriving" of voices and instruments; and the decoupling of the recording from any sonorous unity or "reality effect." These methods allow for a flattening, twisting, and metamorphosing of space and time in ways that trouble a sense of the record as a simple document and the voice as a personifying figure. To "shake, rattle, and roll," "to twist," to move, to "get gone," to "rock and roll" are not just openly secret calls to dance and desire. They also call up the surface distortions in sound that use electronics and communications media against themselves in order to stage a conflict between voices and noises, between recognition and differentiation.

I want to follow the destabilizing trace of noise in four rock 'n' roll recordings that represent a self-conscious "recognition of absence by which we classify representations *as* representations, recordings *as* recordings" (Lastra 1992: 83). This recognition is folded into and projected outward from the works rather than hidden in the implicit background work of communications and recording engineers. Often through economical experimental methods, rock 'n' roll artists aestheticized the act of constructing and producing sound as such. As both a music and an attitude toward recording, then, there are extreme moments in rock 'n' roll's genealogy that take up the black radical tradition that Fred Moten defines in *In the Break*. In the midst of a "historical reality of commodities who spoke"—the "material heritage" of slavery—rock 'n' roll can manifest "the breaking of such speech" and the "rich content of the object's/commodity's aurality outside the confines of meaning ... by way of this material trace" (Moten 2003: 6). It does this by showing its material traces in an oxymoronic condition of embodiment and disembodiment. On the one hand, it emphasizes the timbre, grain, specificity, and resistant aurality of a particular body's voice, but on the other hand, it emphasizes construction, dissolution, and the dissipation of the figure of voice.

Antoine "Fats" Domino's 1949 "The Fat Man" is a paradigmatic entrance into this economy of voice and noise. One of the first songs described and successfully marketed as a rock 'n' roll recording, this performance combines different strains of black music—boogie-woogie piano, swing jazz, and rhythm and blues—through a new relation to the force of the beat. Domino intensifies and abstracts the repetitive rhythms of boogie-woogie by reducing the music's swing and harmonic range. He freezes "the more fluid boogie-woogie" into a kind of "pounding rhythm" (Doerschuk 1992: 110). Domino was well known in New Orleans for his "hammering" of the piano in performances (Coleman 2006: 7). Though such "hammering" may seem staid to contemporary ears, this inexorable attitude toward the beat becomes an important element in the genre of rock 'n' roll. The continuous repetition of "the riff" rather than the melodic, harmonic, and rhythmic variation typical of jazz performance opens up a new relationship to space and time in song. The rhythmic asceticism puts the beat on display, and at the same time the sense of continuity opens up as a field upon which the voice can be projected.

Rather than a structure complete in its own self-possessed narrative or thematic framework, such a song form emphasizes its constructed and contingent possibilities. The voice, words, and instruments float on a rhythm that seems to exist before and after the song. Within this framework of (spectral) continuity, a fragmentary concatenation of sonic effects—which include the voice—moves over and with the pulse. Domino's singing is smooth and articulated in contrast with the piano's hammering: "They call, they call me the Fat Man" (0:37). In the "solo" section of the song (1:07–1:37), however, this impassive voice gives way to a high falsetto that dramatically departs from the sound of the voice in the rest of the song. The texture changes, and the layers of drums, piano, saxophone, and vocals give way to a single repeated syllable that the singer varies rhythmically and melodically:

wah-wah wah
wah wah
wah wah waaaah wah wah wah ... (1:07–1:15)

The movement from closed to opened mouth sounds (from "w" all the way to "ah") creates a shift in the tonal envelope of Domino's voice. A muffled mid-range gives way to a wider expanse of frequencies.[4] This "wah" functions as broken speech: a baby's cry, a phoneme that is almost "want" and "what," connoting desire, confusion, or estrangement. At the same time, it makes a saxophone-like wail. Through the mediation of recording, the voice can become mutable, sounding like a horn and a cry, in an uncanny assemblage of human and nonhuman elements. This complicated embodiment simultaneously shows off vocality and occludes it—hiding it behind a blur of tones and mimicry.

The movement of voice as a mimetic device, however, also opens up the space for a weird, otherworldly anti-mimeticism. The sound simultaneously offers up the voice *as* a saxophone while refusing that assimilation. The imitation of the instrument is not in the shape of melodic repetition but rather in the shape of a sonic retransmission. Domino's voice is literally instrumentalized—taking up the space and time in which there would typically be a saxophone solo. It thus launches itself into a space between different inventions (and conventions) of voice. The voice imitates the saxophone imitating the voice imitating a cry, and these layers of substitution invite the unsettled instability of noise into the vocal performance.

This is not scat singing in Louis Armstrong's mode because it no longer implies a differentiated set of phonemes that the singer slides between in melodic improvisation. It no longer imagines language itself, through the "syllable," as implying the possibility of its own undoing. Rather, it rejects language for a rescrambling of sonic codes. By throwing the voice out into the vocalized space of the instrument so that it might bring back other sounds into its range, it breaks up the "meaningful," "intentional" sounds of voice, on the level of the production of the voice in recorded sound. At this moment, even the indexical qualities that might point back toward "the fat man," the singer claiming his voice in the song, become muddled and distorted. A poetics of noise emerges in these relays. Self-consciously transformed into something other than voice, these sounds move between different orders of recognition and representation. Noise emerges not in the speech sounds themselves—nor in the musical, melodic logic of the passage—but rather in the defamiliarization and mis-recognition that stem from the metamorphosis within the projected voice.

Such moments of undecidable, misheard metamorphosis—a kind of abstract expressionism in sound—emerge from rock 'n' roll's self-conscious poetics of movement and energy. The turning and twisting of such a poetics become

---

[4] The signature sound of the "wah-wah" guitar pedal is based upon this same ability to adjust the tonal envelope of a note as it is played.

particularly important in Little Richard's 1956 "Tutti Frutti," in which the starkness of this principle of distortion comes to the fore. The song is economical in its means, and the New Orleans instrumental combination of voice, piano, saxophone, drums, bass, and guitar creates, as in Domino's work, a repetitive and powerful beat. Perhaps the most striking distinction between these songs is the difference between what Charlie Gillett has described as Little Richard's "frantic, sometimes hysterical" singing as against Fats Domino's flat expressivity (1996: 25). In Little Richard's case, the distorting effects of the voice are placed in relationship with the recording mechanism. While Dominoe's wah-wah solo figures noise in the ambiguous relay between signifier, instrumental sound, and the performance of voice, in the first seconds of "Tutti Frutti" Richard blasts into an a cappella shout:

Womp bama loo mop b-lomp bomp bomp ... (0:00–0:03)[5]

The sound figure of the voice is undone before it is even introduced. Rather than unweaving a voice already given and identified, as in "The Fat Man," the song begins with the dislocated body of the singer, expressed as an instrumental combination of volume, beat, and timbre. The voice is already a percussion instrument, hammering out a rhythm. Here, the voice *as* drum refuses an entrance into communication in order to record the gesture of a movement. This gesture resists phonetic transcription. Little Richard slides between seemingly opposed plosive and liquid sounds to create an effect that is at once continuous and discrete.

Rather than announcing a constituted "I," the sounds produce an unstated (and unstable) relationship to the listener and to the silent—but soon revealed—band, which responds to Richard's shout with the repetitive spectacle of the beat. In Domino's song the singer claimed a singular (if outwardly given) subjectivity—a name, "the fat man." Here, the singer produces only a very thin mask that theatricalizes a multiplied and unfixed desire.[6] The quick and easy rhyming in the verse lyrics is in the same strained and raspy tone as the introductory mouth sounds:

Got a girl named Sue, she knows just what to do (0:18–0:22)
...
Got a girl named Daisy, she almost drive me crazy (0:49–0:53)

[5] My transcription. Others: "Bop bopa-a-lu a whop bam boo" (Google Lyrics); "Whop bop b-luma b-lop bam bom" (genius.com); "A-wop-bom-a-loo-mop-a-lomp-bom-bom!" (Wikipedia.com).
[6] Famously a song originally about homosexual desire, the form of "Tutti Frutti" (despite the lyric censorship) maintains a queer relationship to language and power. See Tyina Steptoe, "Big Mama Thornton, Little Richard, and the Queer Roots of Rock 'n' Roll."

These name/rhyme combinations continuously force language into the frame of the rhythmic movement and raspy timbre that voice has become—as opposed to forcing voice into the frame of language or meaning in speech and bel canto singing. Names are called up out of nowhere, as if they were continuations of the nonsense sounds of the introduction and chorus.

This rhythmic movement emphasizes the mediation of language through tongue, throat, and lungs as well as rhyme, rhythm, and recording. In doing so, this figure of voice continuously threatens to become non-voice, an other-than-voice, a noise-coming-into-voice. "Tutti Frutti" makes a study of what Roland Barthes, remixing Julia Kristeva, calls the "geno-song" of a performance. This is "volume of the singing and speaking voice" where language forms "a signifying play having nothing to do with communication, representation …, expression" (Barthes 1978: 182). "Tutti Frutti" threatens sense with nonsense, the singing voice with the drum, and progressive narration with the automatism of repetition. But, even as Richard's voice showcases the element of "grain" that Barthes describes as "the body in the voice as it sings" (1978: 188), it also attempts to refuse an individuating or indexical element in the voice.

The method of this refusal is power and volume. For the volume of the voice in the song—the pressure exerted by the singer blowing out—breaks open and troubles its indexical qualities. For this volume is not only a question of performance, it is also a negotiation and improvisation with the microphone and the recording apparatus. Barthes describes the grain as an impersonal movement between materiality and language that is also, however, individual—it indicates a body with no "civil identity" but which is "nevertheless a separate body" (1978: 182). The grain of the voice in "Tutti Frutti," however, is not only attached to the materiality of a particular human body. It also emanates from the concrete layers of mediation and materialization that channel sound and voice in the song. In this way, the song is a kind of concrete poetry. Richard over-performs and overburdens his body and the microphone. Steven Connor discusses the grain of the voice in the singing of crooners like Bing Crosby as a concatenation of subtle mouth sounds "edited out in ordinary listening:"

> The microphone makes audible and expressive a whole range of organic vocal sounds which are edited out in ordinary listening; the liquidity of the saliva, the hissings and tiny shudders of the breath, the clicking of the tongue and teeth, the popping of the lips. Such a voice promises the odours, textures, and warmth of another body.
>
> (Connor 2000: 38)

These differentiating accidents of vocal sound are blasted away in Little Richard's performance, and instead of the subtlety of mouth sounds, there is instead a shouting that tests the limits of both the body and the recording mechanism. At 1:35, when the voice enters after the saxophone solo, the sound distorts as Richard screams close to the microphone. By projecting too much volume, too much power in the voice, and too close to the microphone, the electromagnetic transducers write not the voice's projection but rather their material limits. The distortion of the voice-microphone assemblage produces a figure of noisy energy that throws off the "calibration between sound and space" usually effected by timbre (Smith 2008: 119). Within the inarticulate and overburdened sound of the voice is an operation that binds the body to the recording apparatus in a way that produces a body but without its separable, indexical qualities—a body of noise.

If, as Moten suggests, a black avant-garde extends from the recognition that the commodified object speaks and breaks open that speech, Domino's and Richard's works ask us to hear a sonic materiality that extends beyond the reach of identification implicit in the ascription of voice to objects, as in the phonographic recording. Simon Frith contends that "[r]ock 'n' roll faith is faith in the music's black elements, in its sense of performance, its physical energy, its directness, its vocal and rhythmic techniques" (Frith 1981: 20). When black voices are consistently heard as noise under conditions of white supremacy (Stoever 2016: 12), the black elements in rock 'n' roll also conflict with the social and medial processes that suggest voices have a certain shape and a certain timbre as a form of identity. The black "elements" of rock 'n' roll then are those that are not only interior to vocal production but also the exterior, medial sounds that break up and distort voice in the act of recording. In these sounds—in the very status of rock 'n' roll as a recorded art and an African-American art—the force of noise continuously moves from marginal spaces into seemingly "essential" and organized ones. Ashon Crawley, writing on Blackpentecostal breath—a Blackpentecostalism deeply influential on Little Richard and other early rock 'n' rollers—describes how "the sound of the drum, the sound of the voice, the sound of the flesh when clapped, slapped, carries" (2017: 170). What this shouting, moving vocalization carries "is the sociality of otherwise form:" a life outside of violent coordinates of normative reason (Crawley 2017: 171). The reproduction of blackness within rock 'n' roll's sonic field of voice and noise calls into question what Adorno describes as the "illusion of 'here-ness', of closeness, of authenticity" in radiophonic and phonographic music (Adorno 2009: 95). The boundary-crossing of rock 'n' roll very importantly worked *within* the spatializing, territorializing aspects of electro-acoustic mediation in a way that self-consciously emphasized its otherness, its "out-there-ness."

In this way, the literal production (or non-production) of space in rock 'n' roll recordings opens vocal performance to noise by drawing out the conditions of identification and subjectivation by which a listener recognizes both themselves and others in sound. In his history of the ventriloquized voice, *Dumbstruck*, Steven Connor uses the term "vocalic space" to denote the "ways in which the voice is held both to operate in, and itself to articulate, different conceptions of space" (2000: 12). As we have already seen, rock 'n' roll phonography rearranges the sounds of the throat and mouth in ways shaped by language, technique, technology, and engineering. The voice in and as a "vocalic space" names not only the intention-bearing sounds of performance but also the accidental and excessive sounds that can enter into that space. Rock 'n' roll performances that disfigure "vocalic space" as noise project the voice as a porous membrane in which other and othering sounds create a value in excess of expression or signification.

In "Johnny B. Goode," recorded by Chess recording artist Chuck Berry in 1958, the guitar—taking over for the horn sections in Fats Domino and Little Richard's recordings—blasts out from the space of the speaker and no longer merely supports the voice of the singer. Together, the overdriven voice and instrument saturate the sound space of the recording, but they remain in a state of tension. The voice is at times overwhelmed by the bright, high frequencies of the guitar. The texture of this guitar sound (a product of amplifier, electric guitar construction, and studio engineering) stands apart from the orchestral mixes of swing bands and jazz, as well as the R&B-inspired bands of Domino and Richard. Perry Meisel hears this work as a "transistorized" jazz (1999: 61). The sound is electronically and metallically produced—a precursor to the sound Bob Dylan imagined in a different context as a "thin ... wild mercury sound" (Rosenbaum 1978: 69).

This synthetic guitar sound produces an alien soundscape—a soundscape impossible except through the power of electricity. Despite differences in rhythm and tone, it parallels the experimental sonorities of electronic music by composers like Varèse and Iannis Xenakis. These purely electric sounds of the amplified electric guitar play with and against the electric noise of the radio and phonographic medium itself. It mimics—through repetitive ornamental figures, Berry's famous guitar "double-stops"—what Theodor Adorno calls the "hear-stripe" of radio, that always audible "electric current" that sounds "vaguely comparable to the noise caused by drawing a long strip through a narrow aperture or rubbing something against a resisting object" (Adorno 2009: 114). Rather than ignoring that "hear-stripe," Berry's song extracts it and amplifies it through the guitar. The music redefines the illusion of a present "here and now" of mass mediated sound by echoing the noisy (and ignored) buzz of the electric medium itself. Rock 'n' roll aspired not to the condition of making music *here* and *now*, but rather to the condition (to use mid-century hipster lingo) of getting *gone*.

Elvis Presley calls to his band after a false start in 1955's "Milk Cow Blues" : "Let's get gone ... real gone!" This theatricalized moment frames what is to come: an up-tempo, jump-beat take on the classic blues song. It also imagines the space of performance turned inward toward the players, rather than outward toward the audience. This inward turn, however, again moves outward because it acts out a fiction of "presence" within the documentation of the performance. As such, it defines the experiments on and with Elvis's voice by Sam Phillips in the 1950s Sun Sessions. In these sessions, the written sounds of rock 'n' roll do not simply document an "immediate" performance of spontaneous discourse. Rather, they emphasize the sonic manipulation of space in a way that activates and upsets a listening for a particular voice located in a fixed imaginary landscape. The experiments with "slap-back echo" on these recordings show this interruption of space-making at work. The "crucial innovation" of Phillips and Elvis was to locate "the singing voice 'inside' echo and reverb, and at the same time [to] dispense with the realist, pictorialist, landscape traditions of echoic/reverberant sound in favor of expressionist, nonliteral zones" (Doyle 2005: 193). Though a heavy echo effect was first produced by Chess Records on the 1952 Little Walter recording, "Juke," the Sun Records use of echo on songs like R&B singer Doctor Ross's "Boogie Disease" (1954) created a "space" that was a pure sonic fantasy or, as Paul Doyle calls it, "an impossible, M.C. Escher-like space" (Doyle 2005: 183).

When applied to Elvis's voice in songs like "Blue Moon of Kentucky" (recorded 1954) the effect is extreme. The echo returns with such force that there are moments (such as the beginning of the chorus at 0:36) where the vocals blur and become incomprehensible. The redoubling echo transforms Elvis's high wails into a distorted scream that overdrives the recording, pushing out the sounds of the rhythm guitar, bass, and electric guitar. This sonic manipulation—not always used to these extremes—creates a space in which the singer's grainy voice indexes not a body but a voice breaking up and feeding back into its recorded reduplication. T. J. Clark describes abstract expressionist painting as a "texture of interruptions, gaps, zigzags, a-rhythms and incorrectnesses" that "signify a making, no doubt, but at the same time the absence of a singular maker" (1999: 332). The distorted voice in "Blue Moon of Kentucky" is not a responsible subjectivity but an enveloping force, connected to electronic impulse rather than a speaker's body.

It is only later, after the fact, that these sounds must be accounted for and made subject to a singer and a song. Lee Medovoi has argued for the ways in which rock 'n' roll arose within a remapping of space by postwar teenage, suburban listeners. The landscapes imagined by early rock 'n' roll—in both the city and country—became valorized because of their difference from suburbia. These songs represented an otherwise space that could express "an antidomestic counterdesire for the extrasuburban" (Medovoi 2005: 110). Even more than the imaginary landscapes conjured lyrically by these songs, this counter-suburban urge results in a surreal, distorted spatialization, produced out of the means of recording itself. The textures of rock 'n' roll did not establish a conventional space from which a voice emanated. Rather "vocalic space" opened up, overwhelmed, and distorted the song (even in competition with the distorted, overdriven sounds of electric guitars). In the midst of the manifold calls of remediated sonic presences or voices, this work of vocal distortion projected an aesthetic resistance of bodies to the metaphorical, institutional registers of voicing that impressed themselves upon listeners. Rock 'n' roll figures prominently in the distortion of voice because of its paradoxical emphasis upon voices as both reified and fetishized embodiments of desire and as cracked and grainy vessels that could twist outside with inside, margin with center. It redirects listening by finding noise in hectic spurts, irreverence, and overdrive. To search for such noise is to reject the voice of authority by asserting a sonority and an embodied life outside of a responsibility for recognition.

Breathing Noise into Projectivist Verse

The oscillation between embodiment and disembodiment in rock 'n' roll noise mixes what we might call the granular and specular registers of sound: the resistant and the ghostly come together. The noise figured by these recorded performances emanates from a poetics of an outwardly projected speech that breaks up and feeds back. It at once takes up the responsibilities of embodiment and the refusal of subjectivity. Projectivist verse and rock 'n' roll, then, are both vectors for a "systematic disorganization" of the mechanisms of voicing in poetry (Creeley and Olson 1987: 1:51). Even as they draw out the possibilities of a speech-based, sound-based oral/aural poetics, they make the voice apparent in its mediation—its distorting possibilities and energies—in ways that complicate this embodiment of presence. Their mediated (and remediated) voices can act as empty placeholders for energies outside of them rather than as channelizing personas or personifications.

As we have seen in Olson's essay on projective verse, the movement in this verse form is toward a recognition of the individuating, indexical quality of what Amiri Baraka hears as "How You Sound:"

> HOW YOU SOUND?? is what we recent fellows are up to. How *we* sound; our peculiar grasp on say, a.) Melican speech, b.) Poetries of the world, c. our selves (which is attitudes, logics, theories, jumbles of our lives, & all that, d. and the final ... The Totality of Mind: Spiritual ... God?? (or you name it): Social (zeitgeist): or Heideggerian *umwelt*.
>
> (Baraka 1960: 424).

In this way, projectivism comes under a generalized figure of personification, but without a singular consciousness or a conventional ordering mechanism to give it coherence. Sound produces a person, but that person is a continuous and unstable "jumble" of elements. The specificity of sound as speech—any speech placed on the page as writing—manifests the difference of an individual as they move through a total field of sound and sense.

In Baraka's essay, a "sound" is connected to speech's transformation in its contact with listening. What one is "touched by (CAN HEAR)" becomes "my poetry" (Baraka 1960: 424). This poetry combines acts of listening, thinking, and making that become "your own voice ... how you sound" (Baraka 1960: 425). For Baraka working in this projective vein, the materiality of a voice is itself broken into a thousand points of contact: a totality of listening that manifests itself in shards of sound in a verse not defined by regularity or even a relationship with regularity. Rather there is sound as the shape of a body's contact with the world. In this way, very different "projective" verses emerge out of different bodies in contact with the world: from Baraka's own exploratory musical and political verse, to Olson's mass scatterings of rhetorical and historical energy, to the radically spare poetics of Robert Creeley and Larry Eigner. To become a self-sufficient poetics is a process made possible by a reduction of the self to sound in speech and on the page.

This idealization of individual presence, however, also has another measuring material alongside the syllable—the breath. As projective verse avoids conventional methods for organizing language sounds, it emphasizes the breath of the poet/performer: "the breathing of the man [sic] who writes, at the moment that he writes" (Olson 1997b [1950]: 242). The breath indicates the presence of body and mind in speech and recording, but it also has another possibility: "to articulate fragility into the system" (McCaffery 2001: 49). As David Appelbaum notes in his study on voice, "breath disrupts the continuous progress of voluntary phonemic production" (1990: 29). The breath—not the syllables between breaths but the cuts and pauses that phrase, collect, and disrupt phonemic patterning—becomes a space in which the automatism of the body overtakes the "celestial, without breath" condition of a voice, for "in voicing, respiration naturally ceases" (Appelbaum 1990: 30).

The sonic production of voice is a disembodied condition of not-breathing, and that condition is emphasized by the "secondary" materials that write voice—from meter, to print, to audio recording. Olson's credo (via Robert Creeley) that "form is never more than an extension of content" (Olson 1997b [1950]: 240) gives way to the possibility of a dislocated, non-projected form that enters the poem outside of its content. Just as Olson holds open the possibility of staring at the recording mechanism in the Goddard College speech that opened this chapter, the breath breaks in projective verse hold open the possibility of interruption in the midst of continuity. These alternate patterns of verse are also "fraught with apprehension, insecurity, and duress" (Mackey 2018: 7). In recordings in controlled environments, such as the studio recording of "The Songs of Maximus" and "The Kingfishers" that Olson made with Robert Creeley at Black Mountain College in 1954, Olson's phrasing follows the line breaks with precision ("Studio Recording at Black Mountain College," Pennsound). Each halted phrase briefly holds open a space of uncertainty, as the speech plays between movement and stasis. Famously, Robert Creeley's recordings also radically perform the line break as breath and as cut. Such pauses for respiration concretize a principle of interruption that breaks up the voice even as it projects itself. The breath, then, provides an entry point for noise. Rather than the index of a bodily presence, it is an index of a process of searching, the automatic activity of an embodied, material recorder. Olson stated later in his career, "[T]here ain't no recording instruments for poets / only their bodies" (quoted in Boer 1991: 6). The breath is not a present body in the text but the trace of the hesitations and silences of the recording body. It makes static.

To read against the grain of Olson's sonic poetics of presence is to fold the hesitation, fragility, and discontinuity of breath into the distended "voice" of the projectivist poet. Olson's poetry does not simply uncover "sound itself" in language but rather uncovers a relationship to sound that, as in rock 'n' roll, simultaneously projects and distorts its organization as "voice." Robert Von Hallberg describes this attitude in his description of Olson's work:

> Olson never conceived of poetry's effect as pleasurable. His own verse tries, at times, to sound more like noise than like music; noise where music is expected lays rhetorical claims to a language distinct from the culture that teaches us what music consists of. A verse that momentarily masquerades as noise asks to be taken completely on its own terms, the way the music of a wholly foreign culture is taken; its implicit promise is that it can provide a system of value and understanding unlike anything known.
>
> (Von Hallberg 1978: 173)

The "masquerade" of noise, however, is not so much a transitional moment as a constant distorting process. The underside of hearing the "music of a wholly foreign culture" as noise is an imperialism in listening that would consistently hear such sounds as "noise." And yet the work produces not the discovery of the nascent "music" in noise but rather the preservation of its difference and its resistant possibilities of distortion and defamiliarization.

Olson's attempt to make a language outside of the language of a culture of "pejoracracy" and "mu-sick" necessitated a poetics of noise. Seth Forrest argues that Olson's style emphasizes "noisier" (from an acoustic standpoint) consonantal clusters (Forrest 2009: 7). Even more, however, Olson draws upon language's sonic materiality in a way that simultaneously realizes and plays against its nominative function. As Carla Billiteri has recently argued, Olson was a "Cratylic" poet: his ideal language had the same objective and phenomenal status as the things it represents (146). In particular, the proper noun's intimacy with the places and things it named made it an important part of speech for Olson (Billiteri 146). Rather than an arbitrary movement of denotation—of difference and deferral—language exists immanently within the phenomenal world. In this way, the *sounds* of language—rather than arbitrary conventions that can be disentangled from their representations—become consonant actions within a complex of intellectual and physiological movements:

> Breath is man's [sic] special qualification as animal. Sound is a dimension he has extended. Language is one of his proudest acts. And when a poet rests in these as they are in himself (in his physiology, if you like, but the life in him, for all that) then he, if he chooses to speak from these roots, works in that area where nature has given him size, projective size.
>
> (Olson 1997b [1950]: 248)

In this "dimension" extended by and through the human body, Olson imagines "roots" where the language rests within the poet. Olson's poetry, Charles Altieri has argued, "emphasizes the etymological rather than the dramatic qualities of language, [in order to] keep the sources of vitality collective; ... the consciousness evoked in the poem depends on the most impersonal, structural dimensions of language" (1974: 183). To speak from these physiological roots is also to speak from the etymological roots of language—an "original" space and time in which word, act, and thing were coincident.

But the syllables can threaten to descend into the abyss of noise, into mere sound, even as the poet points to their seeming rootedness:

> "home," to the shore
> bu-te pu-bu bu-nu-su
> bayt. "house,"
> to the
> shore
> pa-ba pa-'i-to "Phaistos"
> pa, as in a for
> Apple
> tu tuppûh
> and bird or ku is "town:"
> kr-ku (Her headland, over
> the sea-shore.
>
> (*The Maximus Poems* III.50)

On the surface, this poem from 1964 presents the raw materials for a sound poem. In it, Olson records and glosses a few words from an ancient artifact, the pre-Mycenaean "Phaistos Disc" discovered on Crete (Butterick 1981: 556). He traces etymological roots (the origin of the place name "Phaistos") and maps sound onto sense (with phonographic notes: "pa, as in a for / Apple"). In Von Hallberg's terms, the poem is "masquerading as noise" by presenting a language very few readers are likely to know (1978: 173). And yet at the same time it notates a return from sea—home, town, bird, seashore. Michael Davidson has argued that the "interest in etymology among postwar poets is buttressed by a theory of language that treats words as extensions of physical and biological life. Meaning exists within a semiotic DNA, and every utterance taps into that great verbal pool" (1997: 108). Olson hears and attempts to mime the very process by which a word is constructed, by which it moves from a sensual possibility within the mouth to a definition—by which listening produces the syllable, by which noise becomes name.

Out of the contingency of breath and a dispersed searching after how one might sound, syllables emerge that connect language to object and action. Noise, figured as breath, opens language up by cutting, rearranging, and listening again to its sounds. Poetic language takes on the force of action as a system of recording and transmission. Importantly for Olson, this space in which noise is transformed into a syllable on the page is the space of the body. Barrett Watten is reticent about Olson's use of embodiment: "Does the body translate into the form of the poem, or is the world being translated by the body? Rather than submitting to psychology, one could propose a rejection of the body as a final term …. References are toward the world, not to the body of the poet who is consumed by their metaphorical 'inherance'" (1985: 165). Olson's "body"—despite the rooted inherence of language in its physiology—is defined in his poetics by a "breath" that both locates and dissipates such roots. Olson's poetics of presence, then, contains a movement of difference and deferral at the level of sensation. Rather than being contained within the processes of presentation that might personify sound, sounds move from their marginal status into the space of the poem. Neither "sound itself" nor "voice," such language projects a threshold, a space of boundary-crossing in sound.

In "Maximus at the Harbor," the poet hears the ocean speak in a revelation of noise. The sound of flux becomes for him not an untouchable blankness but an opening, a way into the world through the word:

> Paradise is a person. Come into this world.
> The soul is a magnificent Angel.
> And the thought of its thought is the rage
> of Ocean   :   apophainesthai
> roared the great bone on to Norman's
> Woe: apophainesthai, as it blew
> up a pool on Round Rock shoal;

> apophainesthai it cracked as it broke
> on Pavilion Beach; apophainesthai
> it tore at Watch House point
>
> ("Maximus at the Harbor," *The Maximus Poems* II.70)

The Greek "apophainesthai" means an opening out, a revealing, and a "showing" of phenomena. The noisy "rage / of Ocean" is a metaphysical "thought of thought." To "come into this world" is to hear noise and transform it into an opening: a speech, a name, a place, a person. The poem's act of transforming oceanic noise into speech indicates Olson's sense that "myth is mouth / myth is word" (quoted in Boer 1991: 19). Myth is not, as in T. S. Eliot's work, a last desperate grasp of structure against a wave of noise, but rather a mechanism projecting the contingent—but incessantly reiterated—experience of the sensing body. The poem mishears a vocal sound, a Greek word, in an ocean that "roared," "blew up," "cracked," "broke," and "tore." Out of the breaking resistance and mishearing, however, comes revelation. Sound interpenetrates sound, and a process arises by which, in Roland Barthes words, a "listening speaks" (Barthes 1985: 259).

Gloucester's position as a harbor, as an opening in the earth parallel to the opening that is the sensing body, makes it an important space for naming and renaming—a mediating space for history. To Olson, names that composed and compose Gloucester map a space that is not fixed but constantly changing and creating new constellations of meaning. Names—of people, places, objects—do not simply denote; they also enumerate. That is, they also—even in their particularity—expose the serial, repetitive act of shaping mouth to world, of signifying. This is how the "literal is the same as the numeral" for Olson, how the word becomes the "invention of language and power" that defines a culture and a space (Olson 1979: 94). In "Maximus, to Gloucester, Letter 11," Olson retells the fragmented story (originally told in a letter to Creeley) of his first hearing the word "Tragabizanda"—Captain John Smith's name for what is now known as Cape Ann (*The Maximus Poems* I.49). Though the name is that of Smith's "swooning Turkish Princess," Olson also appreciated its value as a disorienting sound: "'Tragabizanda' / was what I heard" (*The Maximus Poems* I.49). It turns out the word is being spoken by a local dramatist practicing for a pageant. The act of Smith's naming, the dramatic reproduction of the name, and Olson's own fascination with its sound coexist in the word. The distortion of sound, place, and name is paralleled by sound's displacement—its movement from Turkey to America within a colonial project of naming a "new found land" and an imperialist project of conquest, war, and appropriation. The figure of John Smith acts as a kind of audio recording that plays back the word regardless of context. What this word presents is a sound that is neither "here" nor "there" but that indexes its own history of distancing even as it adheres to a particular place.

Olson's presentation of language and history in *The Maximus Poems* plays upon the uncertain and constantly changing surfaces of words in relation to place and person. There is a desperate movement at work in the poem: if "ONE PERCEPTION MUST IMMEDIATELY AND DIRECTLY LEAD TO A FURTHER PERCEPTION" (Olson 1997b [1950]: 241), the cuts and pauses of breath function as swerves and starting points. A rhetoric of amplification, in particular, defines Olson's performance in language. "Amplification," long before it was a technical term for an increase in volume via electronic means, was a technical term in rhetoric that meant "to increase, to expand upon" a discourse—by whatever means necessary. Aristotle uses the word (in Greek: *auxesis*) to denote simply talking more or less at length on a particular subject being praised or blamed (Aristotle 1991: 178). It is a technique of addition but also attention, continuation, and delay. Aristotle points out that amplification is intimately related to asyndeton, the removal of grammatical connectives, by far the defining feature of Olson's poetry: " … asyndeta have a special characteristic; many things seem to be said at the same time; for the connective makes many things seem one, so that if it is taken away, clearly the opposite results: one thing will be many" (Aristotle 1991: 256). In Olson, this amplifying power rests in the proliferation of incomplete clauses and phrases that pluralize our attention. Olson echoes this exact sentiment in the preamble to *The Maximus Poems*, underneath the dedication to Robert Creeley: "all my life I've heard / one makes many" (*The Maximus Poems* unpaginated). Rhetoric—as a way of placing sounds in speech and on the page—acts as a sound technology that amplifies the voice of the poet to the point of erasure and invisibility.

Olson's rhetorical amplification is in conversation with the electro-acoustic amplification of voices in the sound culture of mid-century America, what Lytle Shaw calls a culture of "audio optimism" (2018: 150). Olson wants nothing less than a reframing of attention in order to undo the demands of the many voices making phatic, apostrophic calls upon a listener. At the opening of *The Maximus Poems*, he emphasizes the ear's search for "that which will last" in the midst of mass culture:

> By ear, he sd.
> But that which matters, that which insists, that which will last,
> that! o my people, where shall you find it, how, where, where shall you listen
> when all is become billboards, when, all, even silence, is spray-gunned?
> when even our bird, my rooks,
> cannot be heard
> when even you, when sound itself is neoned in?
>
> (*The Maximus Poems* I.2)

The questions become ones of listening: where will "my people" listen? How will they find what "matters," "insists" and "last[s]"? In this way, Olson positions himself in a long line of modernists critiquing mass culture—Pound and Eliot's antipathy toward mass culture (even as they subsume and reimagine it) comes to the fore. The images of billboards, spray guns, and neon create a visual analog to the invading noise figured in modernity: even "sound itself is neoned-in."

This sensory economy, however, has a different direction. Olson sees these visual images as containing, channeling or "neon[-ing]-in" sound and listening. Listening has no place, no location in which it can happen: "where shall you listen?" This is also how the "musickracket / of all ownership" (*The Maximus Poems* I.14) works: it cordons off and territorializes "the ear." To move "by ear" is to produce a way out of the billboard frame or the neon sign. One could read this ear as the figure of a listening renewed by a "return" to orality. However, as an embodiment of printed speech and as a recording mechanism in its own right, this listening ear also counteracts the smooth flow of communication through voice. Lytle Shaw explains how this counter-listening inheres even in Olson's recording for the 1975 Folkways LP, *Charles Olson Reads from Maximus Poems IV, V, VI*: for Olson, "the eternal must remain a mythic process rather than … the sonic elements of the recording that resist his control and intention" (Shaw 2018: 149). Despite Olson's distrust of tape, then, it models an "ongoingness" in which the force of interruption situates "human agency within a larger field" (Shaw 2018: 151). Noise—mediated by a projected voice—crosses over into speech and writing. Like the vocal performances of rock 'n' roll artists, the vocal performances of these poems work at the threshold of listening where noise and voice meet.

Both of these oral poetries, then, seek out noise within a world of voices continuously calling upon the ear—from portable radios, Muzak, television, automobile sound systems, and other media technologies. Noise becomes a disfiguring force that provides a way of attending to a materiality of sound against the constant demand for response in everyday life. These poetries make available—and figure—a sonic, vocalic space in which the distinction between a poetic "set toward the message" and a phatic "set toward the channel" is called into question (Jakobson 1987: 68–9). Even more, in upsetting this distinction, they challenge the possibility of an Althusserian "hail" in which the many various disembodied voices vying for a listener's attention also frame that listener as a certain kind of subject, a certain identity. Sander van Maas calls attention to the "(tele-)technological realm on which the process of interpellative subjectivation depends" (2015: 64), for, in the words of David Wills, "hailing takes place across a telecommunicational void, without a guaranteed response" (quoted in van Maas 2015: 63). The physical embodiment of this "telecommunicational void" is in the act of turning:

> "Before" we hear the "Hey, you," we react to something as simple as its volume, but which represents the apostrophic, perhaps adrenal, surfeit of what hails out of the blue or out of the shadow, from out of dorsal inaccessibility or invisibility, shocking or surprising us into an instinctual repositioning or corporeal rectification "before" it calls us.
>
> (quoted in van Maas 2015: 63)

Noise sounds out a resistance to these spectral vocalic agencies by presenting and emphasizing the failure of the hail and the phatic call in exchange for some other sound and movement. In the case of Olson and other projectivists' poetries, the twisting of voice and noise through the breath and amplification creates a movement that resists the "instinctual repositioning" of the hail. "Corporeal rectification" gives way to the dance or a listening that refuses the specificities and subjectivization of a call. The dissipating effects of noise make "how you sound" radically contingent: even as we can hear in these sounds individuation and specificity, we also hear a figure of freedom in refusal, nonsense, and interruption.

Granite against Granite

In a short 1958 essay on "Sound, Noise, Varèse, Boulez," Morton Feldman describes the excitement of noise: "[It] bores like granite into granite. It is physical, very exciting, and when organized it can have the impact and grandeur of Beethoven ... Sound is our dreams of music. Noise is music's dreams of us" (2000: 16). Feldman's subtle distinction between "sound" and "noise" helps to define a shift in the poetics of noise embedded within rock 'n' roll and projectivist verse. Sound—a sound in itself, a sound as an escape from the conflict of the political—might be a dream, an imaginary landscape, but noise, "music's dreams of us," shows in particular the continued pull of the tactile and violent "boring" of granite into granite, of grain against grain. In the projective poetics that arose in the middle of the twentieth century, the voice becomes a space in which artists can work through a push and pull between inchoate exteriors and differentiated interiors. The unrecognizable is valued, along with the erased and the disfigured. The switch in agency in Feldman's definition is important: music as a structure and form invites the shadowy dream world of noise. Our dream of music is an active one of finding sound, of developing a competence to hear sounds anew. Noise, on the other hand, suggests a resistance. It is "only noise which we secretly want, because the greatest truth usually lies behind the greatest resistance" (Feldman 2000: 17). A noisy "outside" creates its listeners. It reflects back on them and invites a reckoning.

This kind of reckoning—a making known in the midst of a desire to know—is fundamental to a noise that would break into and break up the mediated immediacy of midcentury sound culture. The insurgent strains of early rock 'n' roll and the projectivist poetics of speech and breath both amplified noise within the construction of an "orality" that promised new forms of contact and consumption in postwar America. In seeking out the breakages, distortions, and tensions within the sound projection of voice, these works find and figure the resistance that appears as the body is rematerialized as an apparatus articulating breath and mouth sound to the sound-writing of the page and record. It is *through* their particular performances of writing voices that noise breaks into voice. The voice is not an interior but a mask, a figure that organizes, covers over, and territorializes. Noise in their hands is a remnant of embodiment that refuses both the personification of the mask and the subjectivizing hail that emerges from it. These works reckon with irrelevant, irrational, and accidental sounds in the midst of the consistency of mediated presence.

This turn toward other sounds, toward a music that might dream its listeners rather than discipline its boundaries, opens up the possibility of a new relationship to the historicity of bodies—their material having-been-in-time. James Lastra discusses the "possibility of history" in recordings:

"Perhaps it is in the non-presence of the repetition, of the wearing away of the original surfaces, the decaying remains, that we recognize the possibility of the event itself. Out of the trace, then, is born history ... or the *possibility of* history" (Lastra 1992: 83). Out of the trace is also born the material entanglements of bodies—with institutions, with techniques and technologies, and with each other. The desire for noise is a desire to await something other than what we are.

5

Noise and the City: Writing and Punk Performance, 1965–80

Lou Reed's infamous 1975 album *Metal Machine Music* is where I begin. At once legendarily "unlistenable" and a forerunner of the genre of "noise music," this album comprises more than an hour of guitar feedback that Reed, in the liner notes, describes as "what I meant by 'real' rock, about 'real' things" (Reed 2007 [1975]: n.p.). In contrast to this "reality," the album's multiple layers of interlocking drones, crowded mid- to high-frequency range, seemingly pitch-shifted tape effects and separate stereo channels seem radically "unreal"—a sonic fantasy taking advantage of the effects available to electronic composers but with basic rock 'n' roll equipment: guitars, amps, four-track tape recorder. Described as both the apotheosis and the antithesis of rock 'n' roll, the album certainly has very little to do with even the most intensely noisy rock albums that preceded it (including by bands like The Velvet Underground). No voice, no song structures, no hooks: the sounds proceed by negation. At the same time, the recording builds up a repetitive, insistent layering of frequencies—of different speeds of vibration and their combination—that reveals rock 'n' roll as a form of electronic music. If rock 'n' roll, as we saw in the last chapter, depended from the beginning on its relationship to mediation and recording, Reed's album emphasizes the medium of rock through a saturation of its stereo channels. Described as a pompous joke, a speed freak diary, a legal fiction, a boondoggle, or a functional music meant to create a purely physical reaction (Lester Bangs discusses many of these possibilities in "The Great Album Ever Made" (2003: 195)), *Metal Machine Music* invites the social production of meaning. It is a cipher demanding a response. Someone buys the record and returns it immediately; someone researches the record's avant-garde lineage; someone plays it as a kind of joke or as meditation music; someone listens or someone doesn't ... However, the record produces a figure of noise as a resistance to—and confirmation of—such a demand for a reaction. In place of an anthropomorphic engagement—the call of a technologically mediated voice by the personified "star" Lou Reed or the genre of rock music—there is a "reality" of sound that is provisional, unstable, and yet delimited by the saturated channels in which it is produced. Noise displaces and disfigures the theatrical amplification of subjectivity, replacing it with sheer sonic mediation, inhuman and anti-lyrical nothingness.

In this chapter, I argue that the messy experimentation between and within poetry and music that defined the birth of punk in New York City from the mid-1960s through the 1970s produced a new valuation of noise as a chaotic, fragile, and temporary utopia. In the 1960s and 1970s, the Lower East Side and the East Village in Manhattan gathered a new wave of experimental poets and performers. The loose term "Downtown" describes this set of experimenters, and it includes the second-generation New York School of poets, the "Downtown School" of music represented by composers like John Cage, Morton Feldman, LaMonte Young, and Steve Reich, as well as punk and proto-punk musicians—Lou Reed, Richard Hell, and Patti Smith. A "scene" rather than a specific aesthetic school or movement, the Downtown umbrella gathers together a variety of practices in poetry, music, and art (avant-garde and otherwise) and emphasizes the social and spatial interactions between artists as well as their mutual, if differently inflected, experimentations in language and sound. Incoherence and eclecticism define this scene. I will describe how the mutually emerging and interconnected sound forms of punk rock and experimental poetry produce a figure of noise as a blank or voided social space in which a deeply critical attitude toward language and representation makes way for a new and utopian soundscape.

For the poets of the second-generation New York School and for early performers in the musical genre that would come to be known as "punk," noise delimited a creative, unstable social space. If, as Anthony Giddens argues, place yields to space in a communications-laden and ever faster-paced modernity, the figure of noise for these poets and performers has the value of recuperating a sense of place as an unstable combination of physical embodiment and semiotic flight (Giddens 1990: 17–21). As with the Dadaists earlier in the century, these noise-makers imagined community not in terms of what Benedict Anderson has termed "unisonance"—the instant collectivity of sounding together—but rather in dissonance (Anderson 1983: 145). But as modernist figures of noise emerge as totalities that break into or parasitically infest meaning, the noise figured by these artists dissipates its effects in the chaotic, localized, and unstable spaces of communal feeling.

For Downtown poets and musicians, a poem or a song could become an act of appropriation and reinvention that combined the Situationist concepts of *détournement* and *dérive*, suggesting a movement through the city that does not merely drift through or take place in certain space but *reuses* space in new and idiosyncratic ways. Writers and performers like Clark Coolidge and Richard Hell replace Cage's Zen-influenced mastery of desire that "lets sounds be themselves" (Cage 1961: 10) and instead celebrate a dispersed, oblique play of desire in which mastery is dislocated into the figure of an active, if meandering, engagement with the city. In this situation, the city's heterogenous spaces and sounds do not become the backdrop for a Cagean close listening but rather become ambient intertexts for literary and musical material. Cage's rhetoric of immanence, of aesthetic uselessness, gives way to urgent and immediate use. Noise does not simply exist "in itself;" it names a deforming, critical force that intervenes in the sound-writing of these poets and performers. They rearranged the phonographic texture of poetry and voice by producing noise in the image of the social spaces around them.

Within this culture of experimentation, such social spaces resound with multiple conflicting and overlapping textures and textualities. This cacophony interrupts or even prohibits an "inner voice" and invites its listeners into a public sphere. Roland Barthes writes of this listening that equates "interior" speech and exterior noise:

> One evening, half asleep on a banquette in a bar, just for fun I tried to enumerate all the languages within earshot: music, conversations, the sounds of chairs, glasses, a whole stereophony ... [T]his so-called "interior" speech was very like the noise of the square, like that amassing of minor voices coming to me from the outside: I myself was a public square, ... through me passed words, tiny syntagms, bits of formulae, and *no sentence formed*, as though that were the law of such a language.
>
> (Barthes 1975: 49–50)

The flashes of a possible—but never quite realized—system of language with its words, sentences, and significations haunts the "half-asleep" yet "enumerating" Barthes. This conflicted position of inattention/attention refuses the univocity of the harmonious sentence in favor of a sporadic, discontinuous, and polyvocal texture. The desire to transform the self into a "public square" undoes the filters that define a self and reacquaints the ear with forgotten or unheard textures within listening.

Rather than denying language, noise for the self-dissolving avant-garde of the Downtown scene takes on positive value as "tiny syntagms." These bits of free-floating form call into question totalizing assumptions about sentences as modes of understanding while at the same time manifesting, in moments of possession, a form of life as a "public square" outside of the mirror of the self. Noise becomes the sound of a "blank generation," the resonating fantasy of an empty vessel, a (to follow Richard Hell) "voidoid." Understood as a constantly shifting category of sounds classified by a listener's act of judgment in a given social situation, noise no longer figures an inherent disruption in the system, a depersonalized dis-ease of the body as medium (as with the modernists infected by "da"), or the counter-effects of an intensive technologizing of the body in discourse (as with projectivism and early rock 'n' roll). Instead, for these Downtown sound-makers, the "easily graspable voice dissolves into small recurrent motifs" that become the "building blocks of noise" (Andrews 1998: 75). Noise arises within the sonic remainder of an absence. It is sound that refuses signification in such a way that refusal itself marks and deforms the discourse it surrounds and penetrates. It is, in the words of the Dead Boys song, a "sonic reducer."

In mapping out such a refusal, I will first describe a changing sense—intuited by Barthes in the quote above and realized by Reed's strange experiment in noise—of sound as mass. Listening as a form of "listening again"—to the sounds of infinitely reduplicated recordings or the sounds of a swarming collectivity—produces a different attunement to urban and mediated sound. In contrast (again) to Cage's primordial act of listening in the anechoic chamber, another sensibility arises through a process that embraces sonic mirrors and mirages: the recollected shards of musical and sonic discourse in records but also the intermingled fragments of sonic and poetic codes. Daniel Kane, in *Do You Have a Band?* (2017), has described the entangled genesis of punk and poetry out of the social poetics of New York School and Downtown music. I will further entangle this nexus of poetry and music in their mutual genesis of new noise by taking up the ways in which artists read, recorded, listened to, and created fragmented syntagms, thus producing new scenes of social and sonic articulation.

The editorial work in magazines like Ed Sanders's *Fuck You/A Magazine of the Arts*, Richard Hell's *Genesis : Grasp*, and Bernadette Mayer and Vito Acconci's *0 to 9* sets the stage for mapping linguistic and sonic experimentation onto social life. These textual spaces show how the desire for an imagined community can also produce noise as formal experiment gives way to an interrupted and discontinuous social world. Similarly, the recorded song forms of The Velvet Underground's

"Heroin," Richard Hell's "Blank Generation," or Patti Smith's cover of "My Generation" become, through disorienting sonic layering and vocal performance, sound spaces in which a fragmented exteriority—the murmur of barely heard but enumerated sounds—dislocates itself into the body of the sound text and the performer. The proto-punk production of noise retunes the social element of sense perception so that the nondiscursive, amorphous, "public square" of a reverberating, multifaceted, and chaotic sonic space can rework the possibilities of articulation within a blank, anti-humanist, and yet firmly communal poetics.

Mass Sounds

As we have seen, at mid-century the sheer quantity of sonic mediation transformed the quality of the soundscape of modernity, as artists sought different forms of escape from the insistent call of capitalist desire and authority. The fantasy of "pure sound" at mid-century potentially overwrites the reverberating and clashing density of sonic experience as a collection of possible syntagms, of regurgitated and free-floating fragments that are not simply "pure sounds" but also carriers of incomplete or disrupted meanings. The mediated city is a giant echo chamber—a reverberating mass of glass, concrete, humans, and machines—but Cage's potential expansion of musicality also embeds a phenomenological reduction of sound, a reduction that potentially elides social space—and its differences, contestations, and ambiguities of meaning. Sound art after Cage generally reaffirms not only the radical freedom of his proposals but also the dynamics of sound as a carrier of (sometimes obscured) meaning. The founding of a post-Cagean noise-scape in the city depends less on a radical aesthetic anarchism and more upon the production of noise as a possibility for erasure, destruction, and anti-lyric feeling in the collapsing urban spaces and economies of deindustrializing cities. Whether printing a magazine from a "secret location on the Lower East Side" or playing a punk rock show at an unknown club on the Bowery, Downtown artists used, added to, and echoed the noisy sonic density of ever-changing urban spaces. Contrary to the canonical high modernists like T. S. Eliot who saw and heard the city as anonymous and isolating—and created an art and attendant criticism based upon the depersonalized, monadic isolation of the text—Downtown artists used their crowded, noisy urban environment as a site of *possibility*, a creative communal space. Their various aesthetic productions—little magazines, happenings, poetry readings, musical performances, recordings and more—reflected a social situation of intermingling and intermixing. New York acted as a force field, pushing different people, methods, and arts together in new ways. But in addition to this sociality centered on bars, clubs, and a variety of more or less official art spaces, the crowded city acted as phenomenological force itself, a place in which the attending individual confronts the "mass" in a variety of sensory overloads—particularly in sound.

High modernist theorists like Theodor Adorno and Clement Greenberg and later theorists of postmodernity like Andreas Huyssen interpreted mass culture as a kind of invasive, top-down force that neutralizes dissent and difference.[1] These critics lament the collapse of the distinction between autonomous aesthetic production (avant-garde) and mass produced objects (kitsch). While this analysis of mass culture—and the corporate and formal structures that undergird that political economy—makes accurate political economic claims, these theorists implicitly posit a passive consumerist acceptance of the standardizing signifying strategies of mass culture.

This characterization, however, ignores the ways in which consumers move through and change the strategic grid of top-down cultural production. In the realm of sound, the noisiness of mass culture becomes a productive space for countercultural incitement. The subject must compose itself (in both the literal and idiomatic senses) within the mass of stimuli in the city, where there is a constant call for the attentions of ear and eye—neon signs, honking horns, sirens, moving and speaking bodies, newspaper headlines, street musics, piped Muzaks, subway screeches, and a thousand other perceptions. But "the city" is also a mass of stimuli communicated by media. The experience of "the massive" as an amorphous entity takes on a stochastic inevitability. Neither wholly determined nor absolutely chaotic, it is composed of the slow, repeated buildup of sounds, rhythms, and other perceptions not regulated by a guiding totalitarian impulse but rather by a loosely organized set of mutually overlapping formulas.

This "drift" becomes the subject of much experimental composition at this time, in particular by composers as diverse as Steve Reich, Morton Feldman, LaMonte Young, Julius Eastman, and Iannis Xenakis. These composers created sonorous analogs to the drifting noises of the distended urbanity of postmodernity.

---

[1] See T. W. Adorno and Max Horkheimer, *The Culture Industry*; Clement Greenberg, *Art and Culture*; Andreas Huyssen, *After the Great Divide: Modernism, Mass Culture, Postmodernism*.

In pieces like *It's Gonna Rain* (1965), Reich reimagined the interrelationship of phase patterns in tape music. Feldman explored the possibilities of asynchronous sound events in many of his pieces, including *Durations I–V* (1960–1). Eastman's endurance-based minimalism—in pieces like *Stay on It* (1973) or, later, *The Holy Presence of Joan of Arc* (1981)—opened up rhythmic and melodic cells through repetition and slow transformation over longer durations. LaMonte Young's pieces, in which performers would hold single notes for long periods, emphasized the transformation of timbre over time even when pitch remains strictly limited. Xenakis's *Concrete PH* (1958) and *La Legende d'Eer* (1977–8) were built on the slow transformation of sonic material through stochastic transformation and glissandos. The work of these composers illustrates what Allen Weiss calls "varieties of audio mimesis," the stylized evocation of a landscape—or soundscape—through the matrix of composition (2008: 91). These pieces represent different means for simultaneously atomizing music—breaking it down into individual elements—and of accumulating those atomized fragments or "syntagms" into a non-hierarchical mass of sound over time. The collective of sound emissions oscillates between the expected and the chaotic, the recognizably diffuse and the unexpectedly rebarbative.

Metal Machine Music also fits into this category of sonic evocation. Though we cannot be sure if Reed's name-dropping of Xenakis and other avant-garde writers in a 1976 interview with Lester Bangs was tongue-in-cheek or not, the album partakes of a similar drive toward the accumulation of sounds. But as it evokes space and the stochastic processes of everyday listening, especially in the city, it also intensifies and flattens out these processes. It makes a "wall" of sound. The repeated buildup of individualized sonic elements is not differentiated with space or a "narrative" of transformation. Rather, it blasts out its feedback squalls and fills up all available frequency space. Reed transposes different "speeds" of sound by both manipulating tape speed and using different droning frequencies of guitar feedback. The bright high-frequency tones of the piece embody the observation by Deleuze and Guattari that "the reign of birds seems to have been replaced by the age of insects, with its much more molecular vibrations, chirring, rustling, buzzing, clicking, scratching, and scraping" (1987: 308). If, for Deleuze and Guattari, "birds are vocal, but insects are instrumental: drums and violins, guitars and cymbals," Reed's piece allegorizes and hypertrophies this distinction (1987: 308). As he calculatedly leaves aside the voice—to the dismay of many of his fans who initially bought the record—and erases any sense of the lyrical with blaring frequency density, he works on the edge of the phatic, disappearing the "here" of an I into the "there" of insect-like accumulation and the overlaid speeds of movement.

In other words, Lou Reed twists the musical explorations of his contemporaries into an extreme, a theatrical gesture emphasizing his non-presence and noncompliance to expectations. The record can be, in the words of Lester Young, "The Greatest Album Ever Made" because it presents a kind of blank surface for writing (as Young does in his article on the album) (Bangs 2003: 195). It opens a non-space within the soundscape of "reality" that demands an accounting for and reframing of listening. Similarly, in the Velvet Underground song "Heroin" (1967), John Cale's viola reframes the ethereal harmonies of LaMonte Young's drone music as an invasive attack on the ear and language. As we listen to Lou Reed's blankly intoning voice, the viola moves into the listening space set up by that voice. It creates distortion and interference. We have to "listen through" it to get to Reed's words, even in the controlled environment of the recorded song. It is an imposition that not only mimetically represents the city (imagine the clichéd correspondence between these electronic shrieks and the screech of the subway) but also attempts to efface the space of communication, to create an overflow of sound that troubles and completes Reed's narrative of urban decay in which all the "politicians" are "making crazy sounds."

The "punk" or "proto-punk" sounds of these composers and performers are interventions into a poetics of noise. They reframe sound through chaotic micro-events that present an epistemic or acoustemological shift in perception—at the micro-level of sound production but also in the macro-level of listening. These music-makers use the rebarbative danger of noise to force the ear into new listening situations, new surprises of sound that evoke layers and spaces rather than conversation and discourse. One does not "read" the phrases and harmonies at work but attempts to listen to too much, to tune into an excess of possible significations. This reimagination of sound mass—and the listener's relation to it—figures the precarity of communication within a fragmented and unstable auditory situation. It also suggests ways in which the listener structures such situations: the meaning of sound is socially produced, both in terms of its origin in the social production of space—in cities, in mediums—but also in the sense of the relations between people that demand responsibility and transformation. Poets and musicians in the Downtown scene sought absolution not only from the disciplinary requirements of something like a "structural listening" but also from the disciplinary listening *for* meaning, matter, and clarity.

Noise and the Mimeograph Magazine: *Fuck You: A Magazine of the Arts*

The pleasures of noise interpretively framed by a decentered urban listening also transformed the relationships between text and performance in Downtown poetry. An oral poetics of represented speech and poetic performance connected the "second generation" New York School of poets like Ed Sanders, Ted Berrigan and Alice Notley with the work and theories of vatic poets like Charles Olson and Allen Ginsberg as well as the plain, "unpoetic" talk of poets like Frank O'Hara. Daniel Kane's *All Poets Welcome: The Lower East Side Poetry Scene in the 1960s* (2003) suggests, however, that this emphasis upon orality in the interactions of these many poets of different schools was part and parcel to the transformation of the poetry reading into a scene of community and sociability (1–26). The kind of interactive, social, dialogic orality of these readings sharply differed from the academic model in which an audience sits silently in quiet halls listening to the poet behind a lectern. Out of this noisy oral situation, the Downtown poets imagined poetry less as a medium for voice and more as a space that could reimagine the linguistic basis of context and contact. They saw a need for performance and social interaction, but they also emphasized ephemeral and speedy production that recorded and transcribed such public events. This reimagined oral poetics not only reaffirmed the bodies and presences of individuals and speakers, it also opened up the space for a decentered aural poetics founded on noise rather than voice, on chance encounters and arrangements that exposed the relationship between disparate and half-heard fragments and the busy, loud, crowded public spaces in which they arose.

The first downtown spaces that opened their doors to such outsider poetics were the coffee shops Café Les Deux Mégots and Café Le Metro. For a short while, second-generation New York School poets along with Black Mountain poets like Paul Blackburn and Joel Oppenheimer, Fluxus composer/poets like Jackson Mac Low, and Beat-generation writers like William Burroughs and Ginsberg all mixed in these wide-open performance events. The poet Dan Saxon created instant publications that recorded them. He would have poets write down (or in some cases type) their performed poems on rexograph paper[2] and then bring collated copies to the next week's reading (Kane 2003: 36). This publication

---

[2] Along with the mimeograph, an early form of small-scale copy-making.

series, called respectively *Poets at Les Deux Mégots* and *Poets at Le Metro*, did not function like a typical publication—with rounds of edits and a design team dedicated to achieving a "finished" project. Instead, it quickly recorded an ongoing process. The "published" work combined text and performance in a way that elided the difference between the two: the performance and the record of the performance became intertwined and nearly simultaneous. Just like the tape recorder that Paul Blackburn used to archive many of these readings, the published document could track the ever-shifting, plural, and multiform language of the poets in performance. This act of recording was not so much a preservation of each night's readings (the printing and paper were cheap and decayed easily) as the active establishment of a fluctuating poetic community through the writing and collecting of speech acts.

Saxon's series, along with many other Lower East Side magazines, was part of what has been called a "mimeograph revolution." Using the newly invented mimeograph machine (a forerunner to today's office copy machines), writers could create quick and cheap publications that avoided the inhibiting codes of taste and unofficial censorship that guided mainstream publishing. They could (at least approximately) capture the festive, theatrical, and incantatory gestures that were based on writers' desire for direct expression, personal liberation, and community creation. In addition to Dan Saxon's publications, Ted Berrigan's *C: A Journal of Poetry*, Amiri Baraka (LeRoi Jones) and Diane DiPrima's *The Floating Bear*, Ed Sanders's *Fuck You/a Magazine of the Arts*, Bernadette Mayer and Vito Acconci's *0 to 9*, and many other magazines allowed more poets to publish whatever strange, unacceptable, incomprehensible, or sexually charged material they desired. Sanders famously declared in his magazine, "I'll Print Anything!"

Fuck You/ (1961–5) was a particularly aggressive example of poetic boundary breaking. Ed Sanders may be best known as the founder of the proto-punk band The Fugs, which performed poems by Blake and Swinburne while also making acoustic ballads about drugs and sex. The poets published in *Fuck You/* pushed against cultural taboos, particularly around sex, desire, and queerness. Imagined by Sanders as a "Total Assault on the Culture," the poetry—from Al Fowler's ironically charged poems about incestual desire, to Peter Orlovsky's very matter-of-fact recounting of sex with Allen Ginsberg, to Sanders's own obsession with using the words "cocks," "cunts," and "fucking"—displayed a casual but revolutionary lack of decorum. The instantaneity of the mimeograph medium supported the inclusion of language specifically meant to break taboos, which are not just standards of what can be spoken but also standards of what can be heard. The magazine ended when Sanders was charged with obscenity by the New York City police (Kane 2003: 77–9). Though the court battle was ultimately decided in Sanders's favor—just as at the same moment the more famous case of William Burroughs's *Naked Lunch* was decided in the publisher's favor—the scenes and desires represented in the magazine had the ability to unsettle in its gregarious, polymorphously perverse way.

But *Fuck You/* also contains a sonic force—it amplifies the interjective force of "fuck you" as a break in communication and a moment of violence even as it structures a feeling of fun. The simple breaking of a taboo begins to undo the distinction between acceptable speech and unacceptable noise on both a "moral" level and at the level of the text. Sanders's assault on "public morals" maps the moral directly onto the poetic. The recording apparatus of print could also expand beyond the limitations of speech, and capture other sounds, usually to index specific events. One poem, "Camping Out with Ed Sanders" by Mark Samara reduces language to a series of inarticulate moans. After three lines of "Ooooooooooooh" sounds the poem ends with an increase in volume:

Oooooooooooh, OooooooooooooH, OoooooooooooooooooH!
"Not Bad!"

(*Fuck You/* Vol. 1, No. 5, unpaginated)

In reproducing these sounds (of pleasure, of excitement, of fear?), the poem acts as a sound recorder of empty address. These "Ooooooooooohs" create distended versions of the apostrophaic "O" that begins so many odes and lyrics, but their presentation deflates the intimate and yet public address of the lyric, leaving us wondering about the context and setting. Unlike a Dadaist sound poem, Samara's "Ooooooooooooh" is just situated enough to prompt questions as to how, why, or in what ways a person might make such an address. The poem ends in dialogue—"Not Bad!"—emphasizing the poem's theatrical aspect and furthering the feelings already evoked of friendship, intimacy, and (possibly) sex without supplying direct narration. In magazines like *Fuck You/* and other small, mimeographed poetry publications like Ted Berrigan's *C,* poetry repeatedly turned not toward the unconscious or automatic but rather to the fragmented scene and to surface texture without explanation. A "setting" was no longer described within the poem but inferred from its language and context within a specific scene of address. In this way, poets could both reaffirm a specific connection to others—friendship, intimate address—and reimagine what one could do or say inside the rarefied tradition of "poetry." It could be emptied of its lyric baggage—its generalizing, abstracting, and anthropomorphizing tendencies—and become instead a medium for talking. In this case, the reduction of this medium to its barest elements could frame non-speech sounds as accidental fragments: both gnomic index and "obvious" surface. To play on the Latin etymology of "obvious"—*ob via*, closed way—the site of the social is simultaneously transparent and blocked.

A language of noise, then, exists as a surface texture that invites people into the work of listening together. With poetry that worked on the edges of the sayable—in both "moral" and formal terms—magazines like *Fuck You/*, *Genesis: Grasp*, and *0 to 9* all imagined poetic community not by means of formal coherence but rather through concatenation and resonance. They gathered together eccentric writing and kept its centrifugal force. Little magazines and the coffee shops, bookstores, and alternative spaces associated with them not only provided a space for experimentation but also created a kind of textual glue that connected the various poets living in or around the Lower East Side. Sanders would often dedicate the back page of *Fuck You/* to the various contributors in that number. Rather than a simple enumeration of an author's biography and publication history, these notes told funny stories, gave writers epithets, and provided a series of in-jokes and advertisements that made the magazine work as a kind of "community newspaper" (Kane 2003: 76). The social environment took on textual form and, conversely, text took on social force. The "contextual practice" of *Fuck You/* and the work of poets in the second-generation New York School depended upon "building works not around a central idea, theme, or symbol but by plucking and arranging images, materials, language, or even people from the surrounding milieu" (Fredman 2010: 3).

In this milieu, the noise of the social inhered in texts that arranged language to emphasize both irreducibility and phatic touch. This is language moored not to an intra- or infra-textual organization but rather to a nebulous, intertextual outside, composed of encounters among friends and strangers in spaces differentiated from the administered communications of "mainstream" culture.

Experimentation and Erasure in *0 to 9*

Another magazine that took part in this transformation of the contextual in poetics was the more explicitly "experimental" *0 to 9*, a mimeographed journal edited by Bernadette Mayer and Vito Acconci. *0 to 9* represented a change from the diaristic work of the Beat and New York School as writers like Mayer, Acconci, and Clark Coolidge investigated the range of poetic possibilities in extreme practices of linguistic play. Influenced by the rebarbative repetitions of Gertrude Stein (who also shows up in the magazine), these artists turned away from the explicit social indexing of poets embedded in a milieu or coterie. They instead developed strategies for expanding upon and intensifying the denatured workings of language within the projected space of the poem. Despite the radically different practices on the two sides of this transition, the connecting thread remained an emphasis upon the social production of meaning. Poetry remained a process that was literally worked *out*—in the air, in the community, on the material page, and on the body. In *0 to 9*, the editors and poets accepted that in quick mimeograph production "nothing was perfect" but this served as a way "to get far away from the idea, so promulgated, of the perfection of the poem with white space around it" (Acconci and Mayer 2006: 13). From these various forms of physicality and materiality, these writers and performers focused on the exterior, the stylized, and the performed in order to test poetic making against the material and communicative limits of language. They could reimagine language not as a fixed grammar with sounds that fill in its categorical spaces but as a sonic field available for patterns wholly outside of previous rhetorical strategies of organization. The vocabulary list overwhelms the sentence.

Bernadette Mayer led some of the first workshops at the Poetry Project at St. Mark's Church in the East Village, a community space for poetry events founded in the mid-1960s. In these gatherings she emphasized the word as thing and the poem as constructed object. She led fellow poets to experiment with various automatic processes, cut-up methods, and group authorship. As an editor in *0 to 9* along with Acconci, she championed language-oriented poetic experimentation, which moved away from the "content" of *Fuck You/* and toward the problem of what language could be made to do on the page. Cut-up poems—a Dadaist technique given new life by William Burroughs's and Brion Gysin's cut-ups of recorded speech—were only the beginning. Aram Saroyan's minimalist single-word poems, Dan Graham's diagrams, Sol Lewitt's drawings, Robert Smithson's maps, Jackson Mac Low's reading scores in addition to experiments in repetition from authors like Stein, John Giorno, and Clark Coolidge tested the limits of language in an aggressively formal way that borrowed some of the procedures of science but without its claims toward universal knowledge. These artists investigated the social construction of meaning not as a testing of boundaries of what can be said (a moral position) or the theatrical scene of the said (a poetics of intimate address) but as the outcome of how saying can happen at all.

This transition entailed a shift in emphasis from an oral to aural poetics. For these writers, "the sound of the words [a writer] compiles ... compile a world" (Ratcliffe 2000: 57). The relations between addresser and addressee and between poet and audience shift from one based upon the difficult "obviousness" of the spoken word to the "easy" obscurity of lists and arbitrary patterning. As compilers, they show words listed, stacked, placed in the space of the page. Rosemary Mayer (Bernadette Mayer's sister) literalizes this compiling approach in "FIRECRACKERS/July 4, 1968" (Acconci and Mayer 2006: 74). The author does not collect words but marks. In a grid that extends for fourteen pages, an "x" marks every time a firecracker explodes. Some minutes are so packed full of explosions that a thick black line substitutes for the individualized x's. This ethnographic foray into July 4th celebrations (the recording lasts from 9:19 p.m. to 1:29 a.m.) provides an alternative recording of sound—an array of marks that reduces sound to quantity and duration. In looking outside of sound—and outside of the national holiday as cause for celebration—the recorder introduces a tension between sound and recording, between individual experience and generalizable principle. There is not a hypothesis, just a written record of noise.

Similarly, in the more explicitly "poetic" texts in *0 to 9*, an emphasis upon the act of writing as a performance of a recording allows authors to morph the speaking author into a listening experimenter. Poets experimented with repetition and arrangement as opposed to the immediately felt (if textually motivated) forms of address common in the New York School. The displacement at the center of Jacques Derrida's critique of Western phonocentrism and logocentrism is that the voice—the "inner" voice of "hearing oneself speak"—is always already other than itself (Derrida 1973: 74–87). It is not a self-authorizing presence but rather a spaced (or written) site for "seeing" (not just hearing) a voice, a "scene, a theater stage" (Derrida 1973: 87). If the voice's exteriority is emphasized by the theatrical placement of language sound in New York School poetry, then the poets/multidisciplinary artists in *0 to 9* (and those who would later fall under the rubric of "Language" poetry) redouble the exteriority and otherness of speech. Speech sounds record both a world and a nothing within that world, an outside inside of speech. In this listening as writing, poets dislocate language from context in ways that go far beyond Eliot's call for "difficulty." Rather than resonant juxtaposition, language becomes a material tool for constructing new forms of syntax against normative grammar.

Coolidge, in a talk at the Naropa Institute, describes language as "sounds and matter: emotions, feelings, desires, densities, substance, arrangement. Everything is there" (Coolidge 1978: 155). But this "everything" only ever arrives in provisional concatenations, or vocabularies, imbued with force fields or arrays of meaning rather than specific forms of address. These relations of texture and pattern select for sonic substance and produce a synecdochic relation with a field of noise. In Coolidge's suite of poems, "Nothing I–XIII," the poet makes "nothing" by extracting words from their grammatical context and putting them back together again in ways that resist comprehension:

I.
the a
these but the
any with on I
them even they
for of the every
they I
in the a
and the I then
with with
what that the
to my to in
all the
no my the who
or what any I I the
in not when
the I we
but

(Coolidge 1968: 1)

Without nouns or verbs, and heavy on pronouns, definite and indefinite articles, prepositions, and conjunctions, Coolidge's poem highlights the connective tissue of sentences, the unheard givens in communication. Though seemingly "nothing," the poem produces potentiality as a "something." These "other" parts of language imply—by the force of absence—gaps in communication that also double as its substance. The organizing words without any objects or actions rewrite poetry as "useless" words or the "empty sounds" of noise. The poem invites its audience to create meaning out of this apparent emptiness, to find the social within space. Yet, Coolidge frustrates attempts to fill in these implicit erasures. Shifters that were implemented, previously, to index, combine with, and relate to other words become substantialized as sound forms. The poetic "I" becomes part of an a-grammatical heap of words finding an off-kilter beat rather than a controlling perspective holding forth in the poem. Relations of grammar are mapped onto relations of sound and repetition. We hear the "the" in "these," the stuttering of lines like "to my to in." Coolidge figures noise as the "nothing" of language—the substantialization of the unheard surface of its functioning.

The poem destabilizes the implicit listening situation of poetry. Rather than an address or a theatricalized situation, the words fall upon the page and connect with each other through the possible arrangements of sound that emerge in reading. Peter Szendy, in *Listen: A History of Our Ears*, describes listening in relation to the "phonogrammatization" of music and sound. He notes that in the context of written sound, listening functions by its mediated and "exterior" transposition rather than its movement by a purely "interior" rhetoric. Rather than passive reception, "[l]istening is a configuring on its own, without being mainly subjected to a rhetorically articulated flux that orders it and structures it from the interior of the musical work" (2008: 10). This sense of "listening as a configuring" can be extended to the "rhetorically articulated flux" of other sound forms—not only poems, recorded songs, and other acts of sound-writing but also the "rhetorically" (or architecturally, legally, and economically) organized flux of a city, a party, a performance. Coolidge imagines arrangement in these expanded terms:

> ... look out your window and you see trees, and leaves on the trees, and birds. Now, where are they? What kind of pattern do they make? What sort of arrangement? There seems to be no intelligence behind it but there is an arrangement.
>
> (Coolidge 1978: 153)

Coolidge exposes an act of arrangement in listening in which the work maps onto the contiguous patterns of things in the "actual world," phenomenal as opposed to atomistic objects. Such listening does not establish a fixed channel of communication—as in the classic rhetorical "call" of a lyric poem—that might reduce noise. Rather, Coolidge amplifies an "outside"—the grammatical fragments that nouns and verbs pass "through"—to make noise. He configures listening against understanding (an "intelligence behind it"). Noise lies in the triangulated space and time between nothing and an index, nothing and a signification.

In this reconfiguration of listening sign becomes gesture, sentences disappear and we again occupy Barthes's public space of floating syntagms. The communal world imagined by Coolidge is not one of collective song but rather of improvisatory free play, and it emerges from his roots in avant-garde jazz as a drummer and critic. It also is in conversation with Mayer's experiments. In prompts that asked writers to "systematically derange the language" or "rewrite someone else's writing," Mayer as an instructor also created maps for improvising within the space of reading and writing. Such improvisations produce new sonic possibilities and new potential connections and textures across the fabric of language. They also involve acts of erasure that mark the effect of a listening that finds other connections, working to create new similarities and repetitions across grammatical, textural, and phonetic sequences.

Mayer's work in *0 to 9* also propels itself through structures of repetition, erasure, and play. Against the hallowed, cordoned-off space of the poem, she curates multiple different arrangements of, and therefore ways of conceiving of, "everything"—as in an untitled poem in *0 to 9* No. 5, January 1969 where she invokes "what's thought of as a boundless, continuous expanse extending in all directions or in three dimensions within which all material things are contained at this moment as a sign of the infinitive … " (Acconci and Mayer 2006: 47). The poem is a long "run-on" sentence that prefigures the "everything work" that would be the effort of Coolidge and Mayer in the mid-1970s. Mayer is "putting as much as possible into from a point outside to one inside" (47), and in this collecting, she touches on "people carrying communications back and forth," cardinal directions, measurements, and comparisons between "one of two things" (47). At the end of the piece, she gives directions for measuring one's reading pace. Whether a "slow," "fast," or "average" reader, the poem—one long block of text that seems to fill up the entire page—is difficult to read through and parse. The maximal effects seem directly opposed to Coolidge's sweet nothings. But the desire to bring outside inside functions similarly to Coolidge's erasures: the positive production of words on the page works against the white space that separates the poem from the world. Mayer saturates the channel, exposing us to both the speed of reading and, like her sister's effort to record firecracker noise, to an experience of the phenomena of the world.

Coolidge, Mayer, and others published in *0 to 9* perform a different aurality in the midst of the sound mass of language. Noise violates both limits in Louis Zukofsky's well-known definition of poetry as "lower limit speech/upper limit music" (1978: 138). These limits no longer define the horizon of poetic making because noise lurks at the threshold of all significant sound. Rather than create a poetic "speaker," a theatricalized scene of personal encounter, or a musical order, words give way to the reorganization of language as noises—a-grammatical and anti-rhetorical sound material. Projectivist poets insisted upon an embodied relationship between a subject and history (through an oral interaction), so they had to bring their bodies into the poem. But these Downtown poets and performers retreated from such historicity. For them, the figure of noise demanded, rather, a sonic reduction of their poems to other sounds. The process by which the body projects itself into the poem or the sound recording is burst open by these writers, who do not think of the body as an expansive, integrating force that guarantees the historicity of the poet's making. The body—caught up in the speed of knowing, perceiving, calculating, compiling, configuring—is, rather, a disintegrating figure on the edges of an erasure.

Punk and the Noise of Disarticulation

The search outside of speech for a language with "densities" parallels the move away from the page and toward the possibilities of rock 'n' roll performance. Two of the most well-known punk originators—Richard Hell and Patti Smith—have long been associated with literature and literary forebears. But both poets forged their iconic performance personas not only in imitation of legendary figures of the avant-garde like Rimbaud but also through the poetic language and forms of community that emerged out of the Lower East Side in the 1960s and 70s (Kane 2017: 1). Both authors had a close relationship to the do-it-yourself literary scene of the New York School. Smith's first reading was at the St. Mark's Poetry Project in February 1971, and Richard Hell, under his first name, Richard Meyers, published experimental poets like Clark Coolidge and Bruce Andrews in his literary magazine, *Genesis : Grasp*, in the early seventies. The direct literary connections of these poet-performers—the way they imagined themselves in and through the kinds of work adjacent to their own literary and musical efforts—inform a poetics of noise that complicates a sense of the "immediacy" of performance in punk rock. In particular, both of these poet-performers rethink the place of the voice in relation to the rock song at the foundation of punk. They call up the vatic power of voice only to undercut it. They make voice into the face of noise, a prosopopeia of racket.

In this way, both Hell and Smith build on the power of the metaphor of voice in performance and on record, but in doing so, they also draw attention to the embodied voice's struggle with this metaphor, a product of a body preceded by text and image and yet present only through its spastic and voided elements. If rock's performed voice mediates a power beyond—an energy or transcendence impossible in the text—that "beyond" paradoxically figures in punk as acts of erasure, an undercutting of communication or meaning. The voices of Hell and Smith are thus not so much iconic as anti-iconic. They connect closely with the movement toward "ineptitude" that Paul Hegarty describes as punk rock's signifier of authenticity (2007: 89). Punk demands failure as noise: it is deskilled, simple, and even (in echoes of Tzara and Iggy Pop) idiotic. Punk's musical and theatrical failure may have been most fantastically and spectacularly perpetuated by the Sex Pistols, but the initial movement toward the minor (juvenile) statement (e.g., Hell's "Love Comes in Spurts" or the Ramone's "I Wanna Sniff Some Glue") and anti-product product has roots in the iconoclastic attitudes of the New York School. Richard Hell's poetic emergence as a punk performer in his influential song "Blank Generation" shows a negotiation between contextual practice and anti-cultural pose, while Patti Smith's first performance at the St. Mark's Poetry Project in February of 1971 suggests the ways in which Smith would transition from a localized social space to the disruptive potential of transcendent noise that defines the genre of punk.

Hell's self-published magazine *Genesis : Grasp* has an important place in this story. Even as a teenage writer, he understood the power of little magazines to form communities. He initially started the magazine to "assert myself as a writer, as well as enter or help fashion a community of writers in which I fit" (Hell 2005a, n.p). Bruce Andrews, a contributor in the last issue of *Genesis : Grasp*, recognized the same qualities in little magazines: "the only kind of angle into the small press poetry world was the radical fringe of what was going on at St. Mark's, some loose formulation of experimental poetry which at that point would include concrete, visual, conceptual or sound work" (quoted in Kane 2017: 198). *Genesis : Grasp*, despite its small scale (about 500 copies were made of each issue), fashioned a community out of poetic production.

Within this magazine's imagined community, the scatological combined with the language play of *0 to 9*'s radical poetics. In his editorial choices and in his own poetry, Hell connected his work to a long line of twentieth-century avant-gardism. Hell printed minimalist poems by Coolidge like "urn urn," which consisted of the word "urn" repeated twice, separated by a large white space, and centered in the middle of the journal page (*Genesis : Grasp* 1.4 (1970): 40). He also printed longer poetry by Coolidge that would go on to be published in Coolidge's Harper and Row book, *Space*. The poem "Made Thought" reflects Tristan Tzara's claim that "thought is made in the mouth:"

> made thought which of it
> all of which a kind yet
> best it in and on should must
> whatever it is often once to do
> in a while once is there and in
> as it like it but often ever that it is
> in which in separate that
> often only very not in which way
> all of this but this which s are alike
> or in an only not what made as for
> it in its well as made open as in
> that which it once all but made but
> for all as it is.
>
> (*Genesis : Grasp* 2.1/2 (1971): 61)

Rather than "in the mouth," the thought is made by the play of words as things, organized along lines of sound play, repetition, and nonsense.

Hell would also include his friend, Tom Miller (soon to be Verlaine), who focused on eyes and bodily malfunction. In one alien-Emersonian formulation the poet becomes a "giant eyeball/green, greasy, softly buzzing" (*Genesis : Grasp* 2.1/2 (1971): 59). On the other hand, Hell/Meyers takes flight in "Goodbye:"

> A crumb from the central kernel
> a moment of resolution
> I rise on my toes and the sidewalk
> falls away
> I think the time has come.
> Speed in the air is like a
> gravestone in the ground
> a floe whose snow
> shutter
> keeps clicking faster and faster
> in a smaller and smaller space
> like my memory
>
> I'm Gon.
>
> (*Genesis : Grasp* 2.1/2 (1971): 26)

To be "gon" in this way is to lose memory in the smaller and smaller space of the photographic click. A surrealist Zeno's paradox, the mapping of image to reality in ever more infinitesimal units results in a state in which memory and space disappear in their moment of capture. This is a poetics of spatio-temporal deformation that challenges any "moment of resolution," even if "the time has come."

At this point in Hell's poetic career, he was searching for a visceral, "direct" poetry, a "muscular poetics committed to immediacy, visuality, and shock value" (Kane 2017: 109). That poetry was found in a variety of experiments with the page as a material opening and constraint, particularly in Hell's work under the pseudonym Ernie Stomach. Under this name, Hell wrote visually playful work like the poem "Hello, I" published in the last issue of *Genesis: Grasp*. "Hello, I" consists simply of "Hello, I" printed halfway down the journal's page and flush against its right boundary. The words, pushing against the edge of the paper, use that edge to figure a larger communication that begins but remains emphatically off the page. The phatic acknowledgment of contact—Hello!—seems to establish a channel to another listener, but the material limits of the page intervene. In this poem, the noise of a space outside of the text is imbricated with the limitations of the medium itself. Simultaneously a "concrete" poem and a joke, "Hello, I" shows Stomach/Meyers/Hell making a sly statement against poetry's literal limits.

With similar intent, Ernie Stomach would create *uh*, a "flip-movie dance alphabet peepshow toy enigma boring book" in January of 1971. This flipbook consists of an alphabet constructed with a stylized font that makes each letter out of a variation on a basic ovoid shape. Flipping through the book, there is no narrative plot as in a child's flipbook but rather a play between the abstract visual shapes and our recognition of them as letters in the alphabet. However, this strange concrete *lettrism* is not all austere constructivism: *uh* in the abstract ovoid alphabet of the book is distinctly penis-shaped. The whole alphabet becomes a variation on penises—a theme often taken up in Hell's poems and songs (Kane 2017: 106). The combination of experimental concrete poetry and the fascination with a penis follows upon Ed Sanders's taboo-breaking moves in the 1960s. In this concrete poem, however, the "enigma" in the book's title is also the movement between registers that do not function by traditional reference. Visual abstraction, phallic representation, and alphabetical matrix all conflict with each other and push the poem away from the page. A concrete action takes place in the cinematic flipping of the book, and this concrete movement of, with, and against the page rearranges form and language as a movement of the eye and ear in an alternative space of reading.

The minimum of figuration in "Hello, I" or *uh* shows the literal and figurative limits of the represented space of the page in relation to a social space off the page. The concatenation of the material of the book, the hand holding it, and the space outside of it figures the concatenation of word, sound, voice, and noise in the performance poetics that would spring from these experiments. One can see how, in a letter written to the poet Bruce Andrews just after the publication of Ernie Stomach's "master" work, Hell is searching for a different aesthetic: "I want each page in the mag to be as direct as possible. I don't want words from the imagination or intellect. I want them from the muscled energy of a being and/or more particularly from the page. I want to turn people on" (Richard Hell to Bruce Andrews, February 12, 1971). In a return letter to Hell, Andrews seems to hit upon the thing Hell is looking for: "I think I know what you want: quick hits, which is only possible with a short and lean (uncomplicated) supercharged poem—EROTIC ROCK 'N' ROLL DOPE poems" (Bruce Andrews to Richard Hell 1972).

Such an attitude suggests the general feeling behind the move by writers like Hell, Verlaine, and Smith from the medium of the page to the mediums of performance and recording in rock 'n' roll. This erotic—bodily, desiring, excessive—movement against the material limits of the page is transformed into an experience of voice, rhythm, and timbre that suffuses the relationship between addressor and addressee, singer and audience with energy and intensity. But this vocal "erotics" also produces deformation, silence, and blankness. The punk embrace of performance was not simply the return of a bardic oral tradition or a naive sense of rock 'n' roll projectivism: it actively renegotiated those traditions through a figure of noise as sonic reduction, mess, and accident.

Hell's song "Blank Generation" has an important place in the genealogy of punk because of its influence on performance style, sound, and lyric in later iterations of the genre. Hell played the song in the different bands he formed: Neon Boys, Television, and then Richard Hell & the Voidoids. Though not officially released until 1977 (after Hell had left Television and formed the Voidoids), the song was an important part of Television's set in its beginning years. Its simple descending riff, inspired by the Rod McKuen's 1959 parodic novelty song, "I Belong to the Beat Generation," was one step away from the bare minimalism of the Ramones and the Sex Pistols. As the song "opened up a space where a new rebellious (if cynical) sensibility … could be cultivated" (Kane 2017: 115), it also defined the sound of that sensibility in noise.

"Blank Generation" combines relatively staid strophic forms with blasts of trebly guitar, a simple and aggressive backbeat, and Hell's own nasal, over-the-top delivery. While the lyrics and formal structure of "Blank Generation" are not particularly extreme in relation to Hell's written poems, the vicious tone of the performance defines the critical punk attitude against previous poetic and musical forms. The song, a hellish birth narrative, emphasizes incompleteness even in the act of generation. Hell writes long verse lines in quatrain form, and the narrator wanders and loses his "train of thought" as he "fall[s] into your arm's tracks/and watch[es] beneath the eyelids every passing dot" (Hell 1977). The movement into the junkie dot world—a world of visuality without vision—mirrors a sense of noise as an aurality without identification, order, or meaning.

If it is, as the song says, "such a gamble when you get a face," that gamble also extends to the metaphoric recognition of the singing voice. The most jarring moment of the song happens when Hell, instead of singing "blank" again, leaves an empty space in the chorus:

> I belong to the blank generation
> I can take it or leave it each time
> I belong to the _____ generation
> I can take it or leave it each time.
>
> (Hell 1977)

Hell's performed silence emphasizes an opposition between "blank" and "_____" that he would often discuss in interviews. "Blank" marked initially a nihilistic and apathetic sense of not caring: "When anything got into the final analysis, I didn't care. That's what the song 'Blank Generation' was about" (McGann and McNeil 1997: 282). And yet at the same time, the empty, open space of the blank created possibility: "To me, 'blank' is a line where you can fill in anything. It's positive. It's the idea that you have the option of making yourself anything you want, filling in the blank" (Bangs 2003: 266). In its recorded performances, the silence of the blank in the song surprises us, creating a space and a cut out of machinic rhythms of the band. This silence is not a Cagean silence—it is not the listener's attention to the plenitude of a total soundscape—it is a bereftness, an absence in which one can disengage or compose oneself. That breach of the song's smooth flow allows for the entrance of sonic accidents that are drowned out by the drumbeat, bass-line, guitar chords, and vocal sounds. On a recently released live version of "Blank Generation" as played by Television at CBGB in 1974, the silence is often quickly filled in by Tom Verlaine's eager guitar (Hell 2005b). The vacuum of sound imposes a sense of *horror vacui* that renders listeners (and fellow players) nervous and expectant. While the song's propulsion moves it into a space "outside", it also includes an anxious interpolation of that outside space, an evidence of otherness within a brief silence.

Hell's vocal timbre parallels this erasure within the act of projecting voice. Influenced by the flat delivery of Lou Reed, the untutored voices of 1960's garage rock, and the crazed theatricality of Iggy Pop, Hell departs from classic rock 'n' roll singing. At least as far back as the blues, rock singing emphasizes the grain and timbre of the voice over purity and diction. However, Hell's voice—like other punk singers—does not produce the "naturalism" of this mode. Where for most popular singers, "inarticulateness, not poetry, is the ... conventional sign of sincerity" (Frith 1981: 36), for Hell an overt stylization overemphasizes the embodied voice. Rock music in general participates in a performed "struggle against words:" "the test of soul conviction is the singer's way with non-words" (Frith 1981: 36). In this struggle, all the sighs, shouts, grunts, etc., of the singer supplement verbal communication to represent a different, "higher," "soul to soul" level of communication. As Richard Middleton suggests, punk played with the contradiction between "style" and "soul-to-soul" spontaneity by pushing through and breaking up the myth of a voice's soul-baring self-expression (2000: 35). Richard Hell's nasally, slurring delivery, his awkward lurch into a different register in the chorus, his grating timbres and wobbly pitch, and the tremendous energy of his outward push and breath all end up alienating voice from a fixed idea of the self and vice versa, even as voice remains central to the act of performance. As Middleton says of Johnny Rotten's singing (which was influenced by Hell through his manager Malcolm McLaren), we are "transfixed by the *performance*," a performance that takes from the codes of vocal soul-baring but that refuses the emotional signification of such transcendence (Middleton 2000: 35). Hell's voice—the archetype of punk vocality—is a performance of performance.

The punk stance toward the sound of the voice is also a criticism of the erotics of unrepresentability, whereby the absent singer's body-in-the-voice, their grain, becomes an object of desire and identification. The punk rock singer blows out this system of voicing. This singing emphasizes distortion and phonic metal to the point of refusing signification. In his diary from the seventies, Hell quotes Baudelaire: "that which is not slightly distorted lacks sensible appeal" (Hell

1990: 99). Hell's vocality seeks this appealing state of distortion, which is not the appeal of "authentic" expression but rather a defiant dedifferentiating impulse. The inarticulate is not the sign of the unrepresentable but an invitation to "do it yourself" or "become your own hero" as Hell put it (Bangs 2003: 265). The inarticulate gesture in the voice opens singing up: everyone can do it, join in, and be their "own hero." Out of vocal noise a community is founded, based not on the circulation of print, nor out of the space of a particular address, but out of the force of a performed defacement. To take the voice outside of itself in this way is to undo the idea of vocal transcendence. The voice remains fleshly, fallible and yet strangely unreal. Even this fallen voice, however, becomes a voice-print, and listeners still hear a unique identifying mark in and on Hell's performances. I am suggesting, however, that Hell's vocal production, through its theatricalization—its doubled sense of being a performance of a performance—retains an excess that continues to play in the gap between voice and identity. Noise remains as that sonic element in the voice that refuses that suture.

Patti Smith and the Generation of Noise

The transformation of voice into noise is not a movement of loss. Within the voided sonic field of the voice, a new sense of social space emerges. The act of dis-identifying voice and reinscribing it with noise becomes an important element in punk and post-punk. In tandem with Hell's move to invite "blankness" into the generation of voice is Patti Smith's simultaneous assumption and destruction of the vatic power of the "rock god." Like Hell, Smith was and remains a writer and a performer, and she was part of the Lower East Side poetry scene before she (along with Television) helped to instigate the punk revolution at CBGB in the mid-1970s. Smith's embrace of noise stems from a struggle over the boundaries of the poem and the possibilities of remaking the figure of voice in a revolutionary and feminine image.

Smith's first performance with guitarist Lenny Kaye on February 10, 1971 has become a legendary event in punk historiography and in the history of the St. Mark's Poetry Project. I would like to avoid a teleological view that hears Smith's early production in relation to her present eminent stature and, instead, return to this first reading as a space of contingency and accident. The gaps or seams in this performance of word and song lead beyond Smith's career and into the work of punk as a genre. Smith has said she was not "content just to read poetry" and that the reading was controversial because she and Kaye "desecrated the hall of poetry with an electric guitar" (Smith 2014). The sound of this "desecration" had, initially, a mimetic purpose: Kaye was asked to accompany Smith on a poem about a car crash, "Ballad of a Bad Boy" (subsequently published in *Early Work: 1970–1972*). The clangs of electric guitar that mark Kaye's entrance into the song/poem as well as the closing screech he creates with aggressive tremolos and pick-scrapes evokes the speed and destruction of a car breaking up. These sounds interrupt and undo the voice's intonation and projection (Smith 1971). Rather than providing (as it mostly has), a rhythmic backdrop, the guitar's inhuman death rattle breaks into the fabric of the performance. The sound has no vocal analog. It figures the end of the voice not in song, rhythm, or tone but in an unpitched wash of frequencies.

In conversation with this figure of noise as both mimetic power and inhuman metallic transformation is an accident that emerges earlier in the set. As Smith concludes a version of the song "Fire of Unknown Origin," Kaye, improvising a repetitive blues riff, keeps going. Smith has to say that she's finished and the audience laughs. The rhythm ends abruptly (Smith 1971). Here, noise enters without the theatrical planning of "Ballad of a Bad Boy." The moment of dissolution exposes an amateurish, improvisatory, and unplanned experimentation. In doing so, it suggests a sudden "fall" from the performed mode of song to the fact of being a body in a room with others—who all have various scripts to perform and play. Smith's undercut vatic utterances suddenly draw the space into them.

As Daniel Kane suggests, Smith was ambivalent about the social poetics of the St. Mark's Poetry Project, and she both rejected and participated in the wider literary and musical scenes around her (Kane 2017: 138). Her desire to emerge as a seer, in the spirit of Dylan Thomas and Allen Ginsberg, not to mention her many rock 'n' roll heroes like Bob Dylan, Jimi Hendrix, Jim Morrison, and Mick Jagger, meant deriding the "namby-pamby" performances of other poets and taking on a new hybrid model of poet-performer-rock star along with a new hybrid model of gender (Kane 2017: 134). However, the unpracticed breakdown in this first reading performance stands in for the limitations of this "heroic" view of the male vatic voice. Noise offers Smith a way to figure not the mythological accession of the male projectivist voice, but rather the productively incomplete accession to voice that a body at the limit makes. She inhabits its cracks, its fissures, its lack of a place. Even as Smith wears the mask of many of her male heroes, then, she dislocates that mask, revealing its limits in a gendered, "visionary" assumption of power.

In this, Smith is following a long line of avant-gardist practice of figuring noise even in the midst of manifesting a new poetic voice. The textual parallels between Arthur Rimbaud and Smith's mid-1970s work suggest that "noise ... for both Smith and Rimbaud [is] a kind of brute matter to which the aesthetic—in the defining dream of the twentieth-century avant-garde—is ordered to return" (Noland 1999: 173). In the case of Smith, the brute sonic mass of noise emerges not only in a textual excess but also in the irruptions of accident in the fabric of the social. Planned accident (the guitar's interruptions) and disorganized faltering (the unpracticed end) converge in noise. For punk, ineptitude became a "strong, fundamentally noisy anti-cultural statement," and the genre thrives on the manifestation of an authenticity of limited skill and limited means (Hegarty 2007: 89). Failures and crashes parallel the self-consciousness of a fragile body in space. The pose of "bad"-ness (as in maladroitness as well as the pose of the countercultural anti-body) becomes an invitation to excess, to pushing the voice too far, to a babble that will not stop, to the racket of the band.

Smith's many citations of canonical rock music, including covers of Them's "Gloria" and interpolations of Jimi Hendrix's "Hey Joe" and Chris Kenner/Wilson Pickett's "Land of 1000 Dances" explicitly take up this form of excess. In the act of citing previous (male) rock music, Smith uses cultural reference as a site of acknowledgment and struggle (Cohen and Coyle 2013: 113). The song becomes not the site of an appropriation so much as an attempt to reframe the tradition of rock as a transcendent revolution, a "religious yearning for communal, non-market aesthetic feeling that official art denied" (Graham 2009: 113). In this way, the accidental, interruptive noise of the social becomes figured as a re-generation of both rock and poetic tradition out of the noise that breaks down bodies, rhythms, and spaces. Smith's 1976 live performance of The Who's "My Generation," added as a bonus track to later releases of *Horses*, manifests—even more than the studio versions of the songs on the album—the frenetic energy that so many critics describe in Smith's music. As the band—with John Cale as a guest performer—speeds through the song, Smith and Cale trade verses in a stuttering, fast-paced style. It is almost as though the speed and distortion of the instruments (particularly of the bass on the recording) force their voices into a mode of stuttering, where the desire to say the word gets in the way of its own pronunciation. Then, in a gesture prefigured by Kaye's guitar breaks from 1971, the band descends into a series of extended wails: glissandos and a breakdown of the rhythmic and tonal form of the song. Smith, babbling from within the noise, sings, "I'm so goooodaaamn youuuung I'm so goooodaaamn yoooung … " until she, along with the band, finally breaks down in exhaustion. The "generation" of this song references a generation—"these stigmas to God [who] are gonna rise up" (quoted in Graham 2009: 112)—imagined not only as a group of people but as a source of production and creativity out of noise.

Smith's optimism toward accident—toward noise as generation—defines a particular sonic ethos of punk. At the same time that Smith projects a voice, she has to undo its effects in exhaustion and erasure. Its very transcendence lies in its abjection. In its ambiguous occupation of the position of the rocker or the projectivist, she does not simply emulate or imitate her heroes but weaves an excess of language (babble) and voice (growling, animalic, stuttering, repetitive) through its elements. She occupies the position of a parasite upon the rock persona while also reimagining noise as a sonic reduction, a sound that forces a "pterodactyl state," a belated but primitive space for hearing again and hearing differently (quoted in Graham 2009: 112).

Other punks would take up and radicalize Smith's example. Performers like the Ramones turned toward the body not as the site of an outward projection of self but as an overdriven medium for adolescent energy: "hey ho let's go!". Punk, at times billed as a "return" to the values of early rock 'n' roll, only ambivalently takes up that position. Rather than nostalgic replication, punk represented a radicalization and rejection of its intimate forebears. So, even as it took up textual experiments that sought to bring reader and listener together in both an imagined and a real social space of language and power, it rejected the limiting effects of the medium of the text. It also refused the implicit rhythmic and vocalic naturalism of much rock 'n' roll and replaced it with sound masses that interrupted and exhausted the potential of song to either simply entertain or to create an "immediate" connection from soul to soul. Smith, Hell, and other early punk singers instead emphasized performance, a radically textualized condition of voice that could break through the mask of vocality and personality of the "rock god."

These punk singers set the stage for even more extreme performances of noise and voice. In New York's No Wave scene of the late 1970s singers like Arto Lindsay of the band DNA used the vocal apparatus as a grunting, growling, chirping, and sound-making machine—but not as a personified voice. He would do everything but enunciate a spoken language. With Lindsay, and artists like him, we encounter the anti-humanism and anti-lyricism figured in Hell and Smith's work but taken to another extreme. Voice and noise, figure and ground, inside and outside blend and unmake each other. Even as the voice itself may be foregrounded in the mix and as the center of attention, the paradoxical quality of the punk performance is that it refuses such foregrounding. Noise opens up the prefiguration of the voice—in both text and performance—to interruption, alteration, and destruction. Its dis-identifying power qualifies punk as an "anti-genre"—a "genre of refusal" (Muñoz 2018: 655). This refusal runs through poetry and punk from this moment in the late sixties and early seventies to the present day. With their enfolding of noise into literary and artistic practice, we see an expansion of the literary text from a formed, neat poem with margins to a "plural body in which ephemeral oral rumors circulate" (de Certeau 1984: 162). In this common space in which bodies can be together within a space of potentiality, "one no longer knows what it is, if not altered and altering voices" (de Certeau 1984: 162).

In these experimental and performance poetics, however, this plural body should be encountered and heard in light of the poet Robert Grenier's famous refusal: "I HATE SPEECH" (Grenier 1971: n.p.). Both the alien language serialism of writers in *0 to 9* and punk's emphasis upon the alteration of voice are against "speech" and "orality" if those terms are taken to be signs of immediacy, of direct address and relation. Rather, the poetics of noise that arises in the movement from poetry to punk amplifies the possibility of community outside of a localized zone of address but still exposed to the social world. Punk mediates noise in part to participate within and to disrupt the commodity form of the rock song—both Hell and Smith are thinking about business as well as form— but also to pluralize the potential of community and to create a "wildness" outside of the social scripts of subjectivity and normativity granted by one's embodiment (Muñoz 2018: 657). By moving within and beyond the concrete social worlds of the Downtown scene, punk suggested instead a disfiguring and generative otherness that could be performed outside of any communal space and yet still manifest in forms of togetherness. Noise does not produce an effect of authenticity but rather an ecstatic displacement, a theatrical standing beside oneself. Noise, figured as a fundamental unreadability, an obscurity within the voice, holds open the potentiality of this paradoxically anti-social but social space.

6

Noise Music, Noise History: Articulations of Sound Forms in Time

In the alignment of punk and a poetic turn to language experiment, figures of noise produce both a communal now—an interruptive force that brings bodies together—and a proleptic remaking of meaning from an imagined community of readers and listeners beyond the "now." The emptying out of voice and a reimagining of the audibility of language's address allows for a disavowal and deferral of the scripts of self that structure everyday life. But how does one dwell within, and even learn from these moments, these flashes of interrupted, even self-less time? In this concluding chapter, I take up sound-makers who figure noise as a myriad condition of address that embeds physiology and history in the act of articulation. Within an expansive sound art, these artists rewrite language, computer code, and visual marking in order to produce an "articulation of sound forms in time." This formulation—taken from Susan Howe's 1987 poem by that name—not only reduces music or poetry to "sound forms" but also calls up the question of "articulation:" the means of forming and concatenating sound in time. The word "articulation" has a rich semantic range: the joints between bones, muscles, and other parts of a body; the connecting points in any structure; the production of speech sounds by movements in the mouth; and, more generally and more recently, the simple materialization of any idea or thought such that articulation is nearly synonymous with saying at all (OED, "articulation").

Perhaps counterintuitively, the sense of articulation as a point of contact, as a hinge between structures of listening to and reproducing speech and language, guides my thinking about the production of noise since the late 1970s and early 1980s. It does so because "articulation" defines a point of contact where both connection and disconnection cohabitate in a trace of sound. The physical medium of signification opens up both a space of communication and a resistance to that communication. Out of the many practices of noise-making that inform contemporary sound art, the poets and musicians Susan Howe, David Grubbs, Tracie Morris, and Florian Hecker defamiliarize acts of articulation—of uniting text and sound, voice and performance—in ways that yield a figure of noise as the uncertainty between contact and failure. In the interplay between writing, sound, and vocal performance in the work of these artists, the processes of articulating sound forms in time and figuring noise conjoin.

By suggesting the ways in which these two processes function together, this group models ways of listening that oscillate or resonate between possible channels for communication and what Christoph Cox has called a sonic flux: the "immemorial sonic flow to which human expressions contribute but that precedes and exceeds those expressions" (Cox 2018: 2). The works of these sound-makers emphasize a movement in listening between an active production of meaning that follows sound's movements in articulation and a sense of passive becoming in the midst of sonic flux. In this way, these artists are all in conversation with the genre of "noise music," an expansive and indeterminate genre that questions the very possibility of listening through the mediations of genre, structure, and significant form. But the intermingling and confusion of voice and noise goes beyond simply a dismantling of listening. These artists also suggest the ways that listening produces or encodes noise. They listen to listening. They figure the figuration of noise.

The projects I discuss in this chapter each use radically different sound forms, but they all revolve around the articulation of sound through voice. Tracie Morris's repetitive and deformed sound poetries; Susan Howe and David Grubbs's collaborative destabilizations of voice, text, and sound; and Florian Hecker's experiments in re-coding written marks and vocal utterances as "chimeric" sound forms all draw attention to articulation as an unstable action that only provisionally joins body, text, audio equipment, electricity, and sound in combinations that move decisively beyond the technology of oral delivery.

In this work, to hear noise is to amplify the resistance of articulation in ways that expose the relationship between articulation, temporality, and history. These artists turn their ears toward an expanded temporality in which noise sounds out of the evacuated scripts of self, being, and society written into historical and cultural time. Sound traces in poetry, electronic sound, and performance dissipate into frequency scatter and let us hear—inside of the decayed, the inchoate, the inarticulate—what persists. As I alluded to in the introduction, these works implicitly ask after what we continue to listen for but cannot hear.

Through sound, they investigate—in stories of sense perception, nationhood, gender, and race—how the seemingly "blank" materiality of sound becomes invested with historical traces and speculative, even utopian, potentialities.

Noise Music and Aesthetic Listening

Susan Howe, David Grubbs, Tracie Morris, and Florian Hecker all work in relation to the experimental and popular genre of noise music, a notoriously shape-shifting tradition that calls into question the very limits of genre. Though precursors, as we have seen, exist throughout the twentieth century, the genre of noise music typically describes a transnational set of sound art practices that stem from a variety of genres: punk rock, free improvisation, industrial music, and experimental electronic music. Noise music typically calls up the sound image of uncompromising, surprising, loud, immersive concatenations of electronically amplified sound. As Marie Thompson has noted, noise music often emerges out of a poetics of transgression by which "noise" represents a distinct and definitive "outside" of music, sound, and social convention (2017: 151). In this way, it becomes closely associated with an imagery of transgression—sadomasochism, violence, fascism, etc.—that very closely resembles the "shock" value afforded to punk through its use of antisocial signifiers. But though an ideology of transgression might be at work in a variety of noise music, a more capacious way of defining its performance is as continuous exposure of "the inherently mediated and material dimension of sound and music" (Thompson 2017: 152). Noise music begins within a space of music- and meaning-making, calling up the noise that resides within milieus and mediums.

In this act of exposure of mediation and listening-as-mediation, noise music refuses the formal expectations of the kinds of organized sound found in music, poetry, and performance. The rubric of noise music includes (to take two extremes) the uncompromising volume and complexity of sound in works like the Chicago musician Kevin Drumm's aptly titled *Sheer Hellish Miasma* (2007) or the nearly inaudible recordings of sine waves, hiss, and pops in works like *Filament 1* (2007) by Japanese experimentalists Otomo Yoshihide and Sachiko M. Speaking of the prolific Japanese noise-maker Merzbow (the "godfather of noise"), Paul Hegarty argues that noise music occupies the "the space of not-music, signaling endlessly (not as beginning or end) the status of music as same/self/subject to noise's otherness" (Hegarty 2002: 198). The otherness of noise music's noise seems to precede genre, as it continually asks the question of music's status and avoids formal rules that might allow listeners to hear in conventionalized ways. It reverses the process of perceiving music out of noise that Simon Frith suggests is the work of genre:

> But just as turning noise into "music" means knowing how to organize the sounds we hear in particular (conventionalized) ways, so to hear music generically (hearing this as punk, this as hard core this as acid this as techno) means organizing the sounds according to formal rules.
>
> (Frith 1996: 91)

In this way, noise music "refuses to be subsumed by genre" (Brassier 2007: 1) because it always exists both before and after a conventionalized, or "generic," listening. The array of possible sound forms circulating within noise music goes beyond any particular salient features.

And yet, importantly, noise music is, as we saw in the case of Lou Reed's *Metal Machine Music*, also a subgenre of popular music, in its "isolating and rarefying of certain tendencies in popular music," not least the use of electro-acoustic amplification and feedback (Steintrager 2011: 124). But despite the centrifugal properties of noise music as performed and recorded, it is still invested with value as it functions within paratextual networks constructed by performance publicity, liner notes, compilations, reviews, venues, and record store sorting labels. A discourse (not least an academic one) describes, adjudicates, and advertises its works. David Novak, in tracing the history and experience of Japanese noise music (and thus of the historical and experiential frame of noise music in general), reads these sonic and cultural practices as specifically in conversation with the transnational networks of exchange and circulation that mediate them. Novak shows how noise "spins out" of the "productive miscommunications" engendered by "circulation at the edge:" the feeding back of global communication into its networks, systems, and procedures (Novak 2013: 19). As the other side of a global—and yet locally distorted—mediasphere, noise music is both a product and a critique of the networks of pop music consumption out of which it arises.

Through its emphasis upon exposing and resisting mediation, noise music also models the continuous reproduction of a gap between sound's production and its transmission and reception. In this way, the genre calls into question the self-organizing address of a public that may or may not become its audience. As Michael Warner notes, the reality of a public lies in the "reflexivity by which an addressable object is conjured into being in order to enable the very discourse that gives it existence" (Warner 2005: 67). The genre of noise music "unendingly" conjures up the object (or figure) of noise in order to reaffirm a public that it also negates and turns away from. It makes thematic the "circularity that is essential to the phenomenon" of a public—or, that is, the group of people who may or may not listen, who may or may not hear noise as an address (Warner 2005: 67). In this way, it both parallels and negates the address of lyric poetry, in which convention produces a system of indirect address, of "overhearing" by which "we regard the event not as communication but as our silent insertion in the self-communion of the speaker, constructing both an ideal self-presence for the speaking voice and an ideal intimacy between that voice and ourselves" (Warner 2005: 81). In this kind of poetic address, the circulation of the poem and even the sense of an "audience" are excluded from the aesthetic event. But the noise of noise music emphasizes its own circulation and negates the "self-presence" of a speaking voice. It becomes an all-over address, a hypertrophy of address, even as it refuses the generic expectations of an audience. Noise music turns away from an audience, not in order to produce an ideal intimacy but to fragment and dissipate an audience's listening.

At once genre and anti-genre, music and the otherness that resides within music's production, noise music produces a version of counterpublic address in which the call for attention is taken up—in total saturation and absorption—but without the representative and conventional forms of identification that might transform the initial phatic address into a poetic figure. If music fundamentally produces an "address in sounds" demanding a kind of "obedience" from an audience, then noise music produces figure upon figure of disintegrating phatic calls that resist listening even in its listening (Lyotard 1991: 167). It foregrounds the exhausting, "trying" work of lending an ear to as-yet-unrecognized or "meaningless" sounds, of straining to hear *something*: an arbitrary collection of textures, timbres, and effects in sound. Salome Voegelin describes listening to Merzbow's *1930* (from 1997) as "the trial of [a] body" as it dissipates into "fragments, everywhere, fast, distinct, rhythmical fragments that fragment me" (Voegelin 2010: 68). Such a trial produces deep affective resonances. In this way, noise music might be heard to produce an "expressive corporeality" that provides "the material for the elaboration of intimate life among publics of strangers" (Warner 2005: 76). But it also forces listeners to create new provisional forms of listening in the midst of a state of constant emergence and emergency. These ways of listening call into question the means by which a listener may be addressed in sound. This shows us that noise music produces an extreme version of what Joanna Demers calls "aesthetic listening," a kind of listening that "heeds intermittent moments of a work without searching for a trajectory that unites such moments" (Demers 2010: 151).

What such a dissipated listening produces is the possibility for new articulations to emerge through free play. Frith—and many other commenters on noise—tacitly accepts a sense of "noise" as a preformation of music, a kind of background out of which music is formed by the mediations of technology, technique, material history, aesthetic theory, and more. This common conception both reflects and supports a sense of noise music as primarily a version of transgression in sound. But the range of noise music—and its possible overstepping and reorganizing of generic distinctions—belies the fixity of such a sense of noise. The phenomenological experience of noise as well as its anti-generic forms of address open out beyond a continuous signification of negation. The sound-makers whose work I describe in the following pages are making noise music, even as they make electronic compositions and poetic performances, because they produce versions of denaturalized noise in the process of materializing, composing, and transforming listening. Their noise works beyond a simple call to a public or the recognition of sonic flux and into systems of mediation and meaning-making.

Voice into History

This wrenching open of listening in noise music—the saturation and withholding of an "address in sound"—deeply informs the ways in which Howe and Grubbs, Hecker, and Morris construct sound forms. I take up the work of these artists through the generic efforts and effects of "noise music"—even if that generic term seems, at first, far away from their practice—because they perform a listening to listening. What most seems to separate their work from the paradigm of noise music is the valuation of voice. In all of their work, to varying degrees, we hear voices—human voices, performed voices, synthesized voices, machine voices, cut-up and detuned and defamiliarized voices, textual voices, encoded voices—a panoply of effects of articulation and disarticulation in the figure of voice. In particular, these works deform the reading voice, the voice that emerges from the transformation of writing into sound through the mediation of codes (of language, speech, and performance) and bodies (of humans, human prostheses, and machines).

Voices become the aftereffects of the dissipated and exploded listening of noise music. The metaphor of intimacy implied by a voice gives way to exhaustive and hypertrophied address of noise. The phatic, wandering, fragmented listening to noise becomes a listening-reading by which voice emerges as more noise, not an a priori given but another (possible) figure within the articulation of technology and body, writing and sound. As the output of a confluence between articulations of sound and the production of noise, this voice/noise emerges as the "immobile mobility" of what Jean-Francois Lyotard calls the "inherent thickness" of the given, a "difference" that continuously falls "into oblivion in the process of signification" (Lyotard 2011: 3).

I use "output" to signal the inhuman process suggested by this dedifferentiation of voice and noise, but through the dissipated address embedded in their articulations of sound, they are also invested in exposing the layered histories of listening at work in the perception of noise. Hecker, Howe, Grubbs, and Morris do not simply present sheer sonic mass or an index of an "immemorial sonic flow." Their figurations of noise encompass both the degradation of signification over a history of transmission and reception—the "loss" of re(re-re- …) mediation—and the polyvalent and unstable materiality that emerges through experimental articulations of sound and writing.

Hecker experiments in the "chimerization" of voice, auditory scene analysis, and the hinge between code and phenomena. His work plays with physiology and cognition in ways that expose what we might call the deep history of listening. Morris's vocal performances simultaneously amplify and unwrite the scripts that inhabit and inform black bodies. Performed without text, her works emphasize how the mutating sonority of dis- and re-articulated language plays with the historical expectations of performance and non-performance, freedom and constraint, listening to or bystanding. Susan Howe's voices emerge from what she calls the "telepathy" to be found in archives, "where a thought may hear itself see" (2014: 24). Her work with David Grubbs not only opens up the archive to the production of an altered and altering history but also exposes the process of reading and performing poetry by articulating new sound forms into and against the "score" of the text. These artists oscillate between reading and sounding, mark and text, knowledge and obscurity, in order to call up the forms of memory and collectivity that continue to haunt our ways of listening to and being in the world.

Hecker and the Chimerization of Voice

Florian Hecker, a German artist whose work in sound perhaps fits most easily within the genre of noise music as I am constructing it here, moves between a variety of institutional spaces and popular venues. From gallery installations at major international museums, to collaborations at a variety of academically sponsored research centers, to performances in dance clubs and noise festivals, Hecker's work reflects the generic confusion and transnational circuits of noise music. Educated in computational linguistics and psycholinguistics, the sound artist uses sophisticated mathematical tools and a variety of analog and digital electronic equipment to radically undo the expected sound forms of music and language. He creates not narrative or improvisational works but "climatic systems" in sound (Mackay 2009: 7). Hecker brings questions of cognition and listening into these systems, where coded algorithms create conditions for exploring and reimagining the sound spaces articulated by electronic instruments, software, and human bodies.

In a major work from 2009, *Acid in the Style of David Tudor* (an homage to Art & Language's *A Portrait of V.I. Lenin in the Style of Jackson Pollack*), Hecker combines mathematical compositional procedures with analog sound equipment (a Roland 303 bass simulator, a Buchla analog synthesizer) in order to create sounds that "vacillate on the edge of objectality, enigmatically quasi-cyclical, integrated and yet protoplasmic" (Mackay 2009: 8). The stream of frequency scatter, however, remains strangely linear and almost textual. As opposed to the thick and all-over texture of sound present in, for instance, *Metal Machine Music*, the work seems to move by "sentences," with many pauses between the different states of sound matter. For the philosopher Robin Mackay, Hecker's most engaged interlocutor and interpreter, these sounds force listeners to ask not only "What is a sound 'of'"—what makes the sound, how did that happen?—but also "What is *a* sound" (Mackay 2009: 8, emphasis in original). This ontological question about the nature of sound also gives way to an analytical one about the sequence of listening: how do we separate "a" sound in the midst of all other sounds? Hecker's sound stream seems to "slow down" the process of listening as we hear figurable entities ("bleeps" and "bloops" we might say) that are also constantly transitioning into other entities—sounds with different envelopes (the "shape" of the sound from its beginning "attack" to its concluding "decay") and different frequency-constructions (pitch and timbre). Are these "the same" sound? Radically different and yet emerging out of each preceding sound,

Hecker's sound forms show how the articulation of a mathematical model and an analog tool can produce a kind synthetic "speech." This articulation includes relations of contiguity and enfolding but also separation and difference.

Despite the radical otherness of these sounds, their speech-like continuity and differentiation also emphasize the "representative" aspect of "of" in the question of "what is the sound of" (Mackay 2009: 1). The iterability of these sounds is also a question of saying or representing. But of what? The "acid" tracks on the album are interspersed with tracks titled "ASA", and these tracks model (or are recordings of) the tone tests used for experiments in auditory scene analysis. Auditory scene analysis maps the ways in which humans "build a picture of the world around us through [an auditory system's] sensitivity to sound" (Bregman 1990: 1). These tracks have the same small set of tones repeated over three minutes. If you listen closely—if you "try" yourself against the sounds to use Salome Voegelin's phrase—you start to hear how repeated tones morph into different orders of sound. You may also simply hear a repeating cluster of tones that, in its minimalist clarity, creates a distinct break with the ever-morphing lines of the acid tracks. Hecker appropriates the psychology of auditory perception to reveal listening's malleability, and he asks us to hear the syntax of the acid tracks on the album as instances where this perceptual malleability is figured in the uncanny continuity/discontinuity of the sounds.

In listening to *Acid in the Style of David Tudor*, I have had to use a metaphorical language of "speech," but Hecker creates similar sonic effects in his series of "chimerizations" of voice, where he takes recognizably vocal sounds and transforms them by recombining them with other acoustic entities. Stefan Helmreich explains chimerization: "auditory chimeras are sound events realized through a technical practice of sieving one sound through another—pressing the 'fine structure' (the second-to-second pitch and texture) of one sound (say, a drum) through the 'envelope' (overall attack, sustain, and decay profile) of another (say, a piano)" (Helmreich 2013: 9). Hecker's *Chimerization* (2013), *Articulação* (2014), and *A Script for Machine Synthesis* (2017) each document this process of chimerization, and their recordings were used for the artist's installations for exhibits in Lisbon, New York, and London. On the first two recordings, Hecker has taken a text by Reza Negarestani, "Nature, its man and his goat", and transformed the voices that read this text using the method of chimerization. The sounds produced displace the voice as a site for the construction of an auditory scene. Hecker "asks auditors to tune in to the new sound that emerges when different sound qualities are pressed into juxtaposition" (Helmreich 2016:

175). The voices remain recognizable constructions, but their timbres disorient our ears, which simultaneously can and cannot hear the voice in the machine's synthetic script. Rather than producing an aesthetics of failure—to use Kim Cascone's phrase to describe the "post-digital" music of glitch—Hecker asks auditors to listen differently (Cascone 2000: 12). Language and voice become sites for playing with an experience of sound where what is otherwise than voice—sounds that produce a background against which it can be heard—is written and incorporated into a listening for voice.

I suggested above that a figure of voice/noise—as a "speech" of iterable but differentiated sounds—undergirds *Acid in the Style of David Tudor*, but in Hecker's chimerizations, the performed voice is actively decomposed by an experience of sound out of bounds. It is this experience that opens out onto a deep history of listening. Despite the fact that Hecker's work is resolutely future-oriented in its impulses, particularly in the creation of human-machine hybrids, the work's exposure of the experience of sound reveals the human ear as a construction and a mediator that negotiates physical and psychological elements in its representations of an auditory scene. As Veit Erlmann describes in *Reason and Resonance*, the study of the ear's functioning is enmeshed with cultural histories that move between the seeming autonomy of reason as against the involvement and co-presence of resonance. The unstable division between object and subject, perceiver and perceived, has long been a feature of philosophical thought (Erlmann 2010: 2). Hecker, in presenting noise music that plays with the very experience of sound at the level of our conscious construction or representation of where and what a sound is, suggests the ways in which "*experience* is far from an obvious, unmediated phenomenon" (Helmreich 2013: 11). The process of artificially reproducing hearing through the decomposition of sound waves into their constitutive parts "fracture[s] any kind of humanist understanding of the voice" (Helmreich 2013: 12) and reveals an expanded sonic field that, through noise, begins to have done with the judgment of noise as transgression.

Morris and the Reconstitution of Noise

If Hecker's noise music reorients our listening to voice through a radical decomposition and rearticulation of sound with mathematical models and machinic hybrids, the US poet, performer, installation artist, and scholar Tracie Morris realizes a movement between articulate and inarticulate voicing in her projections of vocal utterance. Morris began her career as a slam poet and transformed her poetic practice as she considered sound rather than narrative as a connecting thread in her work. She "started to feel it more and more and adjust it within the body" (Morris 2008a: n.p.). The embodied relationship to sound and voice again calls up the body as a carrier of noise, a medium that degrades or otherwise troubles the movement of signification. Morris's work "tries" the body as a site for noise production in the name of undoing language, but even more her sound poetry offers the noise of mediation as coterminous with a history of racialized violence embedded in the cut between voice and noise. As the Canadian Afro-Caribbean poet M. Nourbese Philip suggests in her *She Tries Her Tongue, Her Silence Softly Breaks*, "english / is a foreign anguish" (Philip 2015: 32). The language of oppression, for the enslaved and descendants of the enslaved, is language at odds with black life, and so a valuation of noise is already embedded in black speech. Syncopes, rhythms, and sonic materiality reflect a "noise [that] is essential to [the slave's] speech" (Glissant 1989: 123). Morris's performances—particularly her sound poems that employ deformative repetition such as "Africa(n)", a poem on slavery and its afterlife, and "Resonatæ," her improvisatory "handholding" with Kurt Schwitters from her hybrid book/album *handholding: 5 kinds* (Kore Press, 2016)—work through the violent history and imagined future of a doubled consciousness of speech that is at once voice and noise, sonic plenitude and its absence. Morris's repetitions and improvisations in and through language begin to perform a noise that expresses what Fred Moten calls a "freedom drive" by hearing and relaying the hurt of history (2003: 7). To make noise is to recognize the imposition of an outside, surveilling, and negating white listening upon black speech while also resisting language as a medium for this imposition. Noise poses the question of liberation within and separate from a speech that emerges through a self-reflective hearing already doubled by a racialized language.

This doubly noisy speech is also troubled by writing. Morris has made the decision not to visually represent many of her sound poems and performance poems. To have the poems exist only in performance and as recordings suggests their power in context and with an assembled audience. It also harkens to a long history of African-American oral poetic production. Unlike the scores for performance that Dadaists like Hugo Ball made, these poems exist without a visual or concrete analog that would register their sonic interventions graphically. And yet a poem like "Africa(n)" suggests a phono-graphic logic. In this poem, Morris takes the phrase "It all started when we were brought here as slaves from Africa" and slowly repeats, deforms, and varies it (2008a). Her body becomes the substrate for a phrase "cut" into her, and she is stuck in a skip that itself skips, as individual words and phonemes become repeated over and over inside the performative "script" of the initial phrase. This written/unwritten script becomes the site of a play in articulation. Morris replays these speech sounds and rearranges them into rhythmic sets, short melodic riffs, and sheer repetition.

In working through and over this script, Morris takes up the "stutter of form," in which "speech continues without communicating anything" and "intransitively reaches the limit at which its communication becomes silent" (Dworkin 2009: 168). A stutter breaks up both form and content, and through it "we can hear the body speak" (Dworkin 2009: 168). The body's speech, however, remains ambivalent. It speaks of amplification and energy but also automatism and breakage. The repetitions and stutters recoil from and reproduce the violence of a language against the black body's saying, against its very being. In this way, they perform a resistance to the negating listening already embedded in a language of "foreign anguish". The body continues to say "Here! Here! Here!" in a reiterative phatic call that searches for the possibility of another form of address. As in scat aesthetics as described by Brent Hayes Edwards, Morris produces a resonating proliferation of index that makes palpable an undersound, a sound previously unheard that now can be heard (Edwards 2017: 56). In this case, however, these proliferations function not through the invention of a musicalized language but through an effect on meaning and articulation that is like a glissando. This concatenated slide between forms of articulating and addressing oneself to a single phrase show a spectrum of transformations that disconcert the sonic "object" over time.

In one performance of "Africa(n)," at the Kelly Writer's House in Philadelphia, Morris's chant produces, about three minutes into the poem, an intense bout of microphonic feedback (Pennsound, "Africa(n)," (2008b)). While the feedback ends the reading, breaking off its mesmerizing effects, Morris is quick to hear in it an "energy" that overwhelms and overtakes the reading. The noise of this feedback cuts off the poet but also mirrors the ways in which her own performance cuts off and casts out the script from which it arises. The noise of the mediating, amplifying system—the speaker-microphone assemblage or the language-speech-body assemblage—cuts off saying in noise. But this noise is also a non-speaking speech, a voice unmoored from language and reconstituting itself in and through the differentiating thickness of sound. This voice/noise projects an energy, a practical magic of recovery and reorientation, that issues from the breaking up of speech.

There are many parallels, then, between the oral poetics of Morris and the Dadaist avant-garde tradition that emphasizes the body's dislocation from language and its structures. This project can also involve, as in the case of Hugo Ball's sense of sound poetry as pure *logos*, an absurdist analog to the search for a universal, immediate language. Smith, however, participates in a black avant-garde tradition that works in the "disruption of the Enlightenment linguistic project" of reducing "phonic matter and syntactic 'degeneracy' in the … search for a universal language and … a universal science of language" (Moten 2003: 7). Rather than the progressive, primitive retreat into an "Ur" language, the black avant-garde resolutely pushes language sound into the future, into new forms, creolizations, surpluses, and possibilities for meaning. For Moten, the search for a universal language that could articulate meaning without the noise of mediation and translation is deeply connected to a radical separation of subject and object, an idealist and materialist passing over of the "object who speaks:" the slave (Moten 2003: 1). Phonic materiality and "inarticulate" syntax become figures of noise that trouble the subject's self-possession and present the "dispossessive force objects exert" (Moten 2003: 1).

In her recent *handholding: 5 kinds*, Morris writes with and against five avant-garde literary heroes: Gertrude Stein, Stanley Kubrick, John Akomfrah, John Cage, and the Dadaist Kurt Schwitters. In her "handholding" with Schwitters, she performs a "duet" of sorts with a recording of his famous piece, the *Ursonate* (1922), a sound poem in sonata form that breaks down language sounds into an organized musical composition, with notation, movements, and a cadenza. Schwitters also constructed "Merz" (or "shit") paintings, which included bits of trash and refuse in synthetic abstract compositions. Schwitters's *Merzbau* was a life-long construction of bits and pieces of detritus composed and constructed in his house. The work highlights a general movement in the avant-garde of transmitting an "outside"—trash, the street—into an "inside"—painting, a house. As Schwitters takes the fragments of language—detached phonemes and mouth sounds—into the space of musical composition, he not only emphasizes the sonic material of language but also transforms it into noise. Language, transformed or transmitted as music, makes noise. The contemporary sound poet and performer Jaap Blonk noticed this in his performances of "Ursonate" at punk rock venues: the crowds hated the sound poetry and tried to drown out and attack the poet (Blonk 2009: n.p.). Neither language nor music, the *Ursonate* produces a form of noise music because it tricks and unsettles the listening ear expecting either one of those options.

As the name indicates, however, the "Ur" in Ursonate also harkens after a primitive or originary language preceding poetry and music. Morris takes on this sense of an "Ur" composition by remaining steadfastly "after" the sonata. She is reacting to and improvising with Schwitters's work. In the recordings released by Kore Press, the recording of the composition is not audible, but the silences and gaps suggest a space and time of listening and reacting within the phonographic text. Morris creates an audio palimpsest. Like Schwitters, she uses the voice to sound out a space other than language, but she also adds new layers that overwrite and complicate the audible-inaudible frame of Schwitter's poem. "Ur" sounds become the starting points for other possibilities: scat-singing, humming, and stuttering. In particular, Morris brings the nonsensical poetry of scat—a combination of pitched tones, rhythms, and nonsense syllables—into conversation with its modernist other. But, surprisingly in this context, Morris also synthesizes words out of the non-words of the poem. In her first version of the improvisation, "Resonatæ 1," she seems to move her articulation between the words "forgive" and "fuck it." Other recognizable words pop up and dissipate into hums and inchoate rhythms. Phrases like "see you," "plié," and "rock it a baby" emerge out of improvisations with the "Ur"-text. These fragments of recognizable language double the nonsensical articulation of Schwitters. Morris simultaneously puts together and separates two actions: listening guides an improvisatory speech and speaking deforms the composed musical nonsense. She listens through the nonsense language she hears but also through the English she speaks. In this performance, then, both languages—the avant-garde "Ur" language and a language of imperialism and slavery—are simultaneously conflated and transformed by the mediation of the poet's listening and sounding. Morris takes on a power that reduces these languages and emphasizes their precarity and malleability. The noise they produce is reflected back to Morris's listeners as words and phonemes that have become momentary and unstable articulations in a generative sound-making. This undersound emanates from a body freeing itself from the burdens of avant-garde universalism and the ruins of languages embedded with violence.

It also produces a new collective body that can begin to weave together community out of sonic detritus. The noise of this body becomes the site of a negotiation of freedom but also of address. In heeding the call of Schwitters's poem/sonata, Morris does not simply animate or activate the poem but resonates with it and within it. This resonance, a vibration of the body of the poet as an object, takes on a "voice" that does not have to be grounded by an apostrophic call to an absent other, as in lyric poetry. The lyric animation of an absent other—or the inter-animation of the speaking voice and the silent object of that voice—is undone. This voice simply makes noise as a model of a listening that emerges out of recognition and improvisation, a "handholding" that affirms the mutual materiality of bodies in space, articulating together with and against a history that brought them there. Morris's improvisations invoke the construction of personhood as an art of dismantling and renegotiating the boundaries of bodies and sounds. Noise, particularly for bodies marked as other in a culture of white supremacy, works at the interstices of call and response, self-formation, and reformation.

Howe and Grubbs Reading Noise

If Morris imagines a continuous oral/aural poetics in which the speaking and sounding body plays back an audio archive written on the skin of the performer, she also figures the dissolution of that audio archive as a moment in which noise captures and dissipates that history of violence. The poet Susan Howe takes up a similar history of violence through the physical substrate of texts—particularly the texts that trace a nascent American consciousness in the colonial encounter and Puritan religious and social life. This violence is visually mediated in her texts that cut up, scatter, and layer archival language—diaries, marginalia, pamphlets, and other preserved textual artifacts—all over the page and in opposition to the "dictated rigor and predictable pull of the straight, the dominant Flush left" (Fraser 2000: 177). Her work "unabashedly draws attention to itself as text, written rather than spoken language" (Quartermain 1992: 184). However, her texts also militate against a visual textuality imagined as immediate or concrete because they work by iconoclasm: the "visual violence of the image *breaking*" (Dworkin 1996: 396). In her resolutely textual practice—a practice that Craig Dworkin connects with the medial noise theorized by Michel Serres—Howe "writes from out of the static" in an "ex-static" (non)communication that emphasizes the intertwined, provisional relationship between message and channel (1996: 404).

Howe's material imagination also extends to sound. It is as if, in the process of reading from text to sound, she wants to radically separate the concrete elements of visual and sonic reproduction. Speech sound emanates from a multimedia archive of mouths, texts, and narratives all chaotically "sounding" in collections of languages, libraries, poems, and people. Howe hears a

> Philology heaped in thin
> Hearing.
>
> (Howe 1987: n.p.)

This "philology" is not the discovery of origins but rather the product of wandering in and out of the literal material of history: paper, detritus, grapheme, mark, written word. The visual "noise" of these texts—their illegibility and even unreadability—emerges from Howe's specific attention to the phonographic properties of all the materials at her disposal. Howe sounds out language's persistence in texts and archives:

> Letters are sounds we see. Sounds leap to the eye. Word lists, crosses, blanks, and ruptured stanzas are points of contact and displacement. Line breaks and visual contrapuntal stresses represent an athematic compositional intention.
>
> (Howe 1993: 139)

In seeing letters that sound, Howe attends to the innovations of Dada-inspired *lettrism*. However, the interweaving surfaces of a pulverized language of letters also "represent an athematic compositional intention"—a counter-intention latent within the text. This counter-intention also surfaces as the "impossible" acoustics of texts that seem unreadable and unsoundable. The "dominant Flush left" preserves a system for sounding out the poem that is organized around the straightforward projection of a voice, the monolinear temporal movement of words structured by line breaks, syntax, and punctuation. In this phonographic logic, the line of the poem mirrors the meter or measure of its voicing. The unsaid—the unsayable—is, however, built into this model. Peter Quartermain argues that all poems show a "quite dense play of possibilities, the possibilities afforded by the eye playing with and against those afforded by the ear" (2013: 299). Reading a poem necessarily involves a movement between a particular voicing and the unsayable totality of all possible voicings in the text. Quartermain calls this a "voiced noncommittal crux," and he defines this crux as the "voice of coming-to-speech, that moment on the threshold of speech where syntax as we have been taught it is thrown over as we come to words, as words come to us" (Quartermain 2013: 299).

Howe expands and explodes such a crux: not only in the literal crossing of lines of text upon other lines of text but also in the literal acoustics of writing, overwriting, and marking. In recent talks on the poetry of Emily Dickinson, Howe has taken a position that she remembers hearing in a Joseph Beuys lecture: "every mark on paper is an acoustic mark" (Howe 2017 n.p.; also quoted in Grubbs 2010: 190 as "every mark on paper is an acoustic signal"). In this way, she reads every artifact of mediation—including ink blots, stray marks, blurred words, erasures—as a possible production of sound. This approach radically decenters "the word." Textuality becomes an all-over phonographicity that includes every visual and medial element on the page. Every mark becomes a "noncommittal crux," a crossing whereby sound (any sound) may spontaneously attach to it. The poem is no longer a score for performance but a kind of visual emblem, awaiting not a textual but a sonic explanation. It yokes sound and writing while also inscribing a radical separation between these visual marks and their acoustic production. What does "." sound like? Or even, for that matter, the famous dashes in Dickinson's poems? Much less the heaped language of Howe's poems? Even more, what are the implications of the whole enterprise? As David Grubbs writes,

> What does it mean? … Does it mean that every mark is capable of being translated into sound? Does it mean that every mark waits to be translated into its unique, determinate sound? Should the emphasis … be the suggestion that encoded within visual imagery is the experience of duration?
>
> (2010: 190)

These questions hover in Howe's collaborations with Grubbs, who is a composer, performer, researcher, poet, and sound artist. In *Thiefth* (2005), *Souls of the Labadie Track* (2008), *Frolic Architecture* (2011), and *WOODSLIPPERCOUNTERCLATTER* (2015), Howe and Grubbs have perhaps not definitively answered such questions but provided, instead, an alternative poetics of reading—another method for sounding out the acoustic marks of poems. The sonic range of these collaborations is expansive—Grubbs gathers recordings of a variety of instruments, pianos, drones, electronic sounds, and field recordings while also recording and playing back Howe's voice against her own readings through the texts. Howe provided clues for interpretation because she would not only read the complete letters or words in her texts but also the partially hidden bits of language that could be deciphered through her cut-up methods. In her performance, she would articulate "words in a way that sounds like a razor blade on audio tape" (Grubbs 2010: 187). Grubbs emphasizes this cutting image in their recent *Frolic Architecture* (2011) by recording and collaging Howe's voice with and against her reading of the poems. These layerings do not "complete" the texts. They rather provide an occasion to open up these cuts in the text and to figure noise in the imagined durations of marks on a page. The inclusion of conventionally "musical" improvisational techniques never gives way to a sense of a poetic "setting," in which the voice of the poet becomes a figure against a background of music. As Grubbs emphasizes: "I'm stuck on a motto: no foreground; no background. No accompaniment" (Grubbs 2010: 189). Particularly in *Frolic Architecture*, there is a mutual construction of figures of noise through an act of "sonifying" rather than "personifying" the text. Howe and Grubbs sonify by transforming the visual data of text into sound through an operation that would read all the "acoustic marks" of the page rather than simply projecting a single voice.

I take this term "sonification" from contemporary debates in data representation, as the name of a method used by scientists "to translate relationships in data or information into sound(s) that exploit the auditory perceptual abilities of human beings" (Walker and Nees 2011: 9). Sonification makes certain interpretations in data more noticeable. It is a way of using another sense to separate meaningful messages from the noise of data. In applying the term to the work of Howe and Grubbs, I use it against the grain, as a way of describing the transformation of all acoustic marks into sound matter. Sonification also unmarks the "personification" at work in every figuration of voice—even and in particular the figuration of voice at work in the contemporary poetry reading. As critics like Yopie Prins and Charles Bernstein have shown, the prosthetic extension of voice in text or sound recording necessarily entails the transformation of sonic or textual matter into an imagined utterance indexed to an author, speaker, self, or other being (Prins 2004; Bernstein 2011). The metaphor of poetic voice also "haunts" the situation of the poetry reading, as performers and audiences mediate the sounding out of poetry through such metaphors (Wheeler 2008: 37). Sonification thus undoes figurations of vocality by consciously remediating the poem through a performing body extended and distended by instrumental, musical, and electronic means. It reproduces a spread-out and surface-oriented listening as the irruption of figures of noise that sound out (provisionally, arbitrarily) the iconoclasms of the text.

In *Frolic Architecture*, the arrangement of these figures of noise particularly decenters Howe's voice as Grubbs folds intersecting electronic drones, cut-up snippets of mouth sound, field recordings, and other sound textures into a "reading" of an impossible, unreadable text. The poems that make up *Frolic Architecture* were originally released as a limited edition artist's book with photographs by James Welling and then printed again as the second section in Howe's 2010 book *That This*. Howe composed the work by cutting up and overlaying texts from the journal of Hannah Edwards, the sister of the Puritan theologian Jonathan Edwards, along with "a mix of sources from other conductors and revealers in the thick of things" (Grenfell Press 2010: n.p.). Overlaying strips of text against each other, Howe creates a visual montage in which fragments of intimate language ("what shall I say to you" [Howe 2010: 63, 67]), archival notes (51), number tables (65), books on law (67), and unreadable bits of letters and photocopy static (61) all coincide in amorphous shapes that, with each iteration, move around the space of the page, from center to margin. The visual presentation of the poems on the page make the poem "unreadable." As Howe has said: "*Frolic* was un-readable, you couldn't read it, so of course we had to make it a piece" (Yale Union website 2013: n.p.).

"Unreadability" defines the visual confusion and noise in *Frolic Architecture*, but this term also applies to the expanded sonic architecture of the poem. The unreadable creates an opportunity to read differently—to grant duration to visual marks. On the published recording, Howe's reading of textual fragments (down to the letter) mixes with manipulated recordings of her voice, organ-like drones, field recordings of insects and footsteps, and other electronic sounds. The single thirty minute track opens with a series of pops that emerge from the fragmented mouth sounds of Howe, but they also seem to reference the glitches and failures of mediums. Bodily noise is embedded within the voice. These fragments of vocal scatter, however, are laid over drones that figure, as Grubbs suggests in his questions above, the duration marked by the acoustic page. These drones morph into pops and static. These textures press against the voice and suggest that the page is not simply blank duration but an already-occupied theater of movement, of printed artifacts, and of wandering. At 13:20 in the piece, steps over a gravel surface give way to Howe's voice saying, "pursuing shadows in things," and this may be taken as paradigmatic for the sound recording's project. Things in their phenomenal immediacy—page, visual text, mark—contain revenant frequencies, shadows as relations of resonance and loss.

The recording creates an archive of these shadows out of which "spontaneous particulars" may "telephatically" arise (Howe 2014: 5). The wandering archivist displaces the incantatory prophet. In this way, the drones of *Frolic Architecture* also suggest and displace another drone: the ubiquitous incantatory and monotonous voice of the reading poet. This droning "poet voice," as Marit MacArthur has suggested, has a deep performance history related to "conventions of sermonizing, of reading sacred texts and reciting litanies, some of which tend toward monotony in a precise sense" (MacArthur 2016: 43). These anti-expressivist conventions signify the sincerity of the performer, and they guarantee that she is a faithful medium for a text. Text forces a kind of monotony on the voice, as it explicitly reads and sounds out the marks on the page. Howe and Grubbs redouble and reflect this text-based drone music back onto itself. Howe's voice refuses to mark the movement of a discourse. Her sound-marks spontaneously arise within and through the figured background of drone. In this way, Howe, as in so much of her work, explicitly figures her poetry with and against the puritanical conventions that continue to exert an influence on the meaning of "America." In a noise-making mapped onto an archival practice, Howe embraces uncertainty over revelation, error over "theses that drive off skepticism" (Howe 1993: 117).

To Listen Again

Howe and Grubbs together suggest an alternative, pluralized, and dismembered voicing that arises out of the foreclosed noise of a textual reading. Their collaborations reveal poetry reading as a kind of noise music, in which figures of noise continuously arise within, through, and next to the amplified and intoning voice of the poet. These noises do not address an audience (or, more expansively, an undecided and distracted public) through the present, indexed body of the poet but rather through the medial resistances and constraints of a voicing of text.

The noise-makers in this chapter and in this book work through these resistances and constraints in order to dismember and reconstruct the fabric of sounds in which they find themselves. Their work suggests that noise is not simply an undifferentiated and dedifferentiating force, but a constantly morphing flow heard and heard again through continuously changing channels. Noise is not the automatic metaphysical ground of being but rather an effect of resistance in relationships of addressing and listening, calling and responding. It lurks within all of the dismembered and reconstructed of voices that I have described in this book as the potential outcome of listening differently and of putting bodies, sounds, durations, and histories together in different ways.

For the artists I have discussed, the act of reconstituting and extending articulation between theory and practice, text and body is an act of re-membering. Noise becomes revenant frequency. It becomes the other possibility that haunts the current (auditory) scene or convention of listening. The counter-articulations I have described suggest a process of putting things together differently. This act of rearticulation invites and constructs noise through stuttering bodies, broken conventions, dissipated listening, and chimeric sensation. It follows, for these artists and for a fragmented literary history of noise, upon a new relationship to the otherness of history. What these figures of noise produce is another way of hearing history, of channelizing and reimagining the past as a relation between the phonographically preserved record marked both by texts—and by what Lisa Robertson calls "the multiply layered sonic indeterminacy that is the average, fluctuating milieu of dailiness" (Robertson 2012: 57).

The layered fabric of noise has a history—that history is its fluctuating texture. But even more, the "unreadable" surface of noise may condition and demand a new articulation of history. In this way, noise becomes the sonic equivalent of Benjamin's "wreckage upon wreckage" piling up before the angel facing backward into the past (Benjamin 1968: 257). The "heaped philology" preserved in the ruins of voice models and speculates upon new forms of social response and new ways of making contact and being together. Stuart Hall theorizes articulation as a

> form of the connection that can make a unity of two different elements, under certain conditions. It is a linkage which is not necessary, determined, absolute and essential for all time. You have to ask, under what circumstances can a connection be forged or made?
>
> (Hall 1986: 53)

To figure noise is to encounter the conditions of sensation, mediation, and address in order to begin to forge new connections. These connections—between sound and sense, mouths and language, social bodies and historical narrative—emerge differently when noise changes our attentions and articulations. Out of this difference, out of the disruptive plenitude of noise's undersound, the elsewhere and the otherwise begin to take shape.

References

Acconci, Vito and Bernadetter Mayer, eds. *0 to 9*. New York: Ugly Duckling Presse, 2006.

Adorno, Theodor. *Essays on Music*. Berkeley: University of California Press, 2002.

Adorno, Theodor. "Radio Physiognomies." In *Current of Music: Elements of a Radio Theory*. Edited by Robert Hullot-Kentor. Cambridge: Polity Press, 2009.

Albright, Daniel. *Modernism and Music: An Anthology of Sources*. Chicago: University of Chicago Press, 2004.

Altieri, Charles. "Olson's Poetics and the Tradition." *Boundary* 2 (1974): 173–88.

Altieri, Charles. "From Symbolist Thought to Immanence: The Ground of Postmodern American Poetics." *Boundary* 2 (1973): 605–12.

Althusser, Louis. "Ideology and Ideological State Apparatuses: Notes toward an Investigation." In *Video Culture: A Critical Investigation*. Edited by John Hanhardt. Layton, Utah: Peregrine Books, 1991.

Anderson, Benedict. *Imagined Communities: Reflections on the Origins and Spread of Nationalism*. London: Verso, 1983.

Andrews, Bruce. "Praxis: A Political Economy of Noise and Informalism." In *Close Listening: Poetry and the Performed Word*, ed. Charles Bernstein. Oxford: Oxford University Press, 1998.

Andrews, Bruce. *Letter to Richard Hell*, 1972. Box 5, Folder 155, Richard Hell Papers. Fales Library and Special Collections, New York University.

Appelbaum, David. *Voice*. Albany: State University of New York Press, 1990.

Aristotle. *On Rhetoric: A Theory of Civic Discourse*. Translated by George Kennedy. Oxford: Oxford University Press, 1991.

"The Art of the Jazz. Drummer as Chief Conspirator." *The London Times*. Tuesday, January 14, 1919. Issue 41997. Col D: 11.

Attali, Jacques. *Noise: The Political Economy of Music*. Translated by Brian Massumi. Minneapolis: University of Minnesota Press, 1985.

Ball, Hugo. *Flight out of Time: A Dada Diary*. Translated by Ann Raimes. Berkeley: University of California Press, 1996.

Bangs, Lester. *Psychotic Reactions and Carburetor Dung*. New York: Anchor Books, 2003.

Baraka, Amiri (as LeRoi Jones). "How You Sound?" In *The New American Poetry: 1945–1960*. Edited by Donald Allen. Berkeley: University of California Press, 1999 [1960].

Barbusse, Henri, *Under Fire*. Translated by Fitzwater Ray. New York: EP Dutton & Co, 1917.

Barthes, Roland. "The Grain of the Voice." In *Image/Music/Text*. Translated by Stephen Heath. New York: Hill and Wang, 1978.

Barthes, Roland. "Listening." In *The Responsibility of Forms*. Translated by Robert Howard. Berkeley: University of California Press, 1985.

Barthes, Roland. *The Pleasure of the Text*. Translated by Richard Miller. New York: Hill and Wang, 1975.

Baxendale, John. "'… Into Another Kind of Life in Which Anything Might Happen … ': Popular Music and Late Modernity, 1910–1930." *Popular Music* 14, no. 2 (1995): 137–54.

Benjamin, Walter. "The Storyteller." In *Illuminations: Essays and Reflections*. Ed. Hannah Arendt. New York: Harcourt, Brace, Jovanavich, 1968.

Benjamin, Walter. "Theses on the Philosophy of History." In *Illuminations: Essays and Reflections*. Ed. Hannah Arendt. New York: Harcourt, Brace, Jovanovich, 1968.

Berlin, Irving. "Everybody's Doing It Now." New York: Ted Snyder Co., 1914.

Bernstein, Charles. *Attack of the Difficult Poems*. Chicago: University of Chicago Press, 2011.

Bernstein, Charles. *A Poetics*. Cambridge: Harvard University Press, 1992.

Billiteri, Carla. *Language and the Renewal of Society in Walt Whitman, Laura (Riding) Jackson, and Charles Olson: The American Cratylus*. New York: Palgrave, 2009.

Bjisterveld, Karin. *Mechanical Sound: Technology, Culture, and Public Problems of Noise in the Twentieth Century*. Cambridge: MIT Press, 2008.

Blesser, Barry and Linda-Ruth Salter. *Spaces Speak, Are You Listening? Experiencing Aural Architecture*. Cambridge: MIT Press, 2007.

Blonk, Jaap. "Some words to Kurt Schwitters' URSONATE." 2009. http://www.jaapblonk.com/Texts/ursonatewords.html

Boer, Charles. *Charles Olson in Connecticut*. Middletown: Wesleyan University Press, 1991.

Borden, Mary. *The Forbidden Zone*. Garden City, NY: Doubleday, Doran, 1930.

Brassier, Ray. "Genre Is Obsolete." In *Multitudes*. Hiver-Printemps, 2007. https://www.multitudes.net/Genre-is-Obsolete/.

Brathwaite, Kamau. *History of the Voice: The Development of Nation Language in Anglophone Caribbean Poetry*. Ann Arbor: Michigan University Press, 1984.

Bregman, Albert. *Auditory Scene Analysis: The Perceptual Organization of Sound*. Cambridge: MIT Press, 1990.

Bruns, Gerald. *Modern Poetry and the Idea of Language: A Critical and Historical Study*. New Haven: Yale University Press, 1974.

Bull, Michael. "Soundscapes of the Car." In *Car Cultures*. Edited by Daniel Miller. Oxford: Berg, 2001.

Butterick, Charles. *A Guide to The Maximus Poems of Charles Olson*. Berkeley: University of California Press, 1981.

Byrd, Don. *Charles Olson's Maximus*. Chicago: University of Illinois Press, 1980.

Cabaret Voltaire. Zurich. Reprinted in the International Dada Archive. 1916. http://dada.lib.uiowa.edu.

Cage, John. "Introduction to Themes and Variations." In *Audio Culture: Readings in Modern Music*. Edited by Christopher Cox and Daniel Warner. New York: Continuum, 2004.

Cage, John. *Silence: Lectures and Writings*. Middletown: Wesleyan University Press, 1961.

Cascone, Kim. "The Aesthetics of Failure: 'Post-Digital' Tendencies in Contemporary Computer Music." *Computer Music Journal* 24, no. 4 (2000): 12–18.

Certeau, Michel de. *The Practice of Everyday Life*. Translated by Steven Rendall. Berkeley: University of California Press, 1984.

Certeau, Michel de. "Vocal Utopias." *Representations* 0, no. 56 (1996): 29–47.

Clark, T. J. *Farewell to an Idea: Episodes from a History of Modernism*. New Haven: Yale University Press, 1999.

Cohen, Debra Rae and Michael Coyle. "'Police and Thieves' Citation as Struggle in the Punk Cover Song." *Social Text 116* 31, no. 3 (Fall 2013): 111–22.

Coleman, Rick. *Blue Monday: Fats Domino and the Lost Dawn of Rock 'n' Roll*. New York: Da Capo Press, 2006.

Connor, Steven. *Dumbstruck: A Cultural History of Ventriloquism*. Oxford: Oxford University Press, 2000.

Connor, Steven. "The Modern Auditory I." In *Rewriting the Self Histories from the Middle Ages to the Present*. Edited by Roy Porter. London: Routledge, 1997.

Coolidge, Clark. "Arrangement." In *Talking Poetics from Naropa Institute: Annals of the Jack Kerouac School of Disembodied Poetics*. Edited by Anne Waldman and Marilyn Webb. Boulder: Shambhala Publications, 1978.

Coolidge, Clark. "Nothing I-XIII." *0 to 9*. Ed. Bernadette Mayer and Vito Acconci. No. 4 (June 1968): 1–12.

Coolidge, Clark. *Space*. New York: Harper & Row, 1970.

Cox, Christoph. *Sonic Flux: Sound, Art, and Metaphysics*. Chicago: University of Chicago Press, 2018.

Crawley, Ashon. *Blackpentecostal Breath: The Aesthetics of Possibility*. New York: Fordham University Press, 2017.

Creeley, Robert. *Collected Prose*. Champaign: Dalkey Archive Press, 2001.

Creeley, Robert and Charles Olson. *The Complete Correspondence*. Edited by George Butterick. Boston: Black Sparrow Press, 1987.

Culler, Jonathan. *In Pursuit of Signs: Semiotics, Literature, Deconstruction*. London: Routledge, 1981.

Das, Santanu. *Touch and Intimacy in First World War Literature*. Oxford: Oxford University Press, 2006.

Daughtry, J. Martin. *Listening to War: Sound, Music, Trauma, and Survival in Wartime Iraq*. New York: Oxford University Press, 2015.

Davidson, Michael. *Ghostlier Demarcations: Modern Poetry and the Material Word.* Berkeley: University of California Press, 1997.

Davis, Angela Yvonne. *Blues Legacies and Black Feminism: Gertrude Ma Rainey, Bessie Smith and Billie Holiday.* New York: Vintage Books, 1998.

Deer, Patrick. *Culture in Camouflage: War, Empire, and Modern British Literature.* Oxford: Oxford University Press, 2009.

Deleuze, Gilles and Félix Guattari. *A Thousand Plateaus.* Translated by Brian Massumi. Minneapolis: University of Minnesota Press, 1987.

Demers, Joanna. *Listening through the Noise: The Aesthetics of Experimental Electronic Music.* Oxford: Oxford University Press, 2010.

Derrida, Jacques. "Che cos'e la poesia?" (1988). In *The Lyric Theory Reader*. Edited by Virginia Walker Jackson and Yopie Prins. Baltimore: Johns Hopkins University Press, 2014.

Derrida, Jacques. *Speech and Phenomena and Other Essays on Husserl's Theory of Signs.* Translated by D. B. Allison. Chicago: Northwestern University Press, 1973.

Dickerman, Leah. *Dada.* Washington, DC: National Gallery of Art, 2005.

Doerschuk, Robert L. "Improvisational Piano: Fats Domino, Pt.1: The Nascence of Rock Piano." *Keyboard* 18, no. 4 (1992): 110–11.

Dolar, Mladen. *A Voice and Nothing More.* Cambridge: MIT Press, 2006.

Douglas, Susan. *Listening In: Radio and the American Imagination.* Minneapolis: University of Minnesota Press, 2004.

Doyle, Peter. *Echo and Reverb: Fabricating Space in Popular Music Recording 1900–1960.* Middletown: Wesleyan University Press, 2005.

Dworkin, Craig. "The Stutter of Form." In *The Sound of Poetry / The Poetry of Sound.* Edited by Marjorie Perloff and Craig Dworkin. Chicago: University of Chicago Press, 2009, 166–83.

Dworkin, Craig. "'Waging Political Babble': Susan Howe's Visual Prosody and the Politics of Noise." *Word & Image* 12, no. 4 (1996): 389–405.

Dyson, Frances. "The Ear That Would Hear Sounds in Themselves." *Wireless Imagination: Sound Radio and the Avant-garde.* Edited by Douglas Kahn and Gregory Whitehead. Cambridge: MIT Press, 1992.

Dyson, Frances. *Sounding New Media: Immersion and Embodiment in the Arts and Culture.* Berkeley: University of California Press, 2009.

Edwards, Brent Hayes. *Epistrophies: Jazz and the Literary Imagination.* Cambridge: Harvard University Press, 2017.

Eksteins, Modriss. *Rites of Spring: The Great War and the Birth of the Modern Age.* Boston: Houghton-Mifflin, 1989.

Eliot, T. S. *The Annotated Waste Land with Eliot's Contemporary Prose.* Edited by Lawrence Rainey. New Haven: Yale University Press, 2005.

Eliot, T. S. *Collected Poems of T.S. Eliot.* Edited by Christopher Ricks and Jim McCue. Baltimore: John Hopkins University Press, 2015.

Eliot, T. S. *The Letters of T.S. Eliot*. Vol. 1: 1898–1922. Edited by Valerie Eliot. London: Faber & Faber, 1988.

Eliot, T. S. "Reflections on *Vers Libre*." *The Selected Prose of T.S. Eliot*. Edited by Frank Kermode. New York: Harcourt, Brace, Jovanovich, 1975.

Eliot, T. S. "Ulysses, Order, Myth." In *The Selected Prose of T.S. Eliot*. Edited by Frank Kermode. New York: Harcourt, Brace, Jovanovich, 1975.

Eliot, T. S. *The Use of Poetry and the Use of Criticism*. London: Faber and Faber, 1964.

Ellis, John. *Eye-Deep in Hell: Trench Warfare in World War I*. Baltimore: Johns Hopkins University Press, 1989.

Ellmann, Maud. *The Poetics of Impersonality: T.S. Eliot and Ezra Pound*. Brighton: Harvester, 1987.

Epstein, Josh. *Sublime Noise: Musical Culture and the Modernist Writer*. Baltimore: John Hopkins University Press, 2014.

Erlmann, Veit. *Reason and Resonance: A History of Modern Aurality*. New York: Zone Books, 2010.

Evans, Steve. "The Lipstick of Noise: Project Note." *Poetry Is the Lipstick of Noise: Listening & Linking to Poetry Audio Files*. http://www.thirdfactory.net/lipstick-archive1.html#project

Feld, Steven. "Acoustemology" In *Keywords in Sound*. Edited by David Novak and Matt Sakakeeny. Durham: Duke University Press, 2015, 12–21.

Feldman, Morton. "Sound, Noise, Varèse, Boulez." In *Give My Regards to Eighth Street: Collected Writings of Morton Feldman*. Edited by B. H. Friedman. New York: Exact Change, 2000.

Forrest, Seth. "MU-SICK, MU-SICK, MU-SICK: Olson's Stammer and the Poetics of Noise." *West Coast Line* 43. no. 1 (2009): 4–11.

Foucault, Michel. *The Order of Things: An Archaeology of the Human Sciences*. New York: Vintage Books, 1994 [1970].

Fraser, Kathleen. *Translating the Unspeakable: Poetry and the Innovative Necessity*. Tuscaloosa: University of Alabama Press, 2000.

Fredman, Stephen. *Contextual Practice: Assemblage and the Erotic in Postwar Poetry and Art*. Stanford: Stanford University Press, 2010.

Frith, Simon. *Performing Rites: On the Value of Popular Music*. Cambridge: Harvard University Press, 1996.

Frith, Simon. *Sound Effects: Youth, Leisure, and the Politics of Rock 'n' Roll*. New York: Pantheon, 1981.

Fussell, Paul. *The Great War and Modern Memory*. Oxford: Oxford University Press, 1975.

Garland-Thomson, Rosemarie. *Extraordinary Bodies: Figuring Physical Disability in American Culture and Literature*. New York: Columbia University Press, 2017.

Gascoigne, David. "Boomboom and Hullabaloo: Rhythm in the Zurich Dada Revolution." *Paragraph* 33, no. 2, Rhythm in Literature after the Crisis in Verse (2010): 197–214.

Gates, Henry Louis. *The Signifying Monkey: A Theory of African-American Literary Criticism*. Oxford: Oxford University Press, 1988.
Giddens, Anthony. *The Consequences of Modernity*. Stanford: Stanford University Press, 1990.
Gillett, Charlie. *The Sound of the City: The Rise of Rock and Roll*. New York: Da Capo Press, 1996.
Glissant, Edouard. *Caribbean Discourse*. Translated by J. Michael Dash. Charlottesville: Caraf Books/University Press of Virginia, 1989.
Gobel, Mark. *Beautiful Circuits: Modernism and the Mediated Life*. Columbia: Columbia University Press, 2010.
Goffin, Robert, *Jazz: From the Congo to the Metropolitan*. Garden City: Doubleday, Doran, and Company. 1944.
Gracyk, Theodor. *Rhythm and Noise: An Aesthetics of Rock*. Durham: Duke University Press, 1996.
Graham, Dan. *Rock/Music Writing*. New York: Primary Information, 2009.
Graves, Robert. *Goodbye to All That*. London: Folio Society, 1981: [1930].
Graves, Robert. Interview. *The Listener*, October 1971.
Green, Malcolm, ed. *The Dada Almanac* (1920). Edited by Richard Huelsenbeck. London: Atlas Press, 1993.
Grenfell Press, description of *Frolic Architecture*. 2010. http://www.grenfellpress.com/books/susan-howe-james-welling-frolic-architecture.html
Grenier, Robert. "On Speech." *This 1* (Winter, 1971). Edited by Robert Grenier and Barrett Watten. Lanesville, MA and Iowa City, IA: (n.p.).
Grubbs, David. "Shadowy Hush Twilight: Two Collaborations with Susan Howe." *Chicago Review* 55, no. 1 (2010): 186–91.
Guilbert, Yvette. *How to Sing a Song; the Art of Dramatic and Lyric Interpretation*. New York: Macmillan, 1918.
Guillory, John. "Genesis of the Media Concept." *Critical Inquiry* 36, no. 2 (Winter 2010): 321–62.
Gussow, Adam. *Seems Like Murder Here: Southern Violence and the Blues Tradition*. Chicago: University of Chicago Press, 2002.
Hall, Stuart. "On Postmodernism and Articulation: An Interview with Stuart Hall" Edited by Lawrence Grossberg. *Journal of Communication Inquiry*, June 1 (1986): 45–60.
Harrison, Daphne Duval. *Black Pearls: Blues Queens of the 1920s*. New Brunswick: Rutgers University Press, 1988.
Hartman, Saidiya. *Wayward Lives, Beautiful Experiments: Intimate Histories of Social Upheaval*. New York: W. W. Norton, 2019.
Hatch, David and Stephen Millward. *From Blues to Rock: An Analytical History of Pop Music*. Manchester: Manchester University Press, 1989.
Hecker, Florian. *Acid in the Style of David Tudor*. Editions Mego. 2009.

Hecker, Florian and Robin MacKay. *Sound out of Line: In Conversation with Florian Hecker*, Urbanomic Document, UFD003. 2009. https://www.urbanomic.com/document/sound-out-of-line/

Hegarty, Paul. "Noise Threshold: Merzbow and the End of Natural Sound." *Organized Sound* 7, no. 1 (2002): 193–200.

Hegarty, Paul. *Noise / Music: A History*. New York: Continuum, 2007.

Hell, Richard. *Artifact: Notebooks from Hell 1974–1980*. New York: Hanuman Books, 1990.

Hell, Richard. "Blank Generation." *Blank Generation*. Richard Hell & The Voidoids. Sire Records, 1977.

Hell, Richard. Email Interview with John Melillo. April 5, 2005a.

Hell, Richard. *Letter to Bruce Andrews*, February 12, 1971. Box 5, Folder 153, Richard Hell Papers, Fales Library and Special Collections, New York University.

Hell, Richard. *Spurts: The Richard Hell Story*. Rhino Records, 2005b.

Hell, Richard (as Ernie Stomach). *uh*. Genesis: Grasp Press, 1971.

Hell, Richard [Richard Meyers] and David Giannini, eds. *Genesis : Grasp* 1.1 – 2.1/2 (1968–1971).

Helmreich, Stefan. "Chimeric Sensing." In *Florian Hecker: Chimerizations*. New York: Primary Information, 2013.

Helmreich, Stefan. *Sounding the Limits of Life: Essays in the Anthropology of Biology and Beyond*. Princeton: Princeton University Press, 2016.

Hemus, Ruth. *Dada's Women*. New Haven: Yale University Press, 2009.

Hennings, Emmy. "Maybe the Last Flight." Translated by Christina Mill. In *The Dada Reader: A Critical Anthology*. Edited by Dawn Ades. Chicago: University of Chicago Press, 2006.

Howe, Susan. *Articulation of Sound Forms in Time*. Windsor, Vermont: Awede, 1987.

Howe, Susan. *The Birth-mark: Unsettling the Wilderness in American Literary History*. Middletown: Wesleyan University Press, 1993.

Howe, Susan. "Every Mark on the Page Is an Acoustic Mark." YouTube video. October 11, 2017. https://www.ndbooks.com/article/every-mark-on-paper-is-an-acoustic-mark-by-susan-howe/

Howe, Susan. *Spontaneous Particulars: The Telepathy of Archives*. New York: New Directions, 2014.

Howe, Susan. *That This*. New York: New Directions, 2010.

Howe, Susan and David Grubbs. *Frolic Architecture*. Blue Chopsticks. 2011.

Huelsenbeck, Richard. "Collective Dada Manifesto" (1920b). In *Dada Painters and Poets: An Anthology*. Edited by Robert Motherwell. Cambridge: Belknap Press, 1989 [1951].

Huelsenbeck, Richard. "En Avant Dada" (1920). In *Dada Painters and Poets: An Anthology*. Edited by Robert Motherwell. Cambridge: Belknap Press, 1989 [1920a].

Huelsenbeck, Richard. *Memoirs of a Dada Drummer*. Berkeley: University of California Press, 1991 (1969).

Hughes, Langston. *The Collected Poems of Langston Hughes*. Edited by Arnold Rampersad and David Roessel. New York: Vintage Classics, 1995.

Hughes, Langston. *The Weary Blues*. New York: Alfred A. Knopf, 1926.

Hustwitt, Mark. "'Caught in a Whirlpool of Aching Sound': The Production of Dance Music in Britain in the 1920s." *Popular Music* 3 (1983): 7–31.

Jakobson, Roman. *Language in Literature*. Edited by Krystyna Pomorska and Stephen Rudy. Cambridge: Belknap Press, 1987.

Jones, Dafydd. *Dada 1916 in Theory: Practices of Critical Resistance*. Liverpool: Liverpool University Press, 2014.

Kahn, Douglas. *Noise Water Meat: A History of Sound in the Arts*. Cambridge: MIT Press, 1999.

Kane, Brian. *Sound Unseen: Acousmatic Sound in Theory and Practice*. Oxford: Oxford University Press, 2014.

Kane, Daniel. *All Poet's Welcome: The Lower East Side Poetry Scene in the 1960s*. Berkeley: University of California Press, 2003.

Kane, Daniel. *"Do You Have a Band?" Poetry and Punk Rock in New York City*. New York: Columbia University Press, 2017.

Keegan, John. *The Face of Battle*. New York: Penguin, 1976.

Kenney, William Howland. *Recorded Music in American Life: The Phonograph and Popular Memory, 1890–1945*. New York: Oxford University Press, 1999.

Kittler, Friedrich. *Gramophone, Film, Typewriter*. Stanford: Stanford University Press, 1999.

Kubler, George. *The Shape of Time: A History of Things*. New Haven: Yale University Press, 1962.

Lambrecht, Nora. "'But If You Listen You Can Hear:' War Experience, Modernist Noise, and the Soundscape of The Forbidden Zone." March 8, 2017, Vol. 2, Cycle 1. https://doi.org/10.26597/mod.0005

LaBelle, Brandon. *Acoustic Territories: Sound Culture and Everyday Life*. New York: Bloomsbury, 2010.

LaBelle, Brandon. *Background Noise: Perspectives on Sound Art*. New York: Bloomsbury, 2015.

Lanza, Joseph. *Elevator Music: A Surreal History of Muzak, Easy-Listening and Other Moodsong*. London: Quartet Books, 1995.

Lastra, James. "Reading, Writing, and Representing Sound." In *Sound Theory, Sound Practice*. Edited by Rick Altman. New York: Routledge, 1992.

Leed, Eric. *No Man's Land: Combat and Identity in World War 1*. Cambridge: Cambridge University Press, 1979.

Lord, Albert. *The Singer of Tales*. 2nd edition. Cambridge: Harvard University Press, 2000 [1960].

Lotz, Rainer. "Black Diamonds Are Forever: A Glimpse of the Pre-History of Jazz in Europe." *The Black Perspective in Music* 12, no. 2 (1984): 217–34.

Lyotard, Jean-Francois. *The Inhuman: Reflections on Time*. Translated by Geoffrey Bennington. Stanford: Stanford University Press, 1991.

Lyotard, Jean-Francois. *Discourse, Figure*. Trans. Anthony Hudek and Mary Lydon. Minneapolis: University of Minnesota Press, 2011.

Maas, Sander van. "Scenes of Inner Devastation: Interpellation, Finite and Infinite." In *Thresholds of Listening: Sound, Technics, Space*. New York: Fordham University Press, 2015.

MacArthur, Marit J. "Monotony, the Churches of Poetry Reading, and Sound Studies." *PMLA* 131, no. 1 (2016): 38–63.

Mackay, Robin. "Climate of Bass Hunter." Liner notes for *Acid in the Style of David Tudor*, Florian Hecker. Vienna: Editions Mego, 2009, eMEGO 094.

Mackey, Nathaniel. "Breath and Precarity: The Inaugural Robert Creeley Lecture in Poetry and Poetics." In *Poetics and Precarity*. Edited by Myung Mi Kim and Cristanne Miller. Albany: State University of New York Press, 2018.

Marcus, Greil. *Mystery Train: Images of Rock 'n' Roll Music*. New York: Penguin Books, 1975.

Martin, Meredith. *The Rise and Fall of Meter: Poetry and English National Culture, 1860–1930*. Princeton: Princeton University Press, 2012.

Medina, Mamie, and Edgar Dowell. *That Da-Da Strain*. New York: Clarence Williams Publishing, 1922. Sheet Music.

Meisel, Perry. *The Cowboy and the Dandy*. Oxford: Oxford University Press, 1999.

McCaffery, Steve. "Voice in Extremis." In *Close Listening: Poetry and the Performed Word*. Edited by Charles Bernstein. Oxford: Oxford University Press, 1998, 162–77.

McCaffery, Steve. "Charles Olson's Art of Language: The Mayan Substratum of Projective Verse." In *Prior to Meaning*. Evanston: Northwestern University Press, 2001.

McGann, Gillian, and Legs McNeil. *Please Kill Me: An Oral History of Punk*. New York: Penguin Books, 1997.

McGee, Daniel T. "Dada Da Da: Sounding the Jew in Modernism." *ELH* 68, no. 2 (2001): 501–27.

Mcloughlin, Kate. "Muddy Poetics: First World War Poems by Helen Saunders and Mary Borden." *Women: A Cultural Review* 26, no. 3 (2015): 221–36.

McLuhan, Marshall. *Understanding Media: The Extensions of Man*. New York: McGraw-Hill, 1964.

Medovoi, Leerom. *Rebels: Youth and the Cold War Origins of Identity*. Durham: Duke University Press, 2005.

Meintjes, Louise. *Sound of Africa! Making Music Zulu in A South African Studio*. Durham: Duke University Press, 2003.

Meisal, Perry. *The Cowboy and the Dandy*. Oxford: Oxford University Press, 1999.

Mellers, Wilfred. *Music in a New Found Land: Themes and Developments in the History of American Music*. Oxford: Oxford University Press, 1987.

Melzer, Annabelle. *Latest Rage the Big Drum: Dada and Surrealist Performance*. Ann Arbor: University of Michigan Press, 1980.

Middleton, Peter. *Distant Reading: Performance, Readership, and Consumption in Contemporary Poetry*. Tuscaloosa: Alabama University Press, 2005.

Middleton, Richard. "Rock Singing." In *The Cambridge Companion to Singing*. Edited by John Potter. Cambridge: Cambridge University Press, 2000.

Morris, Tracie. "Africa(n)" Reading for the 3rd Annual Caroline Rothstein Oral Poetry Program at the Kelly Writers House, University of Pennsylvania, October 28, 2008a, *Pennsound*.

Morris, Tracie. "From Sound Making Notes." Liner Notes. *Crosstalk*. Bridge Records, 2008b.

Moten, Fred. *In the Break: The Aesthetics of the Black Radical Tradition*. Minneapolis: University of Minnesota Press, 2003.

Motherwell, Robert, ed. *Dada Painters and Poets*. New York: Wittenborn, Schultz, 1951.

Müller, Friedrich Max. *Lectures on the Science of Language*. London: Longman, Green, and Co., 1885.

Muñoz, José Esteban. "The Wildness of the Punk Rock Commons." *South Atlantic Quarterly* 117, no. 3 (2018): 653–8.

Negarestani, Reza, "Nature, Its Man and His Goat (Enigmata of Natural and Cultural Chimeras)" In *Chimerizations*. New York: Primary Information, 2013.

Nicholls, Peter. *Modernisms: A Literary Guide*. Berkeley: University of California Press, 1995.

Niebisch, Arndt. *Media Parasites in the Early Avant-Garde: On the Abuse of Technology and Communication*. New York: Palgrave Macmillan, 2012.

Noland, Carrie. *Poetry at Stake: Lyric Aesthetics and the Challenge of Technology*. Princeton: Princeton University Press, 1999.

North, Michael. *The Dialect of Modernism: Race, Language, and Twentieth-Century Literature*. Oxford: Oxford University Press, 1998.

North, Michael. *Reading 1922: A Return to the Scene of the Modern*. Oxford: Oxford University Press, 1999.

Novak, David. *Japanoise: Music at the Edge of Circulation*. Durham: Duke University Press, 2013.

Nyman, Michael. *Experimental Music: Cage and Beyond*. Cambridge: Cambridge University Press, 1999.

Olson, Charles. *Causal Mythology*. San Francisco: Four Seasons Foundation, 1979.

Olson, Charles. *The Collected Poems*. Edited by George Butterick. Berkeley: University of California Press, 1997a.

Olson, Charles. *The Maximus Poems*. Edited by George Butterick. Berkeley: University of California Press, 1985.

Olson, Charles. "Projective Verse." In *Collected Prose*. Edited by Donald Allen and Benjamin Friedlander. Berkeley: University of California Press, 1997b.

Olson, Charles. "Reading at Goddard College: April 12, 1962." Pennsound.

Olson, Charles. "Studio Recording at Black Mountain College." (1954) Pennsound.

Ong, Walter. *Orality and Literacy: The Technologizing of the Word*. New York: Routledge, 1982.

Owen, Wilfred. *The Poems of Wilfred Owen*. Edited by Jon Stallworthy. London: Hogarth Press, 1985.

Peress, Maurice. *Dvořák to Duke Ellington: A Conductor Explores America's Music and Its African American Roots*. Oxford: Oxford University Press, 2004.

Peterson, Richard. "Why 1955? Explaining the Advent of Rock Music." *Popular Music* 9, no. 1 (1990): 97–116.

Philip, M. NourbeSe. *She Tries Her Tongue, Her Silence Softly Breaks*. Middletown: Wesleyan University Press, 2015.

Poovey, Mary. *Making a Social Body: British Cultural Formation, 1830–1868*. Chicago: University of Chicago Press, 1995.

Prins, Yopie. "Voice Inverse." *Victorian Poetry* 42, no. 1 (2004): 43–59.

Quartermain, Peter. *Disjunctive Poetics: From Gertrude Stein and Louis Zukofsky to Susan Howe*. Cambridge: Cambridge University Press, 1992.

Quartermain, Peter. *Stubborn Poetries: Poetic Facticity and the Avant-Garde*. Tuscaloosa: University of Alabama Press, 2013.

Rasula, Jed. *Destruction Was My Beatrice: Dada and the Unmaking of the Twentieth Century*. New York: Basic Books, 2015.

Rasula, Jed. "Understanding the Sound of Not Understanding" In *Close Listening: Poetry and the Performed Word*. Edited by Charles Bernstein. Oxford: Oxford University Press, 1998.

Rasula, Jed. "Jazzbandism." *The Georgia Review* 60, no. 1 (2006): 61–124.

Ratcliffe, Stephen. *Listening as Reading*. New York: State University of New York Press, 2000.

Ray, Robert B. *How a Film Theory Got Lost and Other Mysteries in Culture Studies*. Bloomington: Indiana University Press, 2001.

"Rector Calls Jazz National Anthem." *The New York Times*, January 30, 1922. Page 9.

Reed, Lou. Liner Notes. *Metal Machine Music*. Sony Legacy, 2007 [1975].

Richter, Hans. *Dada: Art and Anti-art*. London: Thames and Hudson, 1964.

Robertson, Lisa. *Nilling: Essays on Noise, Pornography, The Codex, Melancholy, Lucretius, Folds, Cities and Related Aporias*. Toronto: Bookthug, 2012.

Rosenbaum, Ron. "Playboy Interview: Bob Dylan." *Playboy Magazine* 25, no. 3 (1978): 61–90.

Rosenberg, Isaac. *The Collected Works of Isaac Rosenberg: Poetry, Paintings, and Drawings*. Edited by Ian Parsons. London: Chatto and Windus, 1979.

Rosenberg, Isaac. *The Collected Poems of Isaac Rosenberg*. Edited by Ian Parsons. London: Chatto and Windus, 1984.

Rothenberg, Jerome. *That Dada Strain*. New York: New Directions, 1982.

Rothenberg, Jerome, ed. *Technicians of the Sacred: A Range of Poetries from Africa, America, Asia, Europe and Oceania*. Second Edition. Berkeley: University of California Press, 1985.

Russolo, Luigi. *The Art of Noises*. Translated by Barclay Brown. New York: Pendragon Press, 1986.

Sanouillet, Michel. *Dada in Paris*. Translated by Sharmila Ganguly. Cambridge: MIT Press, 2012.

Sassoon, Siegfried. *Counter-Attack, and Other Poems*. New York: E. P. Dutton, 1918.

Sassoon, Siegfried. *Memoirs of an Infantry Officer*. London: Faber & Faber Limited, 1930.

Saussure, Ferdinand. *The Course in General Linguistics*. Edited by Charles Bally and Albert Secheye. Translated by Wade Baskins. New York: The Philosophical Library, 1959.

Schuller, Gunther. *Early Jazz: Its Roots and Early Development*. Oxford: Oxford University Press, 1968.

Schwartz, Hillel. *Making Noise: From Babel to the Big Bang and Beyond*. New York: Zone, 2011.

Seldes, Gilbert. "American Noises: How to Make Them and Why." *Vanity Fair*, June 1924.

Serres, Michel. *Genesis*. Translated by Geneviève James and James Nielson. Michigan: University of Michigan Press, 1997 [1981].

Serres, Michel. *The Parasite*. Translated by Lawrence R. Schehr. Minneapolis: University of Minnesota Press, 1982.

Shannon, Claude, and Warren Weaver. *The Mathematical Theory of Communication*. Urbana: University of Illinois Press, 1949.

Shaw, Lytle. *Narrowcast: Poetry and Audio Research*. Stanford: Stanford University Press, 2018.

Sheppard, Richard. *Modernism—Dada—Postmodernism*. Evanston: Northwestern University Press, 2000.

Sherry, Vincent. *The Great War and the Language of Modernism*. Oxford: Oxford University Press, 2003.

Showalter, Elaine. *The Female Malady: Women, Madness, and English Culture, 1890–1980*. New York: Pantheon Books, 1985.

Sieburth, Richard. "Dada Pound." *South Atlantic Quarterly* 83, no. 1 (Winter 1984): 44–68.

Smith, Jacob. *Vocal Tracks: Performance and Sound Media*. Berkeley: University of California Press, 2008.

Smith, Patti. *Early Work 1970–1979*. New York: W. W. Norton, 1994.

Smith, Patti. "Patti Smith's My First Gig: Desecrating a Church with Electric Guitar." NME Youtube Channel. June 12, 2014. https://www.youtube.com/watch?v=tNOuHNlZwEk.

Smith, Patti. "Patti Smith at the Poetry Project." Recorded February 10, 1971.

Southern, Eileen. *The Music of Black Americans: A History*. New York: W. W. Norton, 1997.

Stein, Gertrude. "What Is English Literature?" In *Lectures in America*. Boston: Beacon Press, 1957 [1935].

Steintrager, James. "Metal Machines, Primal Screams, Horrible Noise, and the Faint Hum of a Paradigm Shift in Sound Studies and Sonic Practice." *Musica Humana* 3, no. 1 (Spring 2011): 121–52.

Stephen, Ann. "Blackfellows and Modernists: Not Just Black and White." In *Pacific Rim Modernisms*. Edited by Mary Ann Gillies, Helen Sword, and Steven Yao. Toronto: University of Toronto Press, 2009.

Steptoe, Tyina. "Big Mama Thornton, Little Richard, and the Queer Roots of Rock 'n' Roll." *American Quarterly* 70, no. 1 (2018): 55–77.

Sterne, Jonathan. *MP3: The Meaning of a Format*. Durham: Duke University Press, 2012.

Sterne, Jonathan. *The Audible Past: Culture Origins of Sound Reproduction*. Durham: Duke University Press, 2003.

Sterne, Jonathan. "Sounds Like the Mall of America: Programmed Music and the Architectonics of Commercial Space." *Ethnomusicology* 41, no. 1 (Winter 1997): 22–50.

Stewart, Susan. *Nonsense: Aspects of Intertextuality in Folklore and Literature*. Baltimore: Johns Hopkins University Press, 1979.

Stewart, Susan. *Poetry and the Fate of the Senses*. Chicago: University of Chicago Press, 2002.

Stoever, Jennifer Lynn. *The Sonic Color Line: Race and the Cultural Politics of Listening*. New York: New York University Press, 2016.

Suarez, Juan A. *Pop Modernism: Noise and the Reinvention of the Everyday*. Urbana: University of Illinois Press, 2007.

"Susan Howe and David Grubbs," *Yale Union*. October 2013. https://yaleunion.org/david-grubbs-susan-howe/.

Swensen, Cole. *Noise That Stays Noise: Essays*. Ann Arbor: University of Michigan Press, 2011.

Szendy, Peter. *Listen: A History of Our Ears*. Translated by Charlotte Mandell. New York: Fordham University Press, 2008.

Thompson, Emily. *The Soundscape of Modernity: Architectural Acoustics and the Culture of Listening in America, 1900–1933*. Cambridge: MIT Press, 2002.

Thompson, Marie. *Beyond Unwanted Sound: Noise, Affect and Aesthetic Moralism*. New York: Bloomsbury, 2017.

Tzara, Tristan. "Dada Manifesto" (1918). In *Dada Painters and Poets: An Anthology*. Edited by Robert Motherwell. Cambridge: Belknap Press, 1989 [1951].

Tzara, Tristan. *La premiere aventure céléste de Mr. Antipyrine*, 1916. International Digital Dada Library. http://dada.lib.uiowa.edu.

Tzara, Tristan. "Manifesto on Feeble Love and Bitter Love." In *Dada Painters and Poets: An Anthology*. Edited by Robert Motherwell. Cambridge: Belknap Press, 1989 [1951].

Tzara, Tristan. "Proclamation without Pretension." In *Dada Painters and Poets: An Anthology*. Edited by Robert Motherwell. Cambridge: Belknap Press, 1989 [1951].

Tzara, Tristan. *Seven Dada Manifestos and Lampisteries*. Translated by Barbara Wright. New York: Riverrun Press, 1977.

Tzara, Tristan. "Zurich Chronicle" (1920). In *Dada Painters and Poets: An Anthology*. Edited by Robert Motherwell. Cambridge: Belknap Press, 1989 [1951].

Veit, Walter. "Dada among the Missionaries: Sources of Tristan Tzara's *Poèmes Nègres*." in *Migration and Cultural Contact: Germany and Australia*. Edited by Andrea Bandhauer and Maria Veber. Sydney: Sydney University Press, 2009.

Voegelin, Salome. *Listening to Noise and Silence: Towards a Philosophy of Sounds*. New York: Continuum, 2010.

Von Hallberg, Robert. *Charles Olson: The Scholar's Art*. Cambridge: Harvard University Press, 1978.

Walker, Bruce N., and Michael A. Nees. "Theory of Sonification." In *The Sonification Handbook*. Edited by Thomas Hermann, Andy Hunt, and John G. Neuhoff. Berlin: Lagos Publishing House, 2011.

Warner, Michael. *Publics and Counterpublics*. New York: Zone Books, 2005.

Waters, Ethel, and Charles Samuels. *His Eye Is on the Sparrow: An Autobiography*. New York: Da Capo Press, 1992.

Watten, Barrett. "Olson in Language: Part II." In *Writing/Talks*. Edited by Bob Perelman. Carbondale: Southern Illinois University Press, 1985.

Watten, Barrett. *Total Syntax*. Carbondale: Southern Illinois University Press, 1984.

Weiss, Allen. "Fourteen and a Half Words to Bespeak the Migone." *Christof Migone—Sound Voice Perform*. Los Angeles and Copenhagen: Errant Bodies Press, 2005.

Weiss, Allen. *Varieties of Audio Mimesis*. Berlin: Errant Bodies Press, 2008.

Wheeler, Lesley. *Voicing American Poetry: Sound and Performance from the 1920s to the Present*. Ithaca: Cornell University Press, 2008.

White, Michael. "Umba! Umba! Sounding the Other, Sounding the Same." In *Dada Africa: Dialogue with the Other*. Edited by Ralkf Burmeister, Michaela Oberhofer, and Esther Tisa Francini. Berlin: Scheidegger and Spiess, 2016, 165–71.

Winter, Jay. *Sites of Memory, Sites of Mourning, The Great War in European Cultural History*. Cambridge: Cambridge University Press, 1998.

Worringer, Wilhelm. *Abstraction and Empathy: A Contribution to the Psychology of Style*. Translated by Hilton Kramer. Chicago: Elephant Paperbacks, 1997 [1908].

Zak, Albin J. *The Poetics of Rock: Cutting Tracks, Making Records*. Berkeley: University of California Press, 2001.

Zukofsky, Louis. *A*. Baltimore: Johns Hopkins University Press, 1978.

Index

Note: Locators with letter 'n' refer to notes.

0 to 9 (Acconci) 126, 132, 134–40, 141, 151
4'33'' (Cage) 8–9, 96

a cappella 105
"ABC" poems 92
  abstraction 5, 10, 34, 37, 39, 40, 41, 42, 43, 46–50, 52–4, 56, 58, 65, 66, 78, 79, 83, 85, 89, 97, 102, 103, 104, 109, 134, 143, 165
accompaniment 37, 38, 39, 45, 55, 148, 169
Acconci, Vito 126, 132, 134–5
acousmatic sound 96
acoustemology 5, 130
acoustics 2, 3, 6, 9, 11, 18, 22–3, 31–2, 81, 89–90, 92, 95–8, 100–1, 108, 113, 117, 132, 156, 161, 168, 169–71
address 3, 7, 28, 30, 43, 92, 93, 133, 136, 137, 138, 144, 147, 151, 153, 157–9, 164, 166, 172, 173
Adorno, Theodor W. 68–9, 82, 107–9, 128
African-American music 54–5, 58, 68, 71, 107, 163
African chants 35, 41, 50–1
agency 69, 91–2, 120
"Alexander's Ragtime Band" (Berlin) 55, 57 n. 2
alliteration 3, 23
All Poets Welcome (Kane) 131
Altieri, Charles 114
"American Noise" (Seldes) 74
amplifier 108, 123
analog synthesizer 160
anarchism 127
Anderson, Benedict 124
Andrews, Bruce 140, 141, 144
anechoic chamber 9, 97, 126, 127
"Anthem for a Doomed Youth" (Owen) 22–3

anthropomorphism 24, 30, 47, 65, 80, 91, 124, 134
anti-genre 151, 157
anxiety 22, 82, 83
Apollinaire 44
Appelbaum, David 50, 112
Aragon, Louis 41
Aranda people 53–4
arche-trace 67
Armstrong, Louis 75, 86, 104
Arp, Hans 33, 36, 53
arrangement 4, 48, 81, 131, 136–9, 170
articulation 2, 11, 81, 89, 90, 103, 108, 112, 120, 126, 127, 138, 153–4, 158–9, 161, 164, 165, 166, 172, 173
"Artifice of Absorption" (Bernstein) 5
"Art of Noises, The" (Russolo) 8, 32, 44
assonance 23
Attali, Jacques 4, 7, 8, 31
"At the Somme" (Borden) 26
audile techniques 2
audio technology 88, 100, 112, 117, 129, 154, 166, 167, 169
automatism 24, 25, 31, 40, 42, 62, 64, 82, 106, 112, 164
autonomy 18, 19, 48, 59, 62, 64, 69, 82, 95, 128, 162
avant-garde 1, 9, 27, 33, 48, 51, 54, 89, 96, 101, 107, 123, 124, 126, 128, 129, 139, 140, 149, 164, 165, 166

Bach 55, 56
background noise 3–4, 45
balalaika 36
Ball, Hugo 9–10, 33–8, 41–51, 55, 64, 65–6, 163, 164
"Ballad of a Bad Boy" (Smith, Patti/Kaye) 148
ballads 30, 73, 130, 132
Bangs, Lester 123, 129, 130, 145, 147

banjo 55
Baraka, Amiri (Leroi Jones) 54, 88, 111, 132
Barbusse, Henri 15–16, 17, 21
"barrelhouse" piano 55
Barthes, Roland 106, 116, 125–6, 139
bass 105, 109, 149, 160
Baudelaire, Charles 146–7
beat 21, 30, 42, 56, 58, 77, 82–5, 93, 103, 105, 109, 138
Beat-generation 131, 135, 144
bel canto 106
Benjamin, Walter 20, 173
Berlin, Irving 55, 56, 57–8, 72–3
Bernstein, Charles 5, 91, 170
Berrigan, Ted 131, 132, 133
Berry, Chuck 108–9
Beuys, Joseph 168
Beyond Unwanted Sound (Thompson) 7
Billiteri, Carla 113
bird sounds 129
black art 54
Blackburn, Paul 131, 132
"Black Dada Nihilismus" (Baraka) 54
Black Mountain poetry 112, 131
black music 68, 71, 103
blackness 51, 53, 54, 68–9, 74, 86, 107
Blackpentecostalism 107
Blake, Eubie 71
Blake, William 132
"Blank Generation" (Hell) 126, 141, 144–6
"Blitzkrieg Bop" (Ramones) 150
"Blue Moon of Kentucky" (Presley) 109–10
blues 56, 69, 70–3, 75, 76, 84, 98, 103, 109, 146, 148
body
    (black) female 33–59, 69–70, 72–3, 75, 163–4
    and noise 36, 37, 72–4
    performer's 126–7, 135, 140, 146, 148–51, 164–7, 170, 172
    voice/sound and technology 87–121, 127, 153, 154, 157, 159, 163
Bolderoff, Frances 93
"Boogie Disease" (Ross) 109
boogie-woogie piano 103
"boomboom" 35, 36, 37
Borden, Mary 14, 25–8, 30
Bradford, Perry 71

Brahms 55
Brathwaite, Edward Kamau 76
"Break of Day in the Trenches" (Rosenberg) 28–9
breath 19, 94, 95–6, 106–7, 112–15, 117, 120, 146
Breton, Andre 41
Bridges, Robert 29–30
Brihadaranyaka Upanishad 77, 79, 80
Broadway 71
Brown, Seymour 57 n.2
bruitism 34, 35, 37, 40–6, 48, 51, 55, 56, 58, 64
Buchla 160
Burroughs, William S. 131, 133, 135
Byrne, David 99

C: A Journal of Poetry (Berrigan) 132, 133–4
cabaret 35–40, 46, 55–6, 84, 85
Cabaret Voltaire 34, 36, 44, 51, 52, 55–6
Cabaret Voltaire 39, 44
    editorial manifesto 65
cacophony 98, 125
Café Simplicissimus 36
Cage, John 8–10, 96–8, 124–7, 145, 165
cakewalks 55
Cale, John 130, 149
"Camping Out with Ed Sanders" (Samara) 133
capitalism 56, 127
causality 34–5, 43, 101
CBGB 147
chance operations 34, 40, 98, 131
"Charge of the Light Brigade" (Tennyson) 25
Charles Olson Reads from Maximus Poems IV, V, VI (Olson) 118
Chess Records 108, 109
citation 62–3, 77, 79, 83–4
Clark, Grant 57 n.2
Clark, T. J. 109–10
classical music 44, 55
clubs 55, 84, 127, 128, 160
commodity fetish 69
communications technology 5–6, 10, 89, 90, 96, 98, 100–2, 124, 134
communications theory 89
comparative philology 61, 77–8

Concrete PH (Xenakis) 129
concrete poetry 2, 106, 143
Connor, Steven 15, 106, 108
consonance 23, 49, 75, 113–14
Coolidge, Clark 10, 125–6, 135, 137–42
coon songs 55
cosmopolitanism 29, 30, 68
country music 98
Cox, Christoph 154
Crawley, Ashon 54, 107
"Crazy Blues" (Smith, Mamie/Bradford) 71, 73
Creeley, Robert 88, 111–12, 116, 117
Crisis (periodical) 84
Crosby, Bing 106
Crudup, Arthur 98
cubism 44
Cullen, Countee 85, 86
Culler, Jonathan 30
cuts 112, 115, 117, 135, 158, 163, 167, 169, 170
cymbals 129

"DA" (Eliot) 62, 76–84
"da" sound 61–86
Dada Almanach 53
Dada/Dadaism 9–10, 33–59, 62–86
    Eliot's "DA" 76–84
    form 67
    history and concept 61–7, 77
    Hughes's "Negro Dancers" 84–6
    and jazz 67–70
    Medina's "da-da strain" 68–76
dance music 55, 63
Daughtry, Martin 16
Davidson, Michael 115
de Certeau, Michel 63, 151
dedifferentiation 10, 49, 50, 65, 81, 97, 147, 159, 172
Deer, Patrick 14, 15, 22, 28
Deleuze, Gilles 19, 90, 129
Demers, Joanna 158
depersonalization 50, 56, 126, 127
dérive 125
Derrida, Jacques 19, 136
desire 39–40, 54, 102, 104, 105 n.7, 130, 132, 137, 146
détournement 125

Dickinson, Emily 168–9
DiPrima, Diane 132
disc jockeys (DJs) 91, 100
disruption 22, 41, 58, 62, 126, 165
dissonance 81, 83, 124
distortion 81, 88, 100, 101–2, 105, 107, 110, 113, 116, 120, 130, 146–7, 149
DNA (band) 150
Do You Have a Band? (Kane) 126
Dolar, Mladen 77
Domino, Antoine "Fats" 88, 103–8
double vision 22
Dowell, Edgar 62, 68, 71–2
Downtown/Downtown School 124–31, 140
Doyle, Paul 109
drones 10, 123, 130, 169, 170, 171
drugs 132
Drumm, Kevin 155
drums 37, 41–2, 45, 50, 74–5, 77, 100, 103, 105, 106, 107, 129, 139, 161
Dumbstruck (Connor) 108
Durations I–V (Feldman) 129
Dworkin, Craig 7, 164, 167
Dylan, Bob 108, 148

Eastman, Julius 128, 129
echo 5, 97, 109, 127
eclecticism 35, 36, 46, 58, 124
Edwards, Brent Hayes 164
Edwards, Hannah 170
Edwards, Jonathan 170
Eigner, Larry 111
electricity 108, 154
electro-acoustic mediation 90, 92, 100, 108, 117, 156
electromagnetic transducers 107
electronic mediation 1, 6, 7, 94, 100–2, 108, 110, 117, 123, 154, 158, 160, 169, 170, 171
electronic music 96, 108, 123, 130, 155
Eliot, T. S. 10, 62, 76–84, 116, 118, 127, 136
Ellman, Maud 83
emotion 15, 137, 146
En Avant Dada: A History of Dadaism (Huelsenbeck) 66–7
English Review 26

Ephraim, Jan 52
epic poetry 2, 9, 63, 84, 92, 94
Epstein, Josh 79, 82, 83
Erlmann, Veit 32, 162
Escher, M. C. 109
etymology 78, 92, 114–15, 134
"Everybody's Doing It Now" (Berlin) 55, 56, 57 n.2, 72–3
experimentalism 1, 2, 68, 69, 100, 102, 108, 124, 128, 134, 140, 141, 143, 151, 155, 159
Expressionism 35, 104, 109–10

falsetto 103
Fantastic Prayers (Huelsenbeck) 33, 42
"Fat Man, The" (Domino) 103–5
feedback 1, 6, 74, 95, 123, 129, 156, 164
Feldman, Morton 119–20, 124, 128–9
female body 33–59, 69–70, 72–3, 75, 163–4
field recordings 10, 169, 170, 171
figuration/figure 3–4, 17, 21–2, 23, 30–1, 33, 58, 68, 70, 73, 90, 98, 154, 159, 170
Filament 1 (Yoshihide/Sachiko) 155
"Fire of Unknown Origin" (Smith, Patti) 148
First Celestial Adventures of Mr. Fire-Extinguisher, The (Tzara) 42, 65
First World War 1, 5, 8, 9, 13, 14, 31, 56, 62
"Flanders Fields" (Bridges) 29–30
Floating Bear, The (DiPrima) 132
Fluxus 131
"folk, the" 56
folk songs 36, 37
Folkways LP 118
Forbidden Zone, The (Borden) 26, 27
Ford, Ford Madox 27
form 2, 4, 5, 6, 9, 13–32, 33–3, 37, 40, 44, 46–7, 53–9, 67–70, 74, 76, 79–80, 83, 90, 94, 97–9, 103, 107, 111–12, 115, 120, 123, 126, 134, 141, 144, 145, 149, 151, 154, 164, 165, 173
four-track tape recorder 123
Fowler, Al 130
fragmentation 9, 27, 47, 84
free improvisation 155

free verse poetry 6, 9, 26, 28, 30
Freud, Sigmund 82
Frith, Simon 107, 146, 156, 158
Frolic Architecture (Howe/Grubbs) 169–71
Fuck You/A Magazine of the Arts (Sanders) 126, 132–5
Fugs, the (band) 132
functional music 123
Fussell, Paul 9, 18
Futurism 8, 9, 31, 35, 43–4

Gates, Henry Louis 86
General Course in Linguistics (Saussure) 49–50
Genesis (Serres) 3–4
Genesis : Grasp 126, 134, 140–3
"geno-song" 106
genre 8, 33, 36, 91, 99, 101, 103, 123–4, 141, 147, 149, 151, 154–7, 160
Giddens, Anthony 124
Gillett, Charlie 105
Ginsberg, Allen 131, 132, 148
Giorno, John 135
glissandos 75, 129, 149, 164
"global village" 95, 98, 102
"Gloria" (Them) 149
glossolalia 63
Gobel, Mark 74
Goffin, Robert 74–5
"Goodbye" (Hell/Meyers) 142–3
Graham, Dan 135
grain 40, 56, 68, 88, 93, 102–3, 106, 109–10, 113, 120, 146, 170
gramophone 81, 83, 99
Graves, Robert 13, 16, 17
"Great Album Ever Made, The" (Bangs) 123
Greenberg, Clement 128
Grenier, Robert 151
Grubbs, David 10, 11, 154, 155, 159, 168–72
Grumble, Albert 57 n.2
Guattari, Félix 19, 90, 129
Guilbert, Yvette 39
guitar
  "double-stops" 108–9
  electric 108, 109, 110, 148
  feedback 123

punk style 145–9
rhythm 109
riff 103, 148, 164
rock 'n' roll style 105, 108
sound texture 100, 108
"wah-wah" pedal 104 n.5
Gussow, Adam 73
Gysin, Brion 135

Hainge, Greg 7
harmonic range 8, 55, 58, 72, 103
Hartman, Saidiya 69
Hayes, Brent Edwards 86
Hecker, Florian 11, 154, 155, 158–9, 160–2
"Heebie Jeebies" (Armstrong) 86
Hegarty, Paul 7, 68, 141, 149, 155–6
Hell, Richard 10, 124–6, 140–7, 150–1
"Hello, I" (Hell/Meyers) 143–4
Hendrix, Jimi 148, 149
Hennings, Emmy 33–40, 42, 49
"here and now" 107–9, 117, 130
"Heroin" (Velvet Underground) 127, 130
heteroglossia 44, 51
"Hey Joe" (Hendrix) 149
high-frequency 108, 129
history
    Dada/Dadaism 46, 61–7, 77
    and memory 10
    noise 1–7, 153–73
    rock 'n' roll 98–110
Holy Presence of Joan of Arc, The (Eastman) 129
homosexuality 105 n.7
Horses (Smith, Patti) 149
Howe, Susan 10–11, 153–5, 158–9, 167–72
"How You Sound" (Baraka) 111
Huelsenbeck, Richard 33–8, 41–2, 44, 49–52, 55–6, 64–7
Hughes, Langston 10, 62, 84–6
Huyssen, Andreas 128
hybrid forms 79, 98, 101, 148, 162, 163

iambic pentameter 21, 23
"I Belong to the Beat Generation" (McKuen) 144–5
I Ching 98
"I HATE SPEECH" (Grenier) 151
"I Love the Ladies" (Clark/Schwartz) 56, 57 n. 2

Iliad (Tennyson) 25
Imaginary Landscape No. 4 (Cage) 97
immanence 113, 125
imperialism 8, 50–1, 52, 53, 69, 113, 117, 166
improvisation 14, 18, 74, 95, 104, 106, 139, 148, 155, 160, 163, 165–6, 169
In the Break (Moten) 102
incest 130
industrial music 155
information theory 10, 63, 89
insect sounds 129–30, 171
interference 81, 130
interlocking drones 123
internationalism 35
It's Gonna Rain (Reich) 129
"I Wanna Sniff Some Glue" (Ramones) 141

Jagger, Mick 148
Jakobson, Roman 36, 43, 65, 83–4, 119
Janco, Marcel 33, 36, 41, 44–5
jazz 2, 9–10, 36, 55, 64, 68–76, 86, 99, 103, 108, 139
"jazzbandism" 68
jingoism 35
"Johnny B. Goode" (Berry) 108
Joplin, Scott 55
Joris, Pierre 53
Joyce, James 35
"Juke" (Walter) 109

Kahn, Douglas 4, 9, 51, 89, 96, 98
Kane, Brian 96
Kane, Daniel 126, 131, 133, 134, 140, 141, 143, 144, 148
"Karawane" (Ball) 49
Kaye, Lenny 148, 149
Kenner, Chris 149
"Kingfishers, The" (Olson and Creeley) 112
kitsch 128
Kittler, Friedrich 2, 81
Kristeva, Julia 83, 106

La Legende d'Eer (Xenakis) 129
"L'Amiral cherche une maison a louer" (Tzara) 44–6, 56–7

"Land of 1000 Dances" (Kenner/Pickett) 149
language 2, 3, 11, 14, 17, 18, 74
   Dadaist 33–59, 62–86
   limits of 40, 46, 135, 150
   music and 160
   and noise 19, 25, 37, 48, 77, 134, 162–73
   nonsense 1, 10, 42, 45, 48, 53, 57, 61–86, 102, 106, 119, 142, 166
   organized 28
   poetic 124–6, 130, 132–41, 144, 150
   and power 116, 150
   primitive 50–9, 84
   projective 92–3, 95, 97, 102, 113–18, 135
   Saussurean definition 63
   sonority of 43, 159
   and sound 23, 74, 86, 124, 133
   techniques and technologies 61–86
   theory of 115
   and voice 160–2
Lanman, Charles Rockwell 79
Lastra, James 102, 120–1
Lenin, Vladimir 35
lettrism 143, 168
Lewis, Wyndham 27
Lewitt, Sol 135
Lindsay, Arto 150
line break 93, 112, 168
linguistics 2, 20, 44, 48–9, 50, 61, 63, 64, 79, 80, 81, 83, 102, 126, 131, 135, 160, 165
Listen: A History of Our Ears (Szendy) 138
listening
   aesthetic 155–8
   Barthes on 125, 126
   Cage on 126
   compulsory 93
   double 22, 79
   forms of 3, 77–8, 102, 130
   and noise 2, 4, 6–7, 19, 31–2, 118, 125, 154
   paratactic 97
   phonographic 81–4
   reading and 11
   reconfiguration of 138–9
   sound and 1, 96–7, 115–16, 118, 138, 166, 170
   structural 130, 153
   undifferentiated 81
   in wartime 15–16, 22
Listening to Noise and Silence (Voegelin) 7
"Livery Stable Blues" (Original Dixieland Jazz Band) 75
logocentrism 47, 136
logos 46–7, 164
London Times, The 75
Lord, Albert 94
Loritja people 53–4
"Love Comes in Spurts" (Hell) 141
lullaby 27
Lyotard, Jean-Francois 96, 157
lyrics 10, 14, 29, 30, 57, 62, 68, 71, 72, 100, 105, 110, 124, 127, 133–4, 138, 144, 145, 150, 157, 166

Mac Low, Jackson 131, 135
MacArthur, Marit 171
"Made Thought" (Coolidge) 142
mainstream culture 132, 134
Making Noise (Schwartz) 7
male gaze 40
march music 55
marginalized poetry 1
Marsh, Edward 28
Martin, Dean 98
Marx, Karl 69
mass culture 35, 54, 55, 56, 117–18, 128
mastery 19, 20, 30, 37, 125
Mathematical Theory of Communication (Shannon and Weaver) 89
Maximus Poems, The (Olson) 92–5, 114–18
"Maybe the Last Flight" (Hennings) 39
Mayer, Bernadette 10, 126, 132, 134–5, 139
Mayer, Rosemary 136
McKuen, Rod 144
McLuhan, Marshall 10, 94–5, 98
meaning-making 34, 62, 63, 123, 155, 158
mechanization 56
media 1, 3, 6, 7, 10, 61–8, 79, 81, 88, 94, 102, 118, 128
mediation 3, 6, 7, 9, 10, 20, 22, 54, 61, 63, 67, 79, 80, 81, 82, 86, 88, 90, 91, 94, 97, 100–1, 104, 106, 108, 111, 123, 124, 127, 155, 156, 158–9, 163, 165, 166, 173

Medina, Mamie 10, 62, 68, 69, 71–2, 76, 85
meditation music 123
medium 2, 7–8, 10, 14, 31–2, 43, 53, 61, 67, 74–6, 82–4, 86, 91, 99, 100–1, 108–9, 123, 126, 130–4, 143–4, 150, 153, 155, 163, 171
Medovoi, Lee 110
Meintjes, Louise 5
Meisel, Perry 108
Mellers, Wilfrid 56
memory 10, 18, 19, 82, 94, 143, 159
Merzbow 155, 157
Metal Machine Music (Reed) 123, 129, 156, 160
metamorphosis 102, 104
metaphor 3, 5, 10, 17, 22, 23–4, 30, 89, 90, 96, 110, 115, 141, 145, 159, 161, 162, 170
metaphysics 4, 70, 116, 172
meter/metrical form 1, 9, 13, 18–23, 83, 112, 168
Meyers, Richard 140, 142, 143
microphone 106–7, 164
Middleton, Peter 40
Middleton, Richard 146
military bands 20, 55
military metrical complex 20, 21, 25–6, 28
"Milk Cow Blues" (Presley) 109
Miller, Tom (Verlaine) 142, 144, 146
mimeograph machine 131–5
mimesis 9, 17, 43–4, 129
minimalism 129, 135, 141, 144, 161
minstrelsy 55
mnemotechnics 19
modernism 8, 9, 62, 64, 68, 74, 96
modernity 8, 34–5, 41–4, 47, 50, 53, 56–8, 68, 70, 81–4, 118, 124, 127–9
Monroe, Bill 98
Montage of a Dream Deferred: "Ain't you heard … ?" (Hughes) 85
"Moonlight" (Borden) 27
Morris, Tracie 10, 11, 154, 155, 158, 159, 162–7
Morrison, Jim 148
Moten, Fred 69, 102–3, 107, 163, 165
mourning 22–4
mouth sound 10, 34, 37–45, 48, 52, 59, 78, 88, 103–7, 120, 165, 170, 171

Müller, Max 78–80
murmur 80, 127
musical hall 76
"mu-sick" 88, 92–3, 113
musickracket 92, 118
musique concrete 96
Muzak 89–91, 93, 94, 118, 128
"My Generation" (Smith, Patti) 126–7, 149–50
mythopoeia 63

NAACP 84
Naked Lunch (Burroughs) 133
Nancy, Jean-Luc 6
Naropa Institute 137
nationalism 33, 35, 56
"Nativity Play" (Ball) 46–8
"*Negerlieder*" (Huelsenbeck) 50–1
"Negro Art" (Tzara) 51–3
"Negro Dancers" (Hughes) 62, 84–6
negro rhythm 50–4
neo-classicism 83
Neon Boys 144
new media 7, 81
New Orleans-style 71, 103, 105
New York School 124, 126, 131, 134–6, 140–1
noise
　comparisons to nature 17
　Dadaist 33–59, 124
　"domestication" of 89
　figuration 3–5
　Futurist 43–4
　in information theory 89–90
　in modernism 61–86
　and music 74, 82
　in noise music 162–73
　and poetry, theory and practice 7–11, 124
　punk 123–7, 140–7
　re-versing of 19
　signal and 3
　sound as 61
　sound of 10–11
　static 61, 63
　theory of 65
　visual textuality/reading 167–72
　voicing 5–7
　wartime experiences 13–32

Noise: The Political Economy of Music (Attali) 4
noise forms 3
Noise Matters (Hainge) 7
noise music 2, 5, 7, 8, 10, 43–4, 49, 123, 153–73
Noise/Music (Hegarty) 7
No Medium (Dworkin) 7
nonsense sounds 1, 10, 42, 45, 48, 53, 57, 61–86, 102, 106, 119, 142, 166
"Nothing I–XIII" (Coolidge) 137
Notley, Alice 131
Novak, David 156
No Wave scene 150

Oceanic poetry 35, 41, 50, 51
O'Hara, Frank 131
"Oh Joy" (Tutt Brothers) 71
Okeh 71
Olson, Charles 10, 87–8, 92–5, 111–18, 131, 148
Ong, Walter 10, 88, 94, 95
onomatopoeia 17
"Ooooooooooooh" sound 133
Oppenheimer, Joel 131
oral culture 94
Original Dixieland Jazz Band 75
otherness 50–4, 70, 86, 108, 136, 151, 156, 157, 161, 162, 172
otherworldly 27, 30, 31, 104
Owen, Wilfred 13, 14, 20, 22–5, 27, 28
oxymoron 21

para-linguistic sounds 102
parasite 11, 29, 61, 62, 64–8, 77, 84, 86, 124, 150
Parasite, The (Serres) 63
parlor music 55
Parry, Milman 94
pause 21, 23, 87, 93, 112, 117, 160
"pejoracracy" 92, 113
percussion 45, 74–5, 77, 105
performance
 avant-garde 9
 Dadaist 33–59, 62–86
 noise music 153–73
 projectivist 87–121
 punk 123–51
performance poetry 8, 144, 151

performance style 8, 38, 42, 75, 144
"phatic" element 43, 83–4, 117, 119, 130, 134, 143, 157, 159, 164
phenomenology 2, 3, 7, 15, 96–7, 127, 128, 158
Phillips, Sam 100–1, 109
philology 53, 61, 64, 77–8, 80, 83, 167–8, 173
phonocentrism 136
phonogrammatization 138
phonography/phonograph 2, 7, 10, 11, 22, 61, 62, 68, 76, 78, 81, 82, 83, 85, 86, 88, 94, 98, 99, 107, 108, 114, 125, 166, 168, 173
piano 36, 38, 55–6, 103, 105, 161, 169
Pickett, Wilson 149
pitch/pitch range 8, 71, 123, 129, 146, 148, 160, 161, 166
poesis 19, 68
poetics of witness 13, 25
poetry
 conceptions of 2, 6, 7, 139–40
 concrete 106
 Dadaist 33–56, 62–86
 Downtown 123–51
 lyric 166
 and noise, theory and practice 7–11
 projectivist 87–121
 reading 170
 sound 5–11, 33, 43, 46–50, 51, 154, 163–5
 and sound forms 153–73
Poetry Project 135, 140, 141, 147, 148
Poets at Le Metro 132
Poets at Les Deux Mégots 132
"polis" 95
Pop, Iggy 141, 146
popular song 1, 6, 8, 9, 37, 39, 55–6, 61, 68, 76, 98, 100, 156
portable sound 89, 90, 118
post-literary orality 10
postmodernism 8, 128
Pound, Ezra 94, 118
Presley, Elvis 88, 98, 109
primitivism 4, 42, 50, 51, 54, 68–70, 76–7, 80, 150, 165
Prins, Yopie 22, 91, 170
print culture 22, 53, 61–5, 67, 78, 88, 94, 99, 112, 133, 147

"Projective Verse" (Olson) 88, 93–4, 110–19
projectivist poetry 87–121, 140
protest songs 34, 37
proto-punk 124, 127, 130, 132
punk 2, 5, 10, 123–51, 153, 155, 156, 165

Quartermain, Peter 167, 168
quasi-scat style 62, 86

race 10, 69, 71–4, 85, 155, 163
radio/radio stations 7, 81, 90–1, 95, 98, 100, 107–8, 118
ragtime 1, 36, 54–9, 68, 76, 82
Rainey, Ma 71, 75
Ramones 141, 144, 150
Rasula, Jed 48, 68, 79–80
Reason and Resonance (Erlmann) 32, 162
"Rebecca of Sunnybrook Farm" (Seymour/Grumble) 55, 57 n. 2
recitation 18–19, 40–1, 46, 48, 77
recording
    audio 88, 100, 112, 117, 129, 154, 169
    field 10, 169, 170–1
    rock 'n' roll 98–9
    studio 6, 112
    techniques 10
Reed, Lou 123–4, 126, 129–30, 146, 156
Reich, Steve 124, 128–9
repetition 9–10, 18–19, 23, 26–8, 30, 57, 61, 64, 67, 76, 80, 85, 94, 103, 104, 106, 121, 129, 135, 136, 138, 139, 142, 163, 164
reverberation 22, 97, 109, 127
reversal, of noise 31–2
rexograph paper 131
rhapsody 94
rhyme 1, 3, 23, 94, 106
rhythm 3, 8, 14, 18–20, 25, 27–8, 30–1, 33, 35–6, 41–2, 45, 48–58, 65, 68–9, 72, 74, 77, 80, 82, 85–6, 97–8, 101, 103, 105–10, 119, 128–9, 144, 145, 148–50, 157, 163–4, 166
rhythm and blues (R&B) 98, 103, 108, 109
Richard, Little 10, 33, 44, 55, 88, 105–7
Richard Hell & the Voidoids (band) 144
Richter, Hans 36, 38
Rimbaud, Arthur 140, 149

Rite of Spring (Stravinsky) 82
ritual effects 22–5
Robertson, Lisa 173
rock music 100, 123, 124, 146, 149
rock 'n' roll 2, 10, 88–9, 98–111, 113, 118, 120, 123, 126, 140, 144–8, 150
Rolling Stones 100
Rosenberg, Isaac 14, 28–31
Ross, Doctor 109
Rothenberg, Jerome 53, 68
Rotten, Johnny 146
Russolo, Luigi 8, 44

Sachiko, M. 155
Samara, Mark 133
Sanders, Ed 126, 131–4, 143
Saroyan, Aram 135
Sassoon, Siegfried 14, 18, 20–1, 23, 25, 28
Saunders, Gertrude 71
Saussure, Ferdinand de 49–50, 63
Saxon, Dan 131–2
saxophone 103–5, 107
scat-singing 10, 62, 75, 86, 104, 164, 166
Schaefer, Pierre 96
Schuller, Gunther 56, 70, 75
Schwartz, Hillel 3, 7, 20
Schwartz, Jean 57 n.2, 57 n. 2
secondary orality 88, 94, 98
Second World War 6, 88, 89
Seldes, Gilbert 74
sense-making 2, 22, 64
sense perception 6, 31, 127, 155
Serres, Michel 3–4, 7, 61, 63, 167
sex/sexism 38, 69, 105 n.7, 132–3
Sex Pistols 141, 144
Seymour, Brown 55, 57 n. 2
Shannon, Claude 89
Shaw, Lytle 117, 118
Sheer Hellish Miasma (Drumm) 155
sheet music 68, 71, 88, 99
shell shock 20
Shelley, Percy Bysshe 30, 34
Sheppard, Richard 44
Shuffle Along (Sissle and Blake) 71
silence 3–4, 7–9, 20–1, 24–5, 29–30, 38, 87, 96–8, 113, 118, 144–6, 166
simulator 160
Sinatra, Frank 91

Index

sine waves 96, 155
Sissle, Noble 71
slap-back echo 109
Smith, Bessie 70–1, 75
Smith, Mamie 69, 70–6
Smith, Patti 10, 124, 127, 140–1, 147–51
Smithson, Robert 135
solo 103, 104, 105, 107
"Song of the Mud, The" (Borden) 26–7
"Songs of Maximus" (Olson) 92–4, 112
sonification 170
Souls of the Labadie Track (Howe/Grubbs) 169
sound
    inside 1, 88
    and listening 1–2
    mouth 106–7
    vs. noise 18, 95–8, 101, 119–20
    outside 1, 4, 80, 88
    para-linguistic 102
    in projective verse 92–5, 110–19
    selection and repetition 9–10
    as sound 61
    synthetic 108
    technological apparatuses 1
    texture 99–100, 103
    transmission and reception 6–7
    wartime recognition of 16–17, 22
    as words 61, 167–8
"Sound, Noise, Varèse, Boulez" (Feldman) 119
sound art 2, 7, 95 n.4, 127, 153–5, 160
sound culture 88, 100, 117, 120
sound designers 89
sound effects 1, 48
sound engineering 2
sound forms 11, 14, 18–19, 22–3, 25, 52, 83, 98, 124, 138, 153–4, 156, 158–61
sound poetry 5–11, 33–4, 43, 48, 51, 95 n.4, 154, 163, 164, 165
sound recording 10, 87–121, 96, 133, 140, 170, 171
sound reproduction 2–3
sound traces 11, 154
sound-writing 83, 86, 88, 120, 125, 138
soundscape 1, 10, 23, 62, 81, 95, 108, 124, 127–30, 145
space 5, 8, 15, 18–19, 23, 25–6, 28, 30, 31, 54, 65, 67, 76, 81, 88, 89, 97, 98, 101–4, 103, 108, 109, 110, 112, 114–16, 119, 120, 124–31, 134, 135, 136, 138, 139, 141–51, 153, 155, 165–6, 171
space, production of 108, 130
Space (Coolidge) 142
Stay on It (Eastman) 129
Stein, Gertrude 27, 61, 135, 165
stereo channels 123, 125
Sterne, Jonathan 2, 5, 89, 90
Stewart, Susan 19, 53, 67
Stoever, Jennifer 70, 107
"Storyteller, The" (Benjamin) 20
Stravinsky, Igor 82, 83
Suarez, Juan 81
subversion 4, 38, 39
Sun Records 109
Sun Sessions (Presley) 109
surrealism 17, 42, 82, 110, 143
Swensen, Cole 2
Swinburne, Charles 132
swing jazz 103, 108
syncopation 55–6, 68. *See also* ragtime
syntagms 125–7, 129, 139
synthesizers 35, 96, 158, 160, 166
Szendy, Peter 138

taboo 132–3, 143
tape 6, 87, 102, 118, 123, 129, 132, 169
Technicians of the Sacred (Rothenberg) 53
teleology 4, 7, 147
television 7, 118
Television (band) 144, 146, 147
tempo 91, 109
temporality 17, 21, 30, 44, 154
Tennyson, Alfred Lord 25
"That Da-Da Strain" (Medina) 62, 68–76, 85
That This (Howe) 170
Them (band) 149
therapeutic effects 20, 22, 24, 25, 32
Thiefth (Howe/Grubbs) 169
Thomas, Dylan 148
Thompson, Emily 82
Thompson, Marie 7, 155
timbre 65, 102–3, 107, 129, 144, 146, 157, 160, 162
time 8, 11, 18, 21, 22, 28–32, 35, 42, 57, 67, 87–9, 92, 102–4, 114, 153, 154

Tin Pan Alley 55, 56, 99
"Toto Vaca" (Tzara) 53
"Tradition and the Individual Talent"
    (Eliot) 82
transgression 4, 8, 155, 158
transistorized devices 90, 102, 108
trombone 58, 75
truth-telling 13–14
Tutt Brothers 71
"Tutti Frutti" (Little Richard) 105–7
Tzara, Tristan 9–10, 33–7, 41–6, 49, 51–8,
    64, 65–6, 82, 141–2

"umba" chant 37, 42, 50
Under Fire (Barbusse) 15–16, 17
undersound 2, 5, 76, 85, 164, 173
Understanding Media (McLuhan) 94
"Understanding the Sound of Not
    Understanding" (Rasula) 79–80
unisonance 25, 124
"Up and Down" 71
"urn urn" (Coolidge) 141–2
uselessness, aesthetic 125
utopia 124, 155

van Maas, Sander 119
Varèse, Edgard 96, 108
vaudeville 71, 75–6
Velvet Underground 123, 126, 130
ventriloquism 108
"verse without words." *See* sound poetry
versification 8, 9, 13, 21–2
vibration 3, 7, 74, 123, 129, 166
viola 130
Voegelin, Salome 7, 157, 161
voice
    ambient 91–2
    crux 168
    grain/grainy 102–3, 106, 109
    indexical element 5, 98, 106, 107, 109,
        111, 112, 133–4
    "inner" 136
    mechanics 19
    and noise 5–7, 14, 75–6, 97, 101–10, 154
    in noise music 158–62
    performer's 100–1
    radio production 89–92

singing 30, 106, 109, 145
style 146
vaudevillian style 71, 75–6
"Voice, The" (Sinatra) 91
voice inverse 22
voice production, mechanics of 106
"voidoid" 126, 144
volume 90–1, 98, 105, 106, 107, 119, 133,
    155
Von Hallberg, Robert 113, 114

"wah" sound 103–4
Walter, Little 109
Warner, Michael 156, 159
war poems 9, 13–32
    therapeutic effects of 20
Waste Land, The (Eliot) 62, 76, 77, 79,
    81–3
Waters, Ethel 69, 71, 73, 75, 76
Watten, Barrett 115
Wayward Lives, Beautiful Experiments
    (Hartman) 69
Weary Blues, The (Hughes) 84
Weaver, Warren 89
Weiss, Allen 62, 129
Welling, James 170
Whitman, Walt 26
Who, The (band) 149
Wiggin, Kate Douglas 57 n.2, 57 n. 2
Williams, Clarence 71
Williams, William Carlos 94
Wills, David 119
WOODSLIPPERCOUNTERCLATTER
    (Howe/Grubbs) 169
Wordsworth, William 100
Worringer, Wilhelm 52

Xenakis, Iannis 108, 128, 129
xenoglossia 51

Yoshihide, Otomo 155
Young, LaMonte 124, 128, 129, 130

Zen 97, 125
Zeno's paradox 143
Zukofsky, Louis 139

www.ingramcontent.com/pod-product-compliance
Lightning Source LLC
Chambersburg PA
CBHW070637300426
44111CB00013B/2139